IN THAT DAY

An Exposition of the Final D

according to Zechariah

IN THAT DAY:

An Exposition of the Final Destiny of Israel according to Zechariah

James Ayre

Myrtle Vale, England

Horseshoe Cottage
Old Greenlaw Farm
Duns
Berwickshire TD10 6UP
Tel Greenlaw 206

01361 810 206

First published June 1986

Horseshoe Cottage
Old Greenlaw Farm
Duns
Berwickshire TD10 6UP
Tel Greenlaw 206

~~eadle Hulme~~,
~~SK8 7PX~~

01361 810 206

ISBN 0 948731 00 1

Printed in England by Stanley Press Ltd, Dewsbury

CONTENTS

Preface

Introduction: The Fact of Israel Today 1

PART A: A NIGHT OF VISIONS 9

1 Vision 1 Israel in the Depths 15
2 Vision 2 Four Horns and Four Smiths 32
3 Vision 3 A Man with a Measuring Line 44
4 Vision 4 Take Away the Filthy Garments 55
5 Vision 5 The Candlestick and Olive Trees 78
6 Vision 6 The Flying Scroll 93
7 Vision 7 The Woman in a Tub 101
8 Vision 8 Four Chariots Four Winds 111
9 The Next Morning 124
10 Justice and Mercy 132
11 The Promise to Bless 150

PART B: THE END OF THE AGE

12 Alexander the Great: a Christ-Type Conqueror 165
13 Christ the Cornerstone, Nail, Battlebow, and Absolute Monarch 184
14 Israel Cast Off: the Idol Shepherd 203
15 Grace and Supplication for the Remnant 227
16 Israel: Scattered, Cleansed, and Reconciled 247
17 The Last Days for Israel and for the Whole World: The Day of the Lord 262

PREFACE

It is with diffidence that I am allowing this study to reach a wider public. It originated as sixteen talks given to my Thursday Fellowship group at Cheadle Parish Church. It is no literary gem; it is not meant to be; it has been left quite deliberately in the rough hortatory style in which it was delivered, but which has the advantage at least of retaining something of the vitality and perhaps the occasional vividity of the spoken word.

The study of Old Testament prophecy concerning the future of the Jew, Israel after the flesh, has languished considerably since the Second World War. There are several possible explanations. One is that men of the Reformed school regard the restoration of the Jew to his land, and a millenial Kingdom, as a challenge to the concept of the Church as the Israel of God, and an impingement on the doctrine of justification by faith alone. It is perhaps salutory to remind ourselves that the sub-apostolic Fathers were, almost to a man, pre-millenialists, as the term goes. It was Augustine, chiefly, who abandoned this interpretation and who has influenced eschatological study ever since. But surely, with the birth of the modern State of Israel in 1948, Christians must once again begin asking questions of the Bible, if our God is to be the God of history in any real sense.

It is in pursuit of this line of reasoning that the study of Zechariah has been conducted. Today the Middle East is in turmoil: it has become potentially the most dangerous spot on earth; at the heart of it is the enigmatic, intransigent Jew. Has he any significance in these days of dire global danger? Is his return a precursor of the final clash of nations, and of the return of Christ? Many believe so, and many have, for the last two hundred years, looked for today's happenings to take place. It is we who must take up this study more seriously, for there **are** signs of the times to be looked for; there **are** notes of both alarm and hope to be heard. Perhaps this study will be of some help.

I have used the 1882 Revised Version of the Bible throughout because it has been generally considered the most accurate word-for-word translation of the Hebrew and Greek of all the fine translations published in the last hundred years. I am grateful to the Academic Division of the Oxford University Press for permission to quote from the Revised Version.

Finally, I have no other qualifications for daring to express myself on this subject than a lifelong study of prophecy, an intimate knowledge of Israel, the land, some Hebrew, a love for the much maligned ancient people of God, and many Jewish friends - as well as concern for the Arab peoples, especially those I once represented as Chairman of the International Christian Committee for Israel dealing with Arab refugees.

ACKNOWLEDGEMENTS

I have read prophetic studies for more than fifty years and I owe an enormous debt of gratitude to so many writers whose thinking I have absorbed. I am reminded of F.W. Pitt of the Advent Witness, Mark Kagan, the expositor, and Brigadier-General Frost who, with others, inspired my young mind. I must pay tribute to Adolf Saphir, to Schorr and Baron, as well as to Darby and Kelly, the Brethren writers. Others who have contributed to my education are Dr. Basil Atkinson (the historicist), Sale-Harrison, and the German, Sauer; and I must also acknowledge G.H. Lang, and particularly A.C. Gaebelein, a contributor to the Schofield Bible. Perhaps the most cogent exegete of them all regarding the thousand years was Canon E.A. Litton in his 'Introduction to Dogmatic Theology'.

J.A.
Cheadle, March 1986

INTRODUCTION: THE FACT OF ISRAEL TODAY

The book of the prophet Zechariah, allowing for the gap between the first prophecies and the second part, was written about 500 BC. There is no prophet more startlingly contemporary than Zechariah. Luther called him 'the quintessence of the prophets' but even Luther could not have suspected how quintessential Zechariah has become today. Indeed, he has become more relevant than ever in the last fifteen years.

The book is a condensed and concentrated prophecy which begins with the return from exile. The Jews went into exile to Babylon in 586 BC, and then began the Times of the Gentiles as the Glory of the Lord went up from the Mount of Olives (Ezekiel 11 verse 23) and the Jews were virtually finished as a nation, only a remnant returning seventy years later through the inspired act of Cyrus the Persian. Only forty-eight thousand people came back: they settled and had a tumultuously short period of four hundred years to bring forth the Christ before going back again into exile, this time for nearly two thousand years. And so the prophecy begins with the return from Babylon, but also spans that long period starting with the coming of Christ and His rejection, and the dispersion of the Jews for a further eighteen hundred years (and all the suffering in that time) to the eventual regathering of Israel; and finally, the prophecy ends with the returning Glory. So we have a huge 'rainbow' dealing specifically with Israel, and only incidentally touching the fate of the Gentile nations - the Goyim as they are known in Hebrew.

This book, as many writers have said, is second only to Isaiah in its clear reference to the Messiah. In the first place it concerns itself with His first coming in humiliation. It speaks for instance of the Lord Jesus 'Just and lowly, having salvation, riding upon an ass and upon the colt of an ass'. Zechariah also says: Give me the price of what you think of me; and they sold me for thirty pieces of silver. The prophet goes on to say that He was pierced by His own people (albeit with a Roman spear), and that the sword of God's wrath would smite the good Shepherd. There is no question of the identity of the person; the sword of God's wrath falls upon the good Shepherd in vicarious suffering, not for Himself but for others. Zechariah also speaks of the Messiah as 'The Man that is God's Fellow'. Nowhere else in the Scripture is such an expression found! Moses is God's servant; Abraham is God's friend; but the statement, that This Man is God's own Equal is amazing! The book speaks of the Messiah as 'the Branch of the Lord' and in His final triumph as 'bearing the Glory'. It also says, 'And He shall sit upon His throne as a priest': this prediction that a priest-king will rule is astonishing, but it is the very fulfilment of Psalm 110 and Melchizedek, that mysterious figure to whom Abraham the father of the faithful offered tithes. Indeed, the distinctness of the Messiah is remarkable.

The second mark of the clarity of the prophecy is the light that it throws on the last days. To the unprejudiced, that is, scholars who accept the prophecy at face value as a whole, and not the critics who bring in the theory of anonymous writers (higher critics), the book illuminates the last days. It is to the spiritually alert that the book is addressed, those who can read the signs of the times today. Many of us have a simple personal faith; we pray and believe that we are saved; we feel that the world is going on and on to destruction but that WE are saved. Many Christians lead this cocooned kind of life, but Christ urges us to observe and be aware of the signs of the times: to look upon the world, to look upon history, to look upon the political events; to look upon the Jew as God's timepiece! to regard these as footsteps in the sands of time. You can then hear the rustle of God's robe, and this book throws more light on the last days than perhaps any other book in the Bible.

This book distinctly foretells of the last days of Israel, the last great national trauma, and fate of the Goyim. With regard to Israel, consider that only one hundred years ago Israel was dispersed. If we had lived in 1850, Israel was nothing; of no consequence whatsoever, and she had been nothing for eighteen hundred years. There were just ghettos of Jews scattered around the world, despised, disliked, their hope cut off, of no value, socially ostracised and regarded as mere money-makers; but surviving, however, incredibly. How did they survive? There were no substantial physical links between the ghettos in Europe, in North Africa, in America and elswhere, but however incredibly they suffered they still survived. A hundred years ago the Church regarded herself as the Israel of God (Galatians 6 verse 16) and as having inherited all the spiritual promises of Israel. If we read the Old Testament in the Authorised Version most of the headings above chapters which relate to physical Israel read 'The Church is promised ...' but the Bible is not talking about the Church, which only came into existence about eight hundred years later. So, we may ask, why these headings? and the answer is that the Church has left the curses to the physical people of Israel whilst arrogating to herself the spiritual promises - having decided that God's covenant with the ancient people was ended.

Thirty years ago I was invited to go from Israel to Geneva, where Karl Barth was to have led a symposium just on the word and meaning of 'Israel' in the light of the regathering. He died before the symposium was held, but at least the idea of a symposium made it clear that fresh thinking was now being applied to the meaning of 'Israel', that word the Church was so certain it had defined!

The Jewish nation was but an interesting, stubborn, and despised anachronism a hundred years ago: it had no future, except in the theology of the Puritans. The Puritans reading Romans, especially Romans 11 - where Paul talks about the mystery of Israel and of their being cast-off and then being grafted back in, of the fulness of the Gentiles and of all Israel being saved - the Puritans believed that in the last days before Christ came there would be a spiritual revival among the Jews. In other words, many Jews would be converted to Christ and THAT was the only hope so many of the godly Puritans gave to this stubborn and despised race. An exception was the famous Puritan, Joseph Meade who, as early as the mid-seventeenth century suggested that there was a national future for this people.

So to summarise; more than a century ago here was a nation, almost an anachronism, scattered all over the world and with no nationhood, no land, no government, no power and, in spite of the fact that every year they drank the Passover wine and said, 'Next year in Jerusalem' (they had been saying this for more than eighteen hundred years) it was certainly not very hopeful; especially when what you say over and over again never comes to pass! Yet they hoped against hope.

And then ... there was a stirring of dry bones! (Ezekiel 37). A man named Herzog arose, and in central Europe began to talk to other Jews about nationhood, about getting together, about becoming an entity, about work, and about a political identity. Jews from Austria and Russia and Germany and France met in congress and said: If we are to lead a **normal** life (normality was the ambition of these early Zionists) we must get together, and in order to achieve normality we must have a land and we must work that land; we must not be just money-makers and lawyers and doctors; we must be the labourers and the policemen, the stevedores and the doers of the work; no nation is a nation without grass roots; we must be workers and not be just on the periphery of things as we are today. The Jew! who has ever seen a Jew sweeping the streets in his local town? They do not do things like that; but who has never seen a Jewish doctor or laywer? And so Herzog, and Lilliental, and Achad Ha'am and other great men arose a hundred years ago and urged these ideas, and the flame of Zionism began to burn.

But where shall we go? they asked. They applied to the

British Government for a part of Uganda to make a Jewish national home there. The British had just taken over Uganda and were not opposed to the idea and did not resent the notion of carving it up! Fortunately they did not proceed with this idea, or Idi Amin might have got them! In the end sentiment took over. It was not religious sentiment, for this movement was almost anti-religious. The leaders were the Maschilim, those intellectuals who revived interest in Hebrew as a living language; and Chaim Weizman the English chemist of Russian origin, who was in part responsible for the Balfour Declaration of 1917 on Palestine, was a Maschil and a Zionist, and he became the first president of Israel.

The leaders and the movement as a whole had no faith in the rabbis. They did not believe in the Bible - in the ordinary sense of that word, believe. They did not refer to God as leading them: the movement was purely idealistic, political, and philosophical in its conception and energy. But nevertheless they said: No, if we are to get a land and try to become a people again, let us go back to Palestine; and they said this although the Turks were rulers of the land at that time.

So Jews began to go to Palestine in what is called in Hebrew the Aliya, the Going Up. Men like Ben Gurion, Ben Svi, and Moshe Sharet came from lives of privilege in Europe to Palestine whilst it was still under the Turks, and worked with their bare hands and feet like labourers; and labourers they were indeed, carving out for themselves little orange groves, and clearing swamps and dying (especially at Hadera) in their thousands from malaria. They took over sandy wastes and made them bloom. Where Tel Aviv stands today was formerly a total desert outside Jaffa, and for a vivid account of those early days you should read, "A village beyond Jordan". When Gordon, one of the Olim Hahadshim (The Immigrants) and a considerable philosopher, was spreading manure on the land of a new kibbutz, he is reported to have said, Now I have a right to live! meaning, **this** is normality, Avoda, Work.

So there was a stirring of the dead bones! Now who

said that? Ezekiel said it in chapter 37. Can these bones live? Thou knowest, O Lord God ... full of bones, dry bones, very dry. That was the fate of Israel for eighteen hundred years; very dry! And they stood upon their feet; Ezekiel saw them; and they became flesh and sinew and they came together! Of course you know the bit of history that follows because you yourselves are living history; God has worked in your day. The Jews became a nation in 1948. For the first time in two thousand years Israel (not Judah as it was first intended to call the nation, but the name was changed to Israel by a dint of inspiration) - Israel is a land with a parliament and a language, which in itself is an absolute miracle, for like Latin, Hebrew was almost a dead language but they revived the language also. And now Israel has an army and has Jerusalem too, and that dream 'next year in Jerusalem' has become a fact; actually theirs to live in once again. Today three to four million Jews live in the Promised Land, and all this after nearly two thousand years!

Now by any standards this is a miracle. How did they retain their purity? How did they retain their identity and their passion, their Torah and their Talmud, their religion, their hope? How is it that the Jews were not wiped out altogether? The pogroms and the persecutions were horrendous. We think of Hitler but millions were killed before Hitler. Down the centuries the Jews were slaughtered in numbers like one hundred thousand, then one hundred and forty thousand, and so on and yet! they are now back and they are a miracle! I must insist that by any theological standards, by any historical standards, by any political standards we are facing something which should make us say, My word, this MUST be significant. We must not just read of Israel as if she has been there all our lives, because she was only put there in 1948.

But more ... more of a miracle because Israel has become THE SIGN OF OUR TIMES. Our Lord said, When you see these things begin to come to pass, lift up your heads. Two or three years ago the guns of the American warships were hitting Lebanon again and the Middle East is still aflame. We have poor Lebanon twisted and torn and smashed to pieces: we have Egypt in the south, brooding under its new president and no one really knows what is in his mind. We have Syria, full of hate and backed by Russia. We have Libya under a fanatical Moslem who is trying to revive Moslem dreams along the North African coast. We have Jordan poised precariously and the whole Middle East in turmoil, and the cause? The cause since 1948 is the nation of Israel.

I was living there when they had the Sinai war. I went back in 1967 when the Israelis took Jerusalem. I had just been to Israel in 1973 when Egypt broke over the borders, shocked the Israelis to the core and killed two thousand of them. In 1982 under Menachim Begin, Israel invaded the Lebanon. And today, literally today as I write, those great powers USA, Russia, Britain, Italy, and France are all around Beirut, the coast of Palestine, and are all being drawn in. No doubt temporary solutions will be found; but blind intransigent Israel is reaching out for more and more. I was there in December 1982 and was actually on the Golan when Israel took the Golan heights. They are now committed to taking over the West Bank. Within their borders they will have two million Arabs; but they are determined, they are strong; they are possessed by something that they do not understand themselves. I have talked this over with many Jews; it is a sense of destiny, a sense of election but no Elector. They are ready even to pull the house down over their own heads if anything goes wrong. That is how obsessed they are.

So I want to say this to you. The apocalyptic has not only become the possible, it has become the probable and that is very serious. We read the Revelation of St John and do not understand it. We read Ezekiel also: we call their writings apocalyptic visions, frightful visions, and so frightful that they are put into metaphor. We read of The Beast, The Dragon, The False Prophet, Locusts, Vials of Wrath, and so on; but it is no longer poetry, it is fact! It is fact in the Middle East and no one knows the final solution. No one knows the day of the final solution but the Lord and, if I may say, some of His Saints! They do not know the WHEN, but they believe in and know WHAT the end will be.

Are we surpised? The world does not take any notice, but are we surprised as Christians? If we are, it is because we have not read the Book of Zechariah! because this is the exact state of affairs in this book, as we shall find as we study it.

The Book
The book is in four parts. Chapter 1 verses 1 to 6 is a call to repentance; chapter 1 verse 7 to the end of chapter 6 covers the eight visions; chapters 7 and 8 discuss fasts both in the past and the future, as far as these Jews were concerned; and then chapters 9 to 14 form the great climax, the End of the Age.

The Prelude
The first six verses are absolutely in line with the call of God from Genesis 3 to Revelation 20. In the call of God in verse 2 we get, The Lord hath been sore displeased with your fathers. Notice that there is no false compassion; there is no 'humanism'; God is the Judge of all the earth and His judgment begins at the House of God. The prophet begins in a serious vein: God has been very displeased with you. There is no patting the Jews on the back and saying that you are all right because you are Jews and the children of Abraham; God has been sore displeased! But there is also mercy; and in verse 3 the Lord of hosts says, Return unto me and I will return unto you. Here again the name of God in the text is significant. Za'avot in Hebrew means army and He is called here the Lord of Armies; here He is the Warrior God; here God has got His sword at His side.

In the Old Testament there are many names of God: Elohim means The Strong One; Adonai means The Master, The Lord; El Olam means The Eternal God; El Shaddai means the God of Providence; El Elyon means The Most High God; and then you get the great name Yahweh which is The God of Salvation; and Jehovah-jireh, Jehovah shammah and names like that meaning God will provide, God is there, and so on. But here in Zechariah, He is the Lord of Hosts, and God is calling on men to surrender, to repent, and to return.

This message is the consistent message of Scripture, which never tells us to 'realise our potential' or to get together the good that is within us, or that we are all Sons of God. No, never! There is no progress of humanity in Scripture; there is always a decline, morally and spiritually. The one consistent call in Scripture to mankind no matter how sophisticated or how primitive we are is, Repent, and return. We get that in Isaiah 55 verses 6 and 7:

> Seek ye the Lord while he may be found, call ye upon him while he is near:
> Let the wicked forsake his way, and the unrighteous man his thoughts: and let him return unto the Lord ...

Again in Jeremiah 3 verse 12 (how consistent the Scripture is):

> Go, and proclaim these words toward the north, and say, Return, thou backsliding Israel, saith the Lord; I will not look in anger upon you: for I am merciful, saith the Lord, I will not keep anger for ever.
> Only acknowledge thine iniquity ...

And again in Ezekiel 18 verse 30:

> Therefore I will judge you, O house of Israel, every one according to his ways, saith the Lord God. Return ye, and turn yourselves from all your transgressions; so iniquity shall not be your ruin.

I suggest that you get the same message of 'Repent, and Return' in all the minor prophets, Hosea, Joel, Amos, and Zephaniah. Perhaps the most lovely example of this is in Daniel's prayer, when he makes confession of his own sins and the sins of the people.

But they would not! they would not! and our Lord says that of His generation: How oft would I have gathered thy children together even as a hen gathereth her chicks ... but ye would not. Nor would the Jews before the exile, and so you get these startling verses in 2 Chronicles 36 verses 13 to 16, (we are talking now about the fathers who would not hear, who would not return):

> And he also rebelled against king Nebuchadnezzar, who had made him swear by God: but he stiffened his neck, and hardened his heart from turning unto the Lord, the God of Israel.
> Moreover all the chiefs of the priests, and the people, trespassed very greatly after all the abominations of the heathen; and they polluted the house of the Lord which he had hallowed in Jerusalem.
> And the Lord, the God of their fathers, sent to them by his messengers, rising up early and sending; because he had compassion on his people, and on his dwelling place:
> But they mocked the messengers of God, and despised his words, and scoffed at his prophets, until the wrath of the Lord arose against his people, till there was no remedy.

Solemn words indeed from 2 Chronicles: They did not hear, your fathers; they would not hearken till there was no remedy!

According to the rabbis, verse 5 in chapter 1 is a bit of dialogue: Your fathers, where are they? asks God through the prophet Zechariah; and the people answer insolently, And the prophets, do they live for ever? meaning, Well, where are the prophets? Do they live forever? And the answer is: No, good men indeed die; (we read that in Hebrews) but my words live for ever! The grass withereth, the flower fadeth, but the Word of our God shall stand for ever, says Peter. Men must distinguish between the frail messengers of the Word of God, and the infallible Message of the Word of God, and that was Zechariah's reply to the Jews. And that is the message for us as well as for them: God's men may die but God's Word will live and never fail; and the call of that Word to every generation, irrespective of time, is, Repent, and Return!

What did John the Baptist preach? He came preaching out of the desert, Repent ... and do not say to yourselves that we have Abraham to our father; God, even of these stones, is able to raise up children unto Abraham! Our Lord came: and what did He say? Repent, for the kingdom of heaven is at hand. But the Pharisees, that religious sect, just laughed and said: We are the people, we have the Law, nothing can harm us. But Christ replied: You have got exactly the same spirit as your fathers who killed the prophets for giving this message; rather than obey them they killed them; rather than repent ...

And on the day of Pentecost, when the crowd were moved and said, Men and brethren, what can we do? Peter replied: Repent, and be baptized every one of you in the name of Jesus Christ for the remission of sins. So, with the call of Scripture urging God's people to repent and return, let us begin Zechariah's night of visions.

1 VISION 1 ISRAEL IN THE DEPTHS

From verse 7 of the first chapter of Zechariah we are embarked upon eight visions from God to this young man; a young man probably in his teens, as I have said, and very much like Jeremiah. Lord, said Jeremiah, I am a child, I am a na'ar; how can I speak all these words against Your people? Stand up and be not afraid of their faces, says God. You see, God uses young men and God uses old men, and God uses middle-aged men and God uses women! so never be affronted by whom God uses.

So we have eight visions throwing a light on Israel, and Israel is God's first-born - that is the Exodus description of Israel; throwing light on God's first-born, on the nation, on their punishment, on their suffering, and on their ultimate redemption; from the beginning of the Times of the Gentiles (when the Temple and Jerusalem were destroyed in 586 BC, the Jews taken away, and the Glory of the Lord left the city and rested on the Mount of Olives) right until these same Times of the Gentiles are fulfilled. Let us turn to Luke 21 verse 24:

> And they shall fall by the edge of the sword, and shall be led captive into all the nations: and Jerusalem shall be trodden down of the Gentiles, until the times of the Gentiles be fulfilled.

The Times of the Gentiles are a very significant period in the history of Israel. They date, as we have seen, from the departure of God's Glory and the destruction of the Temple, right until the near return of our Lord Jesus Christ; a very, very important period in spiritual history. From 586 BC to this very day, the Gentiles have held sway and Israel has been as nothing on the face of the earth! But there is no question here merely of survival as a nation: not only will Israel survive in their suffering, in their persecution and in their dispersal all over the world; but they are constantly under Divine Supervision. That is the point to grasp! They are constantly at the heart of the Divine Purpose for all time, and incidently, for all nations. In other words the key to all history in a physical sense, is this despised small nation, the Jews. Although God sent them out, dispersed them, harried them, smote them; nevertheless, He constantly kept, and keeps, His eye upon them.

On the twenty-fourth day of Shebat, two months after Haggai's promise that God would bless them, a great vision came to this young man Zechariah and he begins in verse 8: I saw in the night and behold ... This young man was in an ecstatic condition, and yet his mind was highly tuned. If you read Numbers 12 verse 6 you will see the evidence for such a vision:

> And he said, Hear now my words: if there be a prophet among you, I the Lord will make myself known unto him in a vision, I will speak with him in a dream.

So this young man's mind was absolutely highly tuned to the Voice and Vision of Almighty God.

Now there is a doctrine today, a very dangerous doctrine which arises in the charismatic movement, which says that you can pray with your spirit but that your mind is unfruitful. This is a complete mis-understanding of the text, I believe. Nowhere in Scripture is the mind unfruitful. God made the mind! The mind is the fine instrument through which God works. John Calvin the great reformer, says that if one prays in an unknown tongue, the spirit prays but the mind is unfruitful, not to the one who prays, but to the remainder of the Church. So never interpret that as the mind being in abeyance. The mind is highly regarded; the renewing of the mind is essential, and the effect of the Holy Ghost, as Paul says to Timothy, is the power of a sound mind. You never get the pagan concept that the mind goes into abeyance, or that 'I am motivated by forces within which I cannot understand because my mind is blocked off'. Such a concept is very dangerous because in that guise one can start preaching and believing almost anything. So to verse 8:

> I saw in the night, and behold a man riding upon a red horse, and he stood among the myrtle trees that were in the bottom; and behind him there were horses, red, sorrel, and white.

So this young man is caught up in a vision which we must try to understand. The man on the red horse is identified in verse 11 'And they answered the angel of the Lord ...' He is therefore, according to this verse, the angel of the Lord. But who is the angel of the Lord? Now if you trace that expression in Scripture carefully, he is the 'angel of his face' (the Hebrew word is Penaiv) as in Isaiah: I will save you and the angel of his face will be with you to save you. He is the angel of the covenant in Malachi 3 verse 1:

> Behold, I send my messenger, and he shall prepare the way before me: and the Lord, whom ye seek, shall suddenly come to his temple; and the messenger (or angel - the same word Malach is used) of the covenant, whom ye delight in, behold, he cometh, saith the Lord of hosts.

This is surely the same angel of the Lord with whom we meet in Genesis 18, talking with Abraham about the destruction of Sodom and Gomorrah. Three men, says the text, one of them the Lord! The rabbis are puzzled by this theophany and they wonder who is governing in heaven while the Lord talks to Abraham here on earth!

Again, this is surely the same angel of the Lord who called to Moses out of the burning bush in Exodus 3 verse 2, where it would appear that the angel and God are one and the same. And too, I suggest, the same angel appeared to Joshua in Joshua 5 verse 13. He appeared as Captain (or Prince) of the Host of the Lord and Joshua gave worship to Him, 'for the place whereon thou standest is holy', and this is the same injunction as that given at the bush. The man on the red horse is that same angel, and I would contend from Scripture that it is none other than the preincarnation appearance on earth of Jesus Christ, a Theophany as we say; an anticipation of the Incarnation.

A Man on a red horse! Immediately our minds go to Revelation 6 verse 4 where the red horse signifies judgment, 'and power was given to him to take peace from the earth'. Again, in Isaiah 63 verse 1: Who is this that comes from Bozrah with His vestments stained with blood? Now this man is standing among the myrtle trees. What is special about that? to us nothing; but to the Jews everything because according to the rabbis the word Myrtle, which in Hebrew is Hadassa, is a synonym for Israel, The Righteous One. Hadassa also means Esther and is a popular name for girls. So we see God the Son as a Man of War, if we interpret rightly, standing among the small despised and suffering Jewish remnant (the humble myrtle) in the depths; at the bottom; in the pit, for the Hebrew word here, Matsulla (the deeps), is used in this sense in Psalm 88 verse 6:

> Thou hast laid me in the lowest pit, in dark places, in the deeps.

Now translate all this in the light of what we know to have happened. For eighteen hundred years the Jew has lived among the Gentile nations. He has been forbidden to do this, forbidden to do that; he has been persecuted, pushed around, and hated. He has been in the depths! Yet he **is** the myrtle and the Son of God has been standing in his midst the whole of that time observing, observing ... and **that** is the wonder of this prophecy; it is to do with Israel and her destiny.

We are all familiar with Isaiah 43 verse 2: When thou

passest through the waters ... they shall not overflow thee: when thou walkest through the fire, thou shalt not be burned ... but we should remember that this chapter is not meant primarily for the devotional use of the Christian. Such use is legitimate and included for our sakes; but in the first place the chapter is meant as a promise to Israel after the flesh in the Last Days. Though punished for his gross sin and terrible blasphemy, the Jew has never been utterly forsaken; though he has lived at the bottom, in the shade, in the depths, he has been watched over by the Divine Eye, by the Son of God Himself. Moses predicted terrible sufferings in Leviticus 26, all of which were to come true, especially from AD 70. But Moses ends with the promise in verses 44 and 45:

> And yet for all that, when they be in the land of their enemies, I will not reject them, neither will I abhor them, to destroy them utterly, and to break my covenant with them: for I am the Lord their God:
> But I will for their sakes remember the covenant of their ancestors, whom I brought forth out of the land of Egypt in the sight of the nations, that I might be their God: I am the Lord.

This is the hope the Jew has been clinging to for the last two thousand years. If only we could inject a bit of thrill and understanding into this Book and see it from the Jewish point of view, how much more meaningful it would be. So we have white, and red, and sorrel horses; white speaking of victory, red of judgment, and sorrel, a mixture. When these are all taken together it means that God is dealing with the Jew in a mixture of mercy and judgment; in the deeps, in a pit of suffering, oppressed by the nations, but known unto God and kept. But now to the prophet's question in verse 9:

> Then said I, O my lord, what are these? And the angel that talked with me said unto me, I will shew thee what these be.

To whom does the prophet address his question? To the angel; but which angel? He does not ask the angel on the red horse but the angel 'that talked with me'. Let me explain this.

The Hebrew is Dber b'Ani meaning 'spoke in me' and so introduced for the first time is another angel. We have the angel sitting on the red horse, and he is the angel of the Lord surrounded by his couriers who were doing a reconnaissance of the earth; and we have the young man Zechariah, and IN the young man is an angel talking with him. The prophet does not address this angel as Adonai, which is the word for God; he addresses the angel as Adoni, which is the modern Hebrew word Adon for 'husband' or just plain 'Mr'. This is very significant. When you talk of God you use the word Adonai; but when you talk of an 'ordinary man' you use a lesser but similar word Adon, and there is a very big difference between the two.

So this other angel is talking to the young man and interpreting what is being said to him. Dr Pusey says that it is an interior speech going on in the young man: it is an inward speaking angel, giving inner understanding. Again I stress, the mind is not in abeyance; the angel is giving inward understanding of what is going on. The phrase 'the angel who talked in me' is used eleven times to identify this angel who is standing by, or within, Zechariah. This interpreting angel, always addressed as Adoni and not Adonai, is the expounder of the vision to Zechariah, and through Zechariah to Israel, and through Israel and the Bible, to us all.

So the scene is set. The angel of the Lord and his riders are among the myrtle trees, in the depths, in the bottom, and facing Zechariah; and through the interpreting angel Zechariah's question is answered in verse 10:

> And the man that stood among the myrtle trees answered and said, These are they whom the Lord hath sent to walk to and fro through the earth.

Around the angel of the Lord on His red horse are these

men who had returned from a reconnaissance of the earth. The phrase 'to and fro' through the earth is very significant because the Book of Job talks similarly of Satan. God says to Satan: Where have you been? I have been walking to and fro in the earth and up and down thereon, is the reply. A famous expression isn't it? Peter uses the same phrase: The Devil, like a raging, roaring lion goeth about up and down the earth seeking whom he may devour.

But here you have a marvellous picture: this time you have God's riders! you have God's riders who are far more powerful than Satan for, 'he that is within you is greater that he that is within the world'. We concentrate too much on evil and see the Devil everywhere. Of course he is a reality; we get enough evidence of his work without seeking it too closely. But at the same time, for our benefit and encouragement, remember that the riders of God are going to and fro in the earth; and they are reporting back 'to headquarters'; reporting back to the angel of the Lord; reporting continually to the Throne of God.

Now I know that this is a anthropomorphic picture, a picture made for men to understand; but it is vivid, and it is comforting! so if you think of Satan 'whizzing to and fro' and of all the demons that people concentrate on today, remember this, that God's riders are active too: they are reporting continually over the state of Israel; Israel in trouble; Israel in persecution; Israel in loneliness; Israel scattered and in the depths. In verse 11 the riders answer the captain, the angel of the Lord, the angel of Jehovah:

> And they answered the angel of the Lord that stood among the myrtle trees, and said, We have walked to and fro through the earth, and, behold, all the earth sitteth still, and is at rest.

The Hebrew word used is Sheket, meaning Silence. As a command in modern Hebrew it is 'Be Quiet' or more rudely, 'Shut Up'. The riders are reporting to the angel of the Lord, to the Christ of God, that the world is having a marvellous time; that the Nations are all at peace; all at peace except God's own servant Israel - this one little nation which is being tossed to and fro in suffering at the hands of the Babylonians, the Assyrians and later, at the hands of almost every nation upon the face of the earth. In contrast to the Nations, Jerusalem is broken down; the Temple is in ruins; the people are in exile; there is mourning; there are tears; there is despair; they are 'at the very bottom'. But then you come to a remarkable verse, verse 12:

> Then the angel of the Lord answered (this is Christ Himself) and said, O Lord of hosts (Jehovah that is), how long wilt thou not have mercy on Jerusalem and on the cities of Judah, against which thou hast had indignation these threescore and ten years?

How long is this persecution of the beloved people to go on? This is nothing else but the intercession of Christ for Israel. Do not forget that! Never become so anti-Jewish and so self-righteous a Christian as to forget that Christ interceded for Israel. He wept over Jerusalem even while condemning the city, and as He wept over Jerusalem He said (Luke 19 verse 42):

> If thou hadst known in this day, even thou, the things which belong unto peace! but now they are hid from thine eyes.
> For the days shall come upon thee ...

There is this enormous compassion of God and of Christ for the very people who crucified Him, and turned their backs and spat upon Him, and pierced Him: anti-semitism would not grow up if we could only remember that the Lord had this compassion! You get the same attitude in Acts 1 verse 6: Lord, dost thou at this time restore the kingdom to Israel? and does our Lord say, No, you lot of dullards, you have totally misunderstood the Gospel! Does

He say that? Of course not. He says: The times and seasons are in the hands of the Father: you go and preach to all nations. Our Lord does not deny the presupposition that Israel one day **will be** restored. He just says that it is not for you to know when ... it is in the hands of the Father.

And remember too that Paul, in Romans 9, has the same attitude as the Lord. Paul was hated by the Jews; Paul himself could call them terrible names though they were his own people. He could be as bitter as anyone when he was confronting their unbelief and hardness yet, halfway through his ministry, what does he say in Romans 9 verses 2 and 3? - I have sorrow in my heart continually concerning my people Israel; I could wish myself accursed from Christ if they could be saved.

All I am saying here is that our Lord, as the Angel of the Lord, the pre-incarnate Son of God, is praying: How long O Lord ... how long wilt thou have indignation? they have borne it for seventy years. And then when He became incarnate He makes the same intercession; and so does His apostle St Paul when he says, I have sorrow in my heart ... They both looked forward to the day when the Jew would recognise Christ, and when the Jew would be regenerated, and when the Jew would return.

But let me move to what is the theme for the next few chapters, 'the good and comfortable words' and in verse 13:

> And the Lord answered the angel that talked with me (the interpreting angel) with good words, even comfortable words.

Then the interpreting angel urges Zechariah in verse 14 to 'Cry':

> So the angel that talked with me said unto me, Cry thou, saying, Thus saith the Lord of hosts: I am jealous for Jerusalem and for Zion with a great jealousy.

Now jealousy is the other side of love. If you love anyone passionately and entirely, you are tremendously jealous when another seduces them, or takes them away from you or crushes them, aren't you? I am a jealous God, says God; I am jealous for Jerusalem and for Zion; I am jealous with a great jealousy; I am jealous for an earthly people; I am jealous for an earthly city, says God. And in verse 15:

> And I am very sore displeased with the nations that are at ease: for I was but a little displeased, and they helped forward the affliction.

God is very sore displeased with the Goyim. We translate it as Nations, but the word means, The Peoples of the World, The Non-Jews. He is greatly displeased with those who have the nerve to sit back and enjoy themselves, and have peace and comfort and fulness; those that are at rest and are quiet while Israel is tormented.

So the message to the little remnant is: I am sore displeased; I have great anger; I was but a little displeased with Israel, comparatively speaking. Yes, they worshipped idols; they would not keep my laws, and in the end I was so sick of them that I sent them into exile. I burned their Temple down and I broke down their walls but, in a sense, that was nothing compared with what you Gentile nations have done to them. That is the point! I was but a little displeased with Israel, but **you** have multiplied their sufferings in a way that I never called for!

And is it not true that the Nations have continued to exploit God's anger against the Jew, going far beyond the limits of God's wrath? The record is appalling: let me set it out for you. When you consider that it has been done in the name of Christ, our shame should know no bounds:

AD	70	1,100,000	Jews died in Jerusalem;
	135	580,000	Jews were killed under the Bar Kokhba rebellion;
	1096	10,000	Jews were killed in the Rhineland in May and July;
	1290		All Jews were expelled from England and were not allowed back until 1648 under Oliver Cromwell;
	1298	100,000	Jews were killed in Austria, Franconia, and Bavaria in the autumn;
	1306	100,000	Jews were expelled from France;
	1492	300,000	Jews were expelled or killed by Torquemada, head of the Inquisition in Spain;
	1648/58	400,000	Jews died in the war with Russia, Poland, and Sweden;
	19th century		The infamous pogroms took place in Russia; and
	1939/45	6,000,000	Jews were exterminated by the Germans under Hitler.

A detailed summary of Jews killed in Germany and in countries occupied by Germany in the second world war is given by Robert Aron in his book, Les Grands Dossiers de l'Histoire Contemporaine (1962). He gives the total Jewish population in these countries in 1939 as 8,301,000 of which 5,978,000 were killed, or 72%. At the top of his list is Poland, where 2,800,000 were killed out of a total Jewish population of 3,300,000, which is 85%.

Do you see what God is saying? I was but a little displeased: I sent you into exile; I sent you out of your land; but the Nations - you Nations! you went further than I ever would have gone. You have treated this people mercilessly and, what makes it worse today, is you are professed followers of Christ (all these figures are in the Christian era). Little wonder then that the Jews were (as Romans says) in part, hardened. 'In part' indeed! Little wonder that they have become even more bitter and stubborn today; even more merciless themselves in reaction to the bitterness of others and to the terrible treatment that they have had. Now, say that you English were to read **your** history and saw that the English had been treated like this? You would have a chip on **your** shoulder would you not? - as big as a rock! That is the Jewish attitude. Are you surprised that the Jew is more than a little supercilious? that he stands aside when you try to convert him to Christ? Imagine the irony of it! convert me to Christ when you have done all that in the name of this Christ!

Now we know that it cannot have been truly converted men that did such deeds; but nevertheless, the official Church did so act and many Christians today, even in evangelical circles, bitterly criticise the Jew and they just add to what God has done and they help forward the affliction, 'The Ra-a', the badness. Yes, the Jew has been hardened by God, but he has been hardened also by the injustice of the nations who helped forward the affliction. Indeed they did!

So, well in advance, if only Jews had eyes to see and ears to hear, God speaks good and comfortable words to them, and what does He say? He says four things in verses 16 and 17:

> Therefore thus saith the Lord: I am returned to Jerusalem with mercies; my house shall be built in it, saith the Lord of hosts, and a line shall be stretched forth over Jerusalem.
> Cry yet again, saying, Thus saith the Lord of hosts: My cities through prosperity shall yet be spread abroad; and the Lord shall yet comfort Zion, and shall yet choose Jerusalem.

We will take the statements in order.

I am returned to Jerusalem with mercies

Of course we know that this actually happened, so the

prophecy is fulfilled even as it is written here. It took place; there was a measure of relief and comfort. It was a good and comfortable word but in view of the rest of the prophecy, you will see that the return under Sheshbazzar, Joshua, and Zerubbabel was only an interim mercy, a token mercy, for only fifty thousand at most came back from exile to set up a very precarious little nation. You might well ask, Why this interim bit of mercy? And the answer is, To bring forth the Messiah. Then, as the Jew was reverting to his old unbelief and hardness, Jerusalem was again destroyed and the Jew was sent into dispersion, this time of worldwide dimensions.

Although fulfilled in the first instance, God's promise to return with mercies will, as we shall see later on, be fulfilled in the second instance, in full, for God will return to Jerusalem in the last days, In That Day!

My house shall be built in it

And of course, it was! The poor little group of people under Haggai and Zechariah did indeed build a second Temple and the old men wept at the sight of it. It was so insignificant compared to Solomon's; yet this second Temple was later to be taken up by Herod and made into a most glorious edifice. What Haggai had said did indeed happen, for 'the Desire of all nations' appeared in this second despised Temple; the Son of God Himself! Jesus walked in the porches of it.

So the prophecy was fulfilled in history. But what interesting questions now arise! The Jew is scattered a second time for a crime more heinous than idolatry; for crucifying the Son of God! His blood be upon us and upon our children, they said; and for nineteen centuries the blood of Christ has indeed been upon them. I know that modern commentators do not like this: it puts God in a bad light, they think; He is a loving compassionate God; but they do not understand the Scripture. They think that God is All Love but, as Martin Lloyd-Jones has said, What an infamous person God would be if He were All Love; if in the midst of all this wickedness and terribleness and disease all you have got is some supine, silly, All Loving God! It is an aberration to have one attribute, to have one quality of deity raised above the others.

But what interesting questions arise about modern Israel! The Jew has been in the depths for nearly nineteen hundred years: he has been watched over by the the Son of God; he has been tortured and battered, and his affliction increased by the Nations, and now he is back in the land! And will My House be built again? Well, I will leave you to think about this and to think about Ezekiel's Temple (chapters 40 to 48), a meticulously detailed description of a Temple yet to be - in spite of the sceptics.

So God is returned; these are the good and comfortable words. The promise to return with mercies has been fulfilled and **will be** fulfilled, and the promise, MY House shall be built, has been fulfilled and again, **will be** fulfilled if the Hasidim in modern Israel have their way.

A line shall be stretched forth over Jerusalem

This means simply that Jerusalem will be divided into quarters. And today Jerusalem is indeed divided into quarters. I lived in the Musrara district of Jerusalem for example. Then there is the Katamon district and so on, and that is what the prophet is talking about. It is rather like saying that here in Manchester we have a number of districts such as Sale, Eccles, Salford, and Moss Side; that would be 'stretching a line' over Manchester. Where do you come from? ... I come from Wythenshawe or, I come from Didsbury.

Now this is going to happen to Jerusalem: it is going to have living quarters; it is going to be a vital city with suburbs all around. And in fact, let me tell you this, it is happening today! It happened then right down to Our Lord's day, and now since 1967 (which many people think is the beginning date for the end of the Times of the Gentiles) Jerusalem is no longer being trodden down by the Gentiles. It is the capital of the Jewish State! The old city is still full of Arabs, and that problem has got to be worked out.

Will the Jew push those fifty thousand Arabs out of the old city? Will they build a Temple where the Mosques of Omar and El-Aqsa now stand on the Temple site? The temptation must be simply enormous: to have once again a Temple in Jerusalem; to restore to the Cohanim the priesthood. The question is fascinating and such events not at all improbable in modern Israel.

My cities ... shall yet be spread abroad

Note the personal pronoun, My cities! God, I am trying to say, has a vested interest in that land and God has a vested interest in that people, and God has a vested interest in that ancient promise to Abraham, and God has a vested interest in that kingdom promised to David and, most of all, God has a vested interest in confirming His promises that: In thee all the nations of the earth shall be blessed.

We are dealing with the unalterable, the ever-faithful God. Trace the destroyers of the Jews; trace Hitler; trace the lot of them, Babylonia, Assyria, where are they today? God has a vested interest in His people but, and again I must emphasise this, there is no virtue in the Jew per se, no virtue just in Jewish flesh; election does not mean selection; the Jew is not 'good' in himself. But he **is** elect of God and God always honours His promises. So I suggest that the restoration of physical Israel is implied in Matthew 23 verses 37 to 39:

> O Jerusalem, Jerusalem, which killeth the prophets, and stoneth them that are sent unto her! how often would I have gathered thy children together, even as a hen gathereth her chickens under her wings, and ye would not!
>
> Behold, (this is the interim period of nineteen hundred years) your house is left unto you desolate.
>
> For I say unto you, Ye shall not see me henceforth, till **ye** shall say (Who? now answer that question; who shall say? the Jews? there was no one else there: He was talking to Jews in Jerusalem), Blessed is he that

> cometh in the name of the Lord.

You Jews shall say that! Our Lord is distinctly saying: Your house is going to be left desolate until you Jews say, Blessed is he that cometh in the name of the Lord. So the restoration of physical Israel in Christ will come about when the Jewish nation confesses Him; when they shall look upon Him whom they pierced; and when 'the gathering together of the children of God throughout all the world' takes place, for that will be the high point of history. Do you see God's purposes? He has His eye on Israel; He has His eye on you and me. Look at John 11 verses 51 and 52. John is talking about Caiaphas who had just said, It is expedient for you that one man should die for the people, and that the whole nation perish not:

> Now this he said not of himself: but being high priest that year, he prophesied that Jesus should die for the nation;
> And not for the nation only, but that he might also gather together into one the children of God that are scattered abroad.

Caiaphas, poor fellow, did not know that he was prophesying. How could he guess that the Holy Ghost was using him! This is an instance of God using His enemies to say marvellous things but not to know it; they are the only people in the world who do not know it because God blinds them to the truth of their own words.

But are not John's verses wonderful? Christ died for just one nation. He did not die for the British nation, or for the American nation, or for the German nation, or for the Russian nation, or for any other nation. He died for the Jewish nation! He died because they were the chosen of God; they were the first-born of God; God's elect; they had all the sacrifices and the oracles and He died for them. He became the Servant of Jehovah and laid down His life for His people (Isaiah 53). But He also died for the people of God who are scattered throughout the world;

the great multitude of Gentiles from every nation, tongue, kindred, and so on. These two things are not opposed to each other; the redemption of physical Israel (a remnant of physical Israel) and the gathering together of the people of God throughout the world will **both** be fulfilled when the final comfortable words are complete.

What a glorious vision; and what a glorious hope both for Jew and Gentile in Christ. And what an encouragement to every one of us to cry and cry again to all men, that Jesus Christ is Lord and in Him, in Jesus Christ, total restoration will become a fact. Look at Acts 15 verses 15 to 19. The speaker is James the brother of our Lord. Peter had just told him about the Gentiles turning to Christ and James replies:

> And to this agree the words of the prophets; as it is written,
> After these things I will return, and I will build again the tabernacle of David, which is fallen; and I will build again the ruins thereof, and I will set it up:
> That the residue of men may seek after the Lord, and all the Gentiles, upon whom my name is called,
> Saith the Lord, who maketh these things known from the beginning of the world.

That to me is thrilling, absolutely thrilling, and this was spoken when the Gentiles were only just beginning to come into the Church. So one day the Jew is going to be restored, and the people of God throughout the world are going to be gathered together. We will find out how that takes place when we get into the later parts of Zechariah.

VISION 2 FOUR HORNS AND FOUR SMITHS

The second vision begins at verse 18 after the words of comfort which end the first vision. I believe with all my heart that the 'good and comfortable words' apply to the whole nation of Israel, from the day they were uttered to the very last day of that nation's history on earth, and have a special reference to the second coming of Christ. So, let us begin the vision:

> And I lifted up mine eyes, and saw, and behold four horns.

Let me stress again that a man never abdicates his mental faculties when he is dealing with the things of God. Any doctrine which teaches such abdication is, in my opinion, absolutely abhorrent to Scripture. To assert that, My spirit prays but my mind is infertile ... may be **thought** to come from Corinthians, but it is a bad translation or interpretation to think that your mind can go absolutely blank and your spirit, unknown to you, is saying things which you are not aware of. Such a doctrine is very dangerous because the mind (Let this mind be in you that was in Christ Jesus) is never subject to this sort of pagan drunkenness. Even if we are in ecstasy, we are perfectly aware of what we think. And so the words, I lifted up mine eyes and I saw and behold, is a kind of emphasis on the prophet's awareness of what is going on.

He saw four horns which, in Scripture, stand for strength and pride in the natural sense. 'Lifting up your horn on high' comes in the Psalms time and time again, but the word often means strong Gentile powers such as Babylon or Assyria. You get this in Daniel 7 verse 7:

> After this I saw in the night visions, and behold a fourth beast, terrible and powerful, and strong exceedingly; and it had great iron teeth: it devoured and brake in pieces, and stamped the residue with his feet: and it was diverse from all the beasts that were before it; and it had ten horns.

And that is the point! So in verse 19:

> And I said unto the angel that talked with me, What be these? And he answered me, These are the horns which have scattered Judah, Israel, and Jerusalem.

Verses 18 and 19 require very careful examination. In Scripture the number four stands for universality, such as the four corners of the earth, the four seasons, the four winds, the four Gospels, or the four horsemen and so on. Universality is hinted at here, and in a sense, the two verses include all the universal persecution of the Jews. They were persecuted by the Egyptians, by the Philistines, by Moab, and especially by the Assyrians who took all the ten tribes into captivity in 721 BC. However, Judah remained still, as a lamp of God in Jerusalem; and the Glory of God was still in Jerusalem with kings like Hezekiah and Josiah. So the four horns can stand for the persecution of the Jews, whether universal or from any quarter.

Now in chapter 1 Zechariah refers to the former prophets; so what do the former prophets say about the horns? The former prophets are more specific and what they say is especially concentrated in the Book of Daniel. This states that the chief scatterers and the chief persecutors of this nation of Israel are Babylon, the Medo-Persian empire, Greece, and a great unnamed power - four in all. There are the four horns! Some Bible students say that Greece had not risen by then, but Greece is mentioned in Daniel 8; Greece was on the horizon as the rising power, and Daniel refers to the sons of Greece.

And a great unnamed power! Again you get this in

Daniel 2 in the great statue that Nebuchadnezzar dreamed about. He saw a head of gold, a breast and shoulders of silver, a belly of brass, and legs of iron. And God enabled Daniel to interpret the king's dream and to tell him that **he** was the head of gold, and after him would follow an inferior kingdom, the Medo-Persian empire, which would be followed by a third kingdom, the Grecian empire, and after that would follow a terrible kingdom which would divide into two and have feet of iron and clay. So we have it explained to us by the former prophets: all these empires scattered Israel.

Notice the past tense! When Scripture speaks in prophetic terms it uses the preterite, the past tense; it's happened already! For instance, in Isaiah 53 verse 5:

> But he was wounded for our transgressions, he was bruised for our iniquities: the chastisement of our peace was upon him;

All this is in the past tense although seven hundred years had to pass before the prophecy took place. Prophecy is complete; it sees the whole thing from God's point of view. So we do not have to worry about the past tense 'have scattered' Israel, while two of the kingdoms which would scatter Israel were yet to come.

The question immediately comes to mind as to what comfort can arise from the vision of four empires scattering Israel? What comfort can there be for the nation of Israel, this little remnant listening to the prophecy? Just this! look at Psalm 129 verses 2 and 3:

> Many a time have they afflicted me from my youth up: yet they have not prevailed against me.
> The plowers plowed upon my back; they made long their furrows.

This is a psalm of ascents; the whole nation sang this psalm going up to Jerusalem. Here is the tragic history of Israel being sung in a dirge: Ever since I became a nation

I have been afflicted; the plowers have made terrible wounds on the people of Israel, on the nation of Israel; yet they have not prevailed against it! That sums up the whole tragic history of Israel which has been attacked and persecuted from the very day it was born. It was so too with Christ, the last Israelite, the quintessence of all that Israel ever meant to God, the Elect of God; they plowed upon His back and they afflicted Him from the day He was born, and yet they did **not** prevail against Him. That is the comfort to a suffering nation! My history, the Israelite is saying, is studded with persecution, bitterness, wounds, and sorrow, and yet (a shout of triumph) they have not prevailed against me.

So to this remnant trying to build walls, and being attacked on every side (if you read Nehemiah and Ezra) - to this little nation in distress and trouble, the hope and comfort to sustain them as they came back from Babylon was: They have not prevailed against me. But remember, we are trying to bring hope not only to this remnant of Zechariah's time, but to this people all through its history and to this people today; this prophecy is relevant today! Look at Jeremiah 30 verse 11:

> For I am with thee, saith the Lord, to save thee: for I will make a full end of all the nations whither I have **scattered** thee, (same word - the horns are scattering this people) but I will not make a full end of thee; but I will correct thee with judgment, and will in no wise leave thee unpunished.

So it was a great comfort to these people as they looked to a very uncertain future. Would the race be entirely wiped out and dispersed and lost for ever? No, indeed! They were being punished and God would continue to punish them; the former prophets had said so; it was in their very song of ascents. Yet, they would not be entirely wiped out.

It was true then and it gave great comfort. It was also true of the eighteen hundred years' span from AD 70 in which the Jew has been dispersed world-wide. This has only just come to an end; the Jew has gone through terrible trouble and awful persecution, yet has survived.

The cruelty and suffering is quite incredible but we are so used to it that we almost ignore it. When one reads of Jewish sufferings up to AD 1900, and the Czardom pogroms and so on, one can hardly believe that they are still alive today. They used to burn whole villages of Jews on the gallows and the cruelties were appalling. How astonishing that they have now become a nation again with all the trappings of state. No one would have believed it a hundred years ago. Yet it is God who has done this and not the Jews themselves. They shall not prevail against me! And, if it was true in that long span it is true today. There is the state of Israel; she is surrounded by enemies and I am not defending her, for she is guilty of many things. But with God it is never a question of favouritism; it is the faithfulness of God that is all-important and while Israel will not go unpunished, neither will she be prevailed against in a total and final sense.

You know, Hitler spoke of the final solution to the Jewish problem and he put to death nearly six million Jews. He wiped out the Jewish communities in Germany, Poland, Bulgaria, and eastern Europe and destroyed the culture of European Jewry everywhere he went. But, says Scripture, another is going to come and offer another final solution to the Jewish problem; and this one will make Hitler look like a kindly, benign old gentleman! The Scripture refers to this time in Jeremiah 30 verse 7:

> Alas! for that day is great, so that none is like it: it is even the time of Jacob's trouble; but he shall be saved out of it.

So the statement in Psalm 129 'they have not prevailed against me' which was true of all their history until Christ, has been true throughout the great dispersion, including the crimes of Hitler, until this very day. It is also going to be true of The Beast, the Man of Sin, the

Idol Shepherd (these are various names for this great dictator) who is going to come and enter into a covenant with the Jews, and then seek to destroy them entirely. When **he** attacks will he prevail? No! he will not prevail because Israel is indestructible; she is a bush that burns but is never consumed.

All this is scriptural. God's faithfulness and God's promises cannot be shaken by Hitlers, or even ultimately by the Man of Sin, the Antichrist, The Beast, the Little Horn! Oh yes, there will be terrible persecution, and there will be a holocaust, but Psalm 129 will still be true. This is simply because God is not going to let His promises to Abraham, and His promises to all the great prophets be defeated by the wiles and wills of evil men; or be frustrated by the disobedience and wickedness of Israel herself. God **will** fulfil His promises and, as He says so emphatically in Ezekiel: Not for your sake Israel, but for my Holy Name's sake; I am going to be magnified in the earth! One day people are going to sit down and say, What fools we were not to believe the Scripture - it was all there and we left the Bible unopened; or, We went to church but we never read the Old Testament because it was uninteresting.

But I say again, it is not favouritism; election is not selection! election is everything to do with the purposes of God and nothing to do with the person elected. God can elect whom He likes. No merit is involved or implied in the person elected. But with selection, merit is implied. If you happen to be on a selection committee you will try to pick the best person; but God does not pick the best! He picks whom He wills to do His purposes and the person chosen might even be the worst. In fact in Israel's case He tells them in no uncertain terms: You are the most stubborn lot of people I have ever met; you are a thorn bush! So we are not to worship the Jew; rather we must worship or admire God's purposes for him.

The words, Judah, Israel, and Jerusalem, in verse 19 are used as an all-inclusive term because at that time the ten tribes had gone into Assyria and only a few from

Judah had come back to Jerusalem from Babylon; the many had been left behind. So the term is totally inclusive; the whole Jewish nation is scattered but God is going to do a great thing for them. They were scattered ... so that no man did lift up his head.

Verse 21 is another commentary on Jewish existence. They have lived for literally thousands of years in a state of nightmare, despised, degraded, dismissed as nothing, disliked 'so that no man did lift up his head'. And generally speaking, that is true and that has been the fate of the Jew for eighteen centuries in Christendom, and in Moslem and other countries. You know, the Jew does not walk proudly down the street as you do! he is just very discerning. If he has wealth he keeps it to himself; but he does not lift up his head. They have suffered indeed, and yet, they have not been prevailed against even unto this very day!

Who is the great unnamed horn or persecutor or power in the earth? Of course we all think we know (and I think that I know) though it is wrong to be too dogmatic in prophecy which is not specific. Is it Rome? for Rome was indeed the fourth great empire that followed Babylon, Medo-Persia, and Greece.

Rome came with its great discipline, its mighty armies and organisation and swept away Greece and took over the whole of the empires of these former powers. Rome was an enormous ruthless power and, this is the extraordinary thing: Rome has never really died! It collapsed in the West in AD 476, but in AD 395 Rome was divided and half of it put under Constantinople, which was named after Constantine the first Christian emperor of Rome. So the twin focal centres were Rome as the Western Empire and Constantinople as the Empire in the East. Though Rome fell before Alaric the Visigoth in AD 410 and the Western Empire finally collapsed in AD 476, the Eastern Empire went on until AD 1453 when it was conquered by Mehmed II and the Turkish Empire began. Rome therefore had two legs: just as Daniel had said! and although the western leg fell, Rome itself survived in so many ways. The survival was, and is, quite extraordinary and should be carefully noted.

It survived in the administration of the Roman Catholic Church. When Rome fell in the West the Church, which to some degree was respected by the Vandals, Goths, and Huns, kept the whole hierarchical system going. They kept the names used by the Roman governments, so although from a secular viewpoint Rome died, she went on inside the Roman Catholic Church. Then too, the ecclesiastical provinces were generally identified with old Roman states.

Rome survived in the capital city, and it survived in language. The Roman language was Latin, and Latin became the universal language of the Roman Catholic Church until only a few years ago. Mass was always said in Latin. Most of the workers in the Roman Catholic Church and in hierarchical circles used that language, and Popes still give sermons in the language of the old Roman empire. The very word Pontiff is a Roman expression and not a religious one. The term Cardinal (meaning hinge) is also Roman.

It also survived in Law and today our law is full of latin 'tags' and much of our Common Law is based on Roman Law, as is Scottish and German Law. It survives in medicine and botany. You cannot get a plain answer from a botanist or a doctor for example; they use Roman words! It has survived in military academies and in military systems. The very names captain, major, general, infantry, artillery, cavalry, regiment, and army are taken from the terminology of the Roman army, and of course the word Caesar has survived as Czar and as Kaiser. Importantly, Rome has survived in the sense that, as in her day, a man equals 'a citizen', whose duty is to the State! You live for the state and the state has total control over you. This was the Roman ideal and this is going on in many countries today. There is centralisation, discipline, and obedience, and so Rome lives on.

In 1000 BC the city of Rome was but a village; in AD 30 a million people lived in the city; in the Middle Ages it was a small town and today it has several millions. So the fourth empire such as we talk about here is not dead, and even in the Common Market today we have a Treaty of Rome! All I am saying is that we are trying to identify the great unnamed horn that persecuted the Jew and will again persecute the Jew, and it is thought by many prophetic students, that out of the resurgence of Rome will come another little horn, the Antichrist, who will make a covenant with the Jew, and then will set out to destroy him.

Rome is identified in the Bible with the spirit of Babylon which, in Scripture, is always regarded as the great apostasy against God, as in Nimrod the mighty hunter before the Lord. Babylon is the great enemy of God, and all apostasy is summed up in that word Babylon! If you read 1 Peter, it would appear that the epistle is written to those in Babylon; but it is also thought to be a coded word for Rome. In any case, apostate Rome has the spirit of Babylon which is anti-Christ and anti-God. So we end the vision with verses 20 and 21:

> And the Lord showed me four smiths.
> Then said I, What come these to do? And he spake, saying, These are the horns that scattered Judah, so that no man did lift up his head: but these are come to fray them, to cast down the horns of the nations, which lifted up their horn against the land of Judah to scatter it.

Now who are the four smiths? Other Bible versions use the term four craftsmen, or four carpenters. The Hebrew word is Karosh, meaning a man with tools. In modern Hebrew the word Beit Karoshet means a factory. So who are the craftsmen that cut down the horns that scatter the nation of Israel? And we may note that each horn has its own way of scattering or persecuting Israel. Well, as a matter of fact, they are themselves!

There was Babylon; it was cut down by Medo-Persia. There was Medo-Persia; and it was overwhelmed by Greece. There was Greece; and it was shattered by Rome.

And then you get this two-legged unnamed monster; and who is that to be destroyed by? Now refer back to Daniel 7 verses 7 to 14:

> After this I saw in the night visions, and behold a fourth beast, terrible and powerful, and strong exceedingly; and it had great iron teeth: it devoured and brake in pieces, and stamped the residue with his feet: and it was diverse from all the beasts that were before it; (is this Rome?) and it had ten horns.
> I considered the horns, and, behold, there came up among them another horn, a little one, (here is your Beast, your Man of Sin, your Antichrist) before which three of the first horns were plucked up by the roots: and, behold, in this horn were eyes like the eyes of a man, and a mouth speaking great things.
> I beheld till thrones were placed, and one that was ancient of days did sit: his raiment was white as snow, and the hair of his head like pure wool; his throne was fiery flames, and the wheels thereof burning fire.
> A fiery stream issued and came forth from before him: thousand thousands ministered unto him, and ten thousand times ten thousand stood before him: the judgment was set, and the books were opened.
> I beheld at that time because of the voice of the great words which the horn spake; I beheld even till the beast was slain, and his body destroyed, and he was given to be burned with fire.
> And as for the rest of the beasts, their dominion was taken away: yet their lives were prolonged for a season and a time.
> I saw in the night visions, and, behold, there came with the clouds of heaven one like unto a son of man, and he came even to the ancient of days, and they brought him near before him.
> And there was given him dominion, and glory, and a kingdom, that all the peoples, nations, and languages should serve him: his dominion is an everlasting dominion, which shall not pass away, and his kingdom

that which shall not be destroyed.

There it is! Babylon was destroyed by Medo-Persia which in turn was destroyed by Greece, and Greece was destroyed by Rome, but Rome did not die. Rome could well be resuscitated and Rome will be destroyed by One like unto the Son of Man who shall come before the Ancient of Days and be given universal dominion. That, in picture language, sums up what lies before us and it is essentially connected with the fate of Israel. Recall also in Daniel 2 the great image of gold, silver, brass, and iron which was destroyed by a great stone cut out without hands (not a man-made thing) which smashed its feet and ground it to powder, and the stone filled the whole earth. This stone, says Scripture, is the Christ of God, the Stone that the builders rejected.

But think of today; the smiths are still at work, you know. Who put the Jews to death nearly fifty years ago? Hitler! And who destoyed Hitler? It was Russia. And who is going to destroy Russia? You see, God is at work! God is at work in the ordinary workings of everyday history. The Jew is indestructible; those who deliberately persecute him - now do not get a guilt complex; it does not mean that you have got to go about loving and patting every Jew on the back because he is special, he is not! quite often he is not at all nice - but those who set out on an anti-semitic course to destroy Israel per se, will themselves be destroyed.

I tell you this: many people bemoan the fate of Poland today; I do not! I am sick to death with Lech Walesa and Poland! and for this reason: until 1939 the most anti-semitic country in the world was Poland! A Jew who passed a Roman Catholic church in Warsaw and didn't raise his hat to 'The Host' (I have this information from men who lived and worked in Warsaw) would be kicked into the gutter! So, when I reflect on the so-called heartbreak over Poland I look to the immediate past history and say (though I do not rejoice in it): the country which treated the Jewish people in peace time **worse** than Germany was

Poland! Can you wonder that Begin was so furious and hateful of Gentile nations? He was brought up in Poland. His master was Jabotinsky, the man who advocated violence in the Zionist movement; and where was he born? In Poland.

So there are wheels within wheels, Brethren!

3 VISION 3 A MAN WITH A MEASURING LINE

Our third vision begins at verse 1 of chapter 2 and it starts off with the same stress on total cognition:

> And I lifted up mine eyes, and saw, and behold a man with a measuring line in his hand.

Who is this man? Now many critical scholars who hold a different point of view think that it is simply a figure in a story of no particular value. They believe that the Old Testament is an anachronism and that these things were written just for the times and have no significance for us: they forget Luther had said that this Book was the quintessence of prophecy. They say that it is just like 'a householder' in parables told by our Lord, where the character is simply part of the teaching. But in this prophecy you cannot say that, not if the prophecy is to hold together consistently.

In chapter 1 Zechariah says he saw a man riding upon a red horse: and who was that man? He was the Malach Jehovah; He was the angel of the Lord; He was **The Man** on a red horse. And again, in Ezekiel 40 'a man' appears, and in chapters 40 to 48 this man leads the prophet around the glorious Temple of God; building it and giving instructions; 'a man with a measuring line'. Later on in Zechariah God, through the mouth of the prophet, refers to 'the Man who is my Fellow' which is a most startling statement: God is speaking to a Man who is not His Servant, but His Equal! and of course the other prophets take up the same theme. Isaiah says: A man shall be a hiding place and a covert from the wind and the storm. A man! The prophecy does not say God, but a man! but He must have God-like properties if He can be a hiding place from the storm must He not?

And what do we get in the New Testament? Well - Jesus. There is one Mediator between God and man, **The Man** Christ Jesus. And we have Pilate bringing out our Lord after those mysterious interrogations and what does he say? Behold, the man! You know, these words are perhaps the most pregnant words in history. You also hear the Ethiopian eunuch asking Philip: Who is the prophet talking about - himself? this man or some other man? And beginning at the same Scripture Philip preaches unto him Jesus! (Isaiah 53 and Acts 8 verses 28 to 35).

You see, it depends **how** you come to Scripture. If you come to it cynically and regard it simply as a bit of history, then you do not perceive the truth. But if you come to Scripture as a consistent whole, with the belief that the prophets, although separated from each other by centuries, were all moved by the Holy Ghost, then it all makes sense; that same theme: the Glory of God and the purposes of God and the salvation in Christ; the first Coming and the second Coming of Christ; it all makes total, logical, and mental sense as well as spiritual sense. And so to verses 2 to 4:

> Then said I, Whither goest thou? And he said unto me, To measure Jerusalem, to see what is the breadth thereof, and what is the length thereof.
> And, behold, the angel that talked with me went forth, and another angel went out to meet him,
> And said unto him, Run, speak to this young man, saying, Jerusalem shall be inhabited as villages without walls, by reason of the multitude of men and cattle therein.

Verse 3 is interesting. The angel that talked in Zechariah (his teaching angel) left him and ran forward. He was met by another angel bearing a message sent by The Man. The teaching angel was told to run to Zechariah and comfort him about the terrible things that were to come on Israel.

These terrible happenings are best summed up by Hosea. All we normally remember about Hosea is that he married, then divorced, then remarried, then divorced and all the rest of it! Hosea is called the prophet of love and we all get sentimental over Hosea marrying Lo-ruhamah; but what does he say in Hosea 3 verse 4?

> For the children of Israel shall abide many days without king, and without prince, and without sacrifice, and without pillar (a Temple), and without ephod or teraphim.

This means a long, long period of being without any of their precious God-given avenues to grace. In other words, exile! and only after this, in Hosea 3 verse 5:

> Afterward shall the children of Israel return, and seek the Lord their God, and David their king (this was long after David); and shall come with fear unto the Lord and to his goodness in the latter days.

So the teaching angel was told to say to Zechariah: In spite of all the dreadful things that are going to come on Israel Jerusalem will yet again be crowded with men and cattle; you are going to build in the suburbs, on the hills, on the Mount of Olives, and Jerusalem will be as villages without walls!

How hard it must have been for the little remnant to believe that Jerusalem would once again be overcrowded. The prophecy took place to some degree, for Herod's Jerusalem was being extended right up to the time of Christ. But that was only a partial fulfilment of the prophecy, for Zechariah verse 5 says:

> For I, saith the Lord, will be unto her a wall of fire round about, and I will be the glory in the midst of her.

Remember, this is still the man with the measuring line

speaking, so you have an identity between God and him; you have an identity between the angel of the Lord and the Lord Himself, or between Christ and God; they are interchangeable; they both say the same thing; it is coming from the same Source. Jerusalem will overflow with people and God's wall of fire will protect the people in their day of tribulation. This will be a far greater protection than walls of stone; a greater protection than even Elisha had with the chariots of God and angels all around him at Dothan.

And God (or the angel of the Lord) is going to come back and be 'the glory' in the midst of Israel. Refer to Ezekiel 11 verses 22 and 23:

> Then did the cherubim lift up their wings, and the wheels were beside them; and **the glory** of the God of Israel was over them above.
> And the glory of the Lord went up from the midst of the city, and stood upon the mountain which is on the east side of the city.

We are talking here about 'the glory of Israel' leaving Jerusalem; the time when Israel had so rebelled against God that His glory left them, and on that very day the Times of the Gentiles began. There was no glory; Ichabod! for the ark of the covenant had gone. And when Christ, who was the true Glory of God came to the second Temple, He was not received; He was rejected and crucified but, and this is the great promise in verse 5: I am coming back, and I will once again be The Glory in the midst of Israel.

Now again, has that ever taken place? Has it? No! So when is it going to take place? Now if you are going to take Scripture seriously, look at Isaiah 60 verse 19:

> The sun shall be no more thy light by day; neither for brightness shall the moon give light unto thee: but the Lord shall be unto thee an everlasting light, and thy God thy **glory.**

So what am I saying? God makes promises here: He is going to make Jerusalem absolutely prolific; He is going to defend Jerusalem; He is going to be a wall of fire around the city; He is going to be the Glory of Israel once again; He is going to live in the midst - 'thy God, thy glory'. But it has never happened yet.

Now I must break off here and say that you **can** accept some of these prophecies as referring even now to the Church, to believers, and to God's people, because Scripture has many levels of meaning for those who believe. We who have Christ, can say that the secret of life is 'Christ in you, the hope of glory'; 'in whom believing, ye rejoice with joy unspeakable and full of glory'. This is true for the Christian believer; it is true that 'our life is hid with Christ in God'; and that 'the angels of the Lord encamp around those who trust Him'. But in verse 5 of Zechariah, it is **Israel** that is primarily in view!

Has it ever happened like this? Has God ever surrounded Jerusalem with a wall of fire for her protection; has God ever dwelt in the midst of the Jews in Jerusalem as the supreme Glory? And the answer is No! never since the dedication of Solomon's Temple. Recall what happened then. The ceremony was going on; the priests were inside the Temple and suddenly, the Temple was filled with the Shekinah Glory. The Hebrew word Shaken means a neighbour. God was so close that He was in truth a Neighbour, sitting next to them and they were forced out of the Temple because the Glory of God filled it and they were amazed and it was glorious! But the Presence, the Glory! it has never happened like that since. But it **will** happen when Jesus comes again, this same Jesus - 'every eye shall see Him and all flesh shall see it together'. Read Isaiah 4 verses 4 and 5:

> When the Lord shall have washed away the filth of the daughters of Zion, and shall have purged the blood of Jerusalem from the midst thereof, by the spirit of judgment, and by the spirit of burning.

> And the Lord will create over the whole habitation of mount Zion, and over her assemblies, a cloud and smoke by day, and the shining of a flaming fire by night: for over all **the glory** shall be spread a canopy.

Isn't that marvellous? And that, my dear friends, is going to happen. The Glory of Christ is once again going to be experienced by the race that rejected Him. It is not going to be frustrated, says St Paul in Romans 11, by Israel's hardness of heart. But they do not believe, you say; they hate the Christ. But I say that they are deeply perturbed by the Christ! The mysterious Man from Nazareth, say the rabbis. They are disturbed all the time by the Christ and God's plans will not be frustrated by their hardness of heart, or by the ungodliness or anti-semitism or anything else of the Nations. Paul says this in Romans 15 verse 8:

> For I say that Christ hath been made a minister of the circumcision (He came especially to the Jews) for the truth of God, that he might confirm the promises given unto the fathers,

Note that carefully. He did not come to transfer the promises to the Church. He came to confirm the promises given by God unto the Fathers. Jesus Christ had two vocations: firstly He came as the promised Messiah to Israel; but He came also as the One in whom all the nations of the earth would be blessed, in accordance with the promises to Abraham. Paul, that great rabbi, says it all so clearly: that He came for the Truth of God and to **confirm** those promises, not to abolish them.

May I recall what I said in the introduction. It makes nonsense of the text to believe that the promises made to the fathers do not belong to the Jews today. I contend that it is wrong to hand the curses to the Jews and for us to take over the promises. It simply does not make sense of the text to spiritualise it like that. But let us continue with verses 6 and 7 which is an appeal to the Jews still in Babylon to flee from that land:

> Ho, ho, flee from the land of the north, saith the Lord: for I have spread you abroad as the four winds of the heaven, saith the Lord.
> Ho Zion, escape, thou that dwellest with the daughter of Babylon.

This was a timely reminder to the several hundreds of thousands of Jews left behind to get out of Babylon, for there had been two serious rebellions in which the Jews had suffered very much. Both rebellions had been put down by King Darius.

We now come to five very important verses about the appearance of Christ and about the Last Day, and I suggest to you that verses 8 to 12 can be understood only in the light of the doctrine of the Trinity; the Father, Son, and Holy Ghost. It is no wonder that the rabbis stumble over these verses. They cannot understand the way the pronouns get mixed up. He becomes Me and I becomes He, and this interchange of pronouns is very puzzling unless understood in the light of the Trinity. Collectively the verses describe the Person of the Messiah and the course of the events of the Last Day. We will look at the verses in turn starting with verse 8:

> For thus saith the Lord of hosts: After glory (that is, the return of Christ when the Glory comes back to Israel) hath he sent me unto the nations which spoiled you: for he that toucheth you toucheth the apple of his eye.

The Jew is so precious to God because of His covenant to Abraham, that if you touch the Jew you are touching (damaging) your own eye! The words 'hath he sent me' were spoken by our Lord in Nazareth in: The Spirit of the Lord is upon me, because he anointed me (sent me) to preach good tidings to the poor; he hath sent me to proclaim ... (Luke 4 verse 18). In this passage Jesus is being sent. What is extraordinary is that the rabbis themselves recognise that He is sending Himself in a sense! He is sending the Messiah, He is sending His Own, He is sending Himself; Jehovah is sending Jehovah unto the nations which spoiled Israel. And verse 9:

> For, behold, (this is the One who is sent) I will shake mine hand over them, and they shall be a spoil to those that served them: and ye shall know that the Lord of hosts hath sent me.

In other words, the One who is sent has the power of God to punish. He is going to shake His hand in judgment over the nations of the earth and He says: When I judge the nations, you Jews who have been so obdurate and unbelieving in rejecting me shall know that the Lord of Hosts has sent me! They will know **that** in the day Christ comes and fights for Jerusalem. Let us look forward for a moment to the last chapter of Zechariah and verses 3 and 4:

> Then shall the Lord go forth, and fight against those nations, as when he fought in the day of battle.
> And his feet shall stand in that day upon the mount of Olives, which is before Jerusalem on the east, and the mount of Olives shall cleave in the midst thereof ...

Are you getting the picture now of those important words 'After glory' in verse 8? When Christ has come, when Christ returns He is going to be sent to the nations to bring forth judgment upon them, to shake His hand over them: Behold, I will shake my hand over them in punishment and you shall know that day that the Lord of Hosts has sent me! He comes and fights for Jerusalem; it is God who is fighting for Jerusalem; it is Christ who is coming back to the mount of Olives, this same Jesus, and they are identified as one and the same; it is the Messiah, and so the great call in verse 10:

> Sing and rejoice, O daughter of Zion: for, lo, I come, and I will dwell in the midst of thee, saith the Lord.

This is being addressed to Jews and remember, it is still the angel of the Lord who is speaking. This so confuses the rabbis that they have invented a Ben Yusef (a suffering Messiah) and a Ben David (a reigning Messiah); they cannot make head nor tail of it! How is this Man going to be born in Bethlehem as a baby, and how is this Man nevertheless going to rule with a sceptre? So they say, Well, the Messiah must have two aspects - Ben Yusef a suffering one like Joseph, and Ben David a reigning one like King David. But we know that all these facets are wrapped up in one Person; The Man Christ Jesus who came in humility, and suffered and died on the cross, and rose again, and as His angels told the disciples on the Mount of Olives, This same Jesus shall so come again in like manner as ye have seen Him go. And in verse 11:

> And many nations shall join themselves to the Lord in that day, and shall be my people: and I will dwell in the midst of thee, and thou shalt know that the Lord of hosts hath sent me unto thee.

When He comes to save the Jews many nations shall join themselves to the Lord in that day. The Goyim you see, are being included with the remnant that is going to receive the Messiah; those who belong to the Nations but who turn to the Lord. Through the prophet the Lord is saying: You did not know me when I came the first time but you **shall** know me in that day! When I come, when I shake my hand over the nations, and when I dwell in the midst of you, and when nations come unto me you shall know! And of course we are told by Zechariah and by Revelation that the Jews will mourn when they see Him and they will say, This is our God - we have waited long. And they will wail because of Him; because they have been so obdurate down the ages and refused to recognise Him.

Now I say this to you very honestly. If this is not the true interpretation of Zechariah then I cannot see any other meaning (and I have read much) to fit these great words; I really cannot. All the fiddling and trivial explanations have nothing to do with the tremendous words of the prophet. To read them and not to see the import as I have explained to you is, I think, a total waste of time. If the whole prophecy is spiritualised and if He is not going to come and dwell in the midst; if He is not going to fight for them, and be a wall of fire; if He is not going to be the Glory and if nations are not going to come to Him; then why spend our time on it? And of course, that is the reason why many people refuse to bother with it; they refuse because they do not believe it and yet, look at how verse 12 spells out the Last Day:

> And the Lord shall inherit Judah as his portion in the holy land, and shall yet choose Jerusalem.

Could this be more specific? Can you spiritualise this and say that it means something else? It says that the Lord shall inherit Judah in ... where? in Great Britain? No, in the Holy Land; the Lord shall yet choose Jerusalem! So emphatic is all this, and so aware is the prophet (through the angel who spoke with him) of the unbelief that is going to be spread throughout the world, that he says in verse 13:

> Be silent, (the Hebrew is Sheket, Be quiet) all flesh, before the Lord: for he is waked up out of his holy habitation.

In other words, God is starting to move in the history of His people again, and we can hear the trample of His feet. You read this in the newspapers: Israel, Syria, Egypt, Lebanon ... you can hear the mighty God on the march again!

If you do not believe it and you do not believe this prophecy then what a mighty coincidence is taking place today! And what a miraculous deliverance there has been of this people right down the ages and what a strange thing it is that we are reaching a time in history when everything is ripe for the fulfilment of this very prophecy! The threat of nuclear war, pollution, famine, and every other thing that the Scripture speaks about is a sign of the end; and our God is marching on.

Quiet! says the prophet, Listen, you unbelievers, you doubters, you people who sit in judgment on my word ...

How tiresome these little academic German professors and their English counterparts and their copiers can be! They do not take the Word of God seriously. Never forget that our Lord endorsed this prophet Zechariah when He rode into Jerusalem - riding on an ass and on a colt the foal of an ass; and where does that come from? from Zechariah chapter 9 verse 9, the part critics reject!

Be still! I ask you to consider these thoughts and to look at history in a new light; for our God does indeed reign and is reigning today.

4 VISION 4 TAKE AWAY THE FILTHY GARMENTS

Now we have been weighing the good and comfortable words that God spoke in the first vision concerning the return of Israel to her own land, and the return of the Glory that had departed in 586 BC and had never come back. We have thought about the Times of the Gentiles which began when the Glory departed. We have considered in vision 2 the destruction of Israel's persecutors, those four horns who have lacerated God's people far beyond anything He wanted. We have pondered on the fourth horn which could (but only by implication in Revelation) be named as Rome, and that there can be room for the views of certain expositors who believe, for example, that a revived Babylon could be the fourth horn - though I do not favour it.

We have stressed that the Jew in himself is not special; that his preservation throughout the ages is by the grace of God alone and because God is faithful to His promises made to the Fathers. We are aware that there are Jews today, who in their arrogance say that they stand by the grave of their persecutors because of some particular virtue in themselves. They are wrong! for it is the physical return **and** the spiritual regeneration that is stressed in vision 4, and I want to dwell a little on this twin aspect of the redemption of the Jew.

You know, the one aspect without the other is unthinkable. If Israel is going to come back and take her place, she has got to be spiritually renewed. Zechariah is always quoting the former prophets and what is it they say? They all look forward to a day of national repentance, to a day of spiritual rebirth, and to a new covenant. Refer to Jeremiah where he says that the law in the future, the new covenant, will not be written on tables of stone, but 'on the fleshly tables of your heart'. It will be an interior spiritual regeneration, and not just a religious observance of outward rules. And Hosea, who writes very lovingly (and so he should because his wife left him four times and it affects the way a man writes you know!) says in chapter 14 verses 1, 2 and 4:

> O Israel, return unto the Lord thy God; for thou hast fallen by thine iniquity.
> Take with you words, and return unto the Lord: say unto him, Take away all iniquity, and accept that which is good: so will we render as bullocks the offering of our lips.
> I will heal their backsliding, I will love them freely: for mine anger is turned away from him.

So the prophets all look forward to **the** great day of Atonement. You know, Israel has always had an annual day of atonement when the sins of the nation were, for a year, covered (Kippur means 'to cover'). But the prophets looked forward to a great and **final** Yom Kippur; to the complete forgiveness of sins; for chapter 3 verse 9 of Zechariah says, And I will remove the iniquity of that land in one day. Note that statement: in one day! a great national Yom Kippur when all Israel shall be saved, says Romans 11 verses 25 to 27:

> For I would not, brethren, have you ignorant of this mystery, lest ye be wise in your own conceits, that a hardening in part hath befallen Israel, until the fulness of the Gentiles be come in;
> And so all Israel shall be saved: even as it is written, There shall come out of Zion the Deliverer; he shall turn away ungodliness from Jacob:
> And this is my covenant unto them, when I shall take away their sins.

Paul is talking about Israel in verse 25 and as Professor

F.F. Bruce very rightly says, verse 26 **must** refer to physical Israel in the context; it cannot be spiritualised to mean the Church of God; Bruce is very strong on that. So all Israel shall be saved. But then, the horrendousness of sin immediately comes to mind!

Do you ever doubt your own salvation? Do you ever say, Is my salvation in jeopardy? Of course you do and so do I. In a sense we are wise so to doubt. When I think of God forgiving me, I sometimes cannot believe it. It is all right being glib and being triumphal; the evangelical often goes around shouting with total assurance, but sometimes he is covering a doubt in his heart and thinking, Can God really forgive me and all my sins? Who knows a man save the spirit of man? And that is here; it is writ large here! Israel forgiven? yet so guilty and so stained with the blood of her prophets? Just look at Matthew 23 verse 35:

> That upon you may come all the righteous blood shed on the earth, from the blood of Abel the righteous unto the blood of Zachariah son of Barachiah, whom ye slew between the sanctuary and the altar.

Yes, so stained with the blood of her prophets; with rebellion, disobedience, and unbelief which culminated in what? the murder of God's righteous Servant! I am quoting the Old Testament; I am quoting Isaiah 53. In other words, Israel's guilt in slaying God's righteous Servant had been prophesied long before the event.

It was a foregone conclusion that when God's totally righteous Servant came, Israel would do to Him as she had done to all the prophets: she had dismissed them, thrown them down into pits, sent them off into exile, told them to shut up and speak to themselves, and had slain them before the altar. Our Lord said, You just fill up the sins of your fathers. So remember, the Old Testament can interpret its own message. How then can Israel be pardoned? The question is put in all its simplicity in Jeremiah 3 verses 17 and 18:

> At that time they shall call Jerusalem the throne of the Lord; and all the nations shall be gathered unto it, to the name of the Lord, to Jerusalem: neither shall they walk any more after the stubbornness of their evil heart.
> In those days the house of Judah shall walk with the house of Israel, and they shall come together out of the land of the north to the land that I gave for an inheritance unto your fathers.

Notice how similar this message is to that of Zechariah; how totally consistent the Bible is as it preaches this message of return and recovery. Notice also how there can be no possible doubt that the land is Palestine. But now comes that questioning doubt in Jeremiah 3 verse 19;

> But I said, How shall I put thee among the children, and give thee a pleasant land, a goodly heritage of the hosts of the nations?

Indeed, how on earth is this possible? How can God put Israel among the children of a pleasant land? She is wicked, polluted, she is filthy, she is utterly defiant of God. How can He do it? and the answer comes in the continuation of verse 19:

> and I said, Ye shall call me My father; and shall not turn away from following me.

Note the imperative, Ye shall call me ... shall not turn away. Israel will be pardoned for there WILL BE a spiritual regeneration and there WILL BE a change of heart; and God says, I will be able to plant you back again into your land. And in this fourth vision of Zechariah we see something of 'how' it will be done. Let us begin at verse 1 of chapter 3:

> And he shewed me Joshua the high priest standing before the angel of the Lord, and Satan standing at his

> right hand to be his adversary.

The Lord here is Jehovah, The Name; The Name above every name, which if blasphemed was punishable by death. The Old Testament is quite clear about this. Why was Christ put to death? because He took the name of Jehovah when asked by the high priest, Art thou the son of the Blessed, The Name? and the high priest tore his robe at Christ's answer 'I am' and said: How this man blasphemeth!

Joshua is standing before a judgment seat, for the phrase 'stand before' has a judicial meaning in the Bible. But here, Joshua is standing before the angel of Jehovah as Ha Cohen Hagadol, as the High Priest of Israel; as the representative of the nation. It is Israel that is on trial in this vision, and one man stands before the angel of the Lord to await the judgment. He is dressed in filthy clothes; totally filthy clothes, and Satan, which in Scripture means The Adversary, is standing at his right hand. How strange it is that Satan has persuaded us to make fun of him, and so reduce his stature! But here, the very person who caused Israel to sin is now standing at her right hand ready to say to God, You see! this chosen nation of yours, this elect; she is filthy, disobedient, and totally unworthy! Let us look at Psalm 109 verses 6 and 7 just to confirm this:

> Set thou a wicked man over him: and let an adversary stand at his right hand.
> When he is judged, let him come forth guilty; and let his prayer be turned into sin.

That was Satan's intention, to follow the pattern of normal judicial trials and so accuse Israel. Here is a great mystery which no one can really solve. How can this great Adversary of God have access to the very throne of God? and how can he walk in the midst of the angels of God and bring raving accusations against God's elect? How is it that he can challenge and seek flaws in God's righteousness? And he is especially virulent as regards Israel, the Apple of God's Eye!

Exodus is so full of that: Israel was elected to service; Israel was elected to bring God's promises to all the nations; that all the nations in Abraham would be blessed. She was elected to receive, to keep, and to preserve the oracles and the glory, and the covenants and the services, and the promises: this is Romans 9. And she is privileged above everyone, says St Paul. But above all, Israel was elected to bring forth the Messiah. So, you see the strategy of Satan: destroy Israel and you have destroyed all God's promises and purposes for the salvation of all mankind, for Israel is His channel.

So I say this: every effort to exterminate or destroy Israel by any one nation, or by all the Gentile nations, is inspired by Satan. Ultimately, anti-semitism is satanic. But we must get this right. As I have said before, it does not mean that the Jew should be free from criticism and that the unrighteous Jew should go about freely to do evil, simply because he is a Jew. The Jew makes great use of anti-semitism! if you attack him for breaking the law he will say that you are being anti-semitic. Modern Israel reacts in the same way: she does wrong but when she is accused she simply shelters behind the anti-semitic shield. That apart however, people who are anti-semitic ultimately are inspired by Satan himself.

Now Christ is the real Israel, the final Israelite, the only Israelite, 'My Elect One', as God calls Him on the Mount of Transfiguration. And Satan sought to destroy Him and did destroy Him, or thought he had. So the destruction of Israel is high on Satan's agenda; in fact it is probably the very highest thing on his agenda and all this fits in with modern thinking and reading about Israel.

So Joshua, clothed in filthy garments, stands before the angel of the Lord as a prisoner at the bar, so to speak; Israel is at the bar of God! And she is filthy; the Hebrew word Tsoim means the most loathsome, filthy condition. When a word like this is used, there is great hope for us all; you cannot get any dirtier than this word in Hebrew; absolutely filthy! Israel must surely be beyond the pale, and this must have been in Zechariah's mind and must be in most people's minds today. I know many Christians who believe Israel is nothing. She has rejected Christ, she murdered the Son of God, she is finished. And any event today that one tries to explain as prophecy is dismissed as a political accident. You must have heard many Christians who talk like that; but they do not understand the Old Testament.

Is Israel beyond the pale? The message of this vision is, No! Let Satan gloat: let him stand at the right hand saying, Look at this nation, filthy beyond words. But he reckons without God's personal intervention and God's marvellous grace; that wonderful property of God which, though not clearing the guilty, yet, in all justice, is able to forgive and to restore. Mercy and truth have met together and have kissed. The two poles **can** come together; but only in the Cross of Jesus Christ.

Do you wonder why Paul says: I will not preach about anything but the Cross. It is God's way of solving our dilemma; righteousness and wickedness beyond compare can come together in the Cross and be reconciled, and God can forgive the sinner. Why talk about good works and ethics and all the rest of it? They are all attendant truths and we are not to ignore them; but at the heart of things is: 'God forbid that I should glory, save in the Cross'. The Cross is right in the centre; God becomes our own personal advocate and shows us grace. Note how both the Old and the New Testament speak of God justifying us; God justifying sinners; God justifying also a sinful nation. Look at Isaiah 50 verses 7 to 9:

> For the Lord God will help me; therefore have I not been confounded: therefore have I set my face like a flint, and I know that I shall not be ashamed.
> He is near that justifieth me; who will contend with me? let us stand up together: who is mine adversary? let him come near to me.
> Behold, the Lord God will help me; who is he that shall condemn me? behold, they (the condemners) all shall

> wax old as a garment; the moth shall eat them up.

You see what I am saying? It is God who justifies sinners; it is God who justifies the sinful nation of Israel. You get it put in absolutely clear form in Romans 8 verses 33 and 34 where Paul, who was an Old Testament scholar par excellence, says the same thing:

> Who shall lay anything to the charge of God's elect? It is God that justifieth;
> Who is he that shall condemn? It is Christ Jesus that died, yea rather, that was raised from the dead, who is at the right hand of God, who also maketh intercession for us.

So the message of both Testaments is exactly the same: we are sinners, and who justifies us? God; our Lord Jesus Christ. The old nation of Israel is filthy, sinful, gone astray; and who justifies her? Isaiah says, The Lord God draws near and it is He that will justify.

But you see Satan never stops attacking the people of God; to destroy Israel if he can; to condemn those of us who take refuge in Christ. This is our trouble; the Devil is saying to us: You are not worthy to be a Christian, your sins are too many! Then you begin to measure yourself and you fall short of the righteousness of God and you become depressed. But who is it that justifies you? Not an angel, but God; Christ Jesus. Who will lay anything to the charge of God's elect? It is one total message - for Israel as well as for us - and this vision in Zechariah 3 is Israel's reassurance. In Romans 8 Paul is saying, Do not let the Devil get you down; it is Christ Jesus who died and nothing shall separate us from the love of God in Christ Jesus. Paul is full of assurance and we all shout Hallelujah to that; yet we forget that Romans 9, 10, and 11 follow, and the message in these chapters is that God is going to do the very same thing for Israel! Our assurance in chapter 8 is linked with Israel's assurance that she too will be saved. And so to verse 2:

> And the Lord said unto Satan, The Lord rebuke thee, O Satan; yea, the Lord that hath chosen Jerusalem rebuke thee: is not this a brand plucked out of the fire?

Note that in these first two verses the angel of the Lord and Jehovah are interchangeable expressions. In verse 2 it is the Lord, or Jehovah, or the angel of the Lord, who puts Satan to flight. The Hebrew word Yegar means 'to rebuke with force', 'to crush' as it were, the Nations. The phrase comes in Jude verse 9:

> But Michael the archangel, when contending with the devil he disputed about the body of Moses, durst not bring against him a railing judgment, but said, The Lord rebuke thee.

Only the Lord can rebuke Satan; only Christ can rebuke Satan, so to deny the deity of Christ is a most heinous sin. This is the sin of sects like the Jehovah's Witnesses and St John says that such people undermine salvation, because they deny that Jesus is Christ. They deny that He is the eternal Son of God and if they are right, then He cannot rebuke Satan and His cross is not efficacious. St John is most bitter about such heretics because the deity of Christ is totally essential to any scheme of salvation that we find in the New Testament.

In verse 2 the Lord identifies Himself a little further with: Yea, the Lord that hath chosen Jerusalem rebuke thee. It is God in association with Israel; it is God in Christ, it is Jesus the God-Man, the Theanthropos, the God-Son who rebukes Satan and who is to bring us our redemption finally; no other! no created being but the One whose name is Wonderful, Counsellor, Mighty God, the Ever- lasting Father, and the Prince of Peace.

My dear friends, these are not little facts, these are great facts to hang on to: the total deity of Jesus Christ the Eternal Son of God; begotten not made; 'I was with the Father and before Abraham was, I am'. And here Jehovah 'the Lord that hath chosen Jerusalem' is Israel's

Advocate, and that puts God in a special light. It agrees with what Paul says in Romans 11 verse 1: I say then, Did God cast off his people? God forbid. And in verse 2: God did not cast off his people which he foreknew. Paul is living in our age! The crucifixion had taken place; the Jews were being dispersed; but had God cast away His people whom He had foreknown? God forbid! and this is the rabbi speaking; this is the Old Testament scholar speaking.

Then what a lovely phrase in Zechariah, Is not this a brand plucked out of the fire? - something on the way to utter destruction and actually in the midst of the flames; and the mighty God puts in His hand and takes it out! That is what Jesus Christ has done for us, and that is what God is going to do for Israel. She deserved the burning, and like her so do we; we are being consumed by our sins, yet God in mercy and grace and power plucks both us and Israel (these two things are joined) from the burning.

How many times does God keep doing that! If you look in the Old Testament Israel was always in the furnace. Do you remember in Genesis 15 when Abraham had to slice animals in two and a torch and a smoking lamp went between them? It was the Presence of God in the midst of His people long before they had become a nation. And do you remember in Egypt when God said: I will bring you out of the furnace of Egypt? And so He did. And do you remember when the Jews went to Babylon? Did He not bring them out of the heat and fire of Babylon? Look at Isaiah 48 verses 9 and 10 which concern the dispersion:

> For my name's sake will I defer mine anger, and for my praise will I refrain for thee, that I cut thee not off.
> Behold, I have refined thee, but not as silver; I have chosen thee in the **furnace of affliction.**

Notice again that it is only for the sake of God's own Name that He is refraining from utterly destroying His people. And again in Isaiah 43 verses 2 and 3:

> When thou passest through the waters, I will be with thee; and through the rivers, they shall not overflow thee: when thou walkest through the fire, **thou shalt not be burned**; neither shall the flame kindle upon thee.
> For I am the Lord thy God, the Holy One of Israel ...

And in Isaiah 4 verses 2 to 4:

> In that day shall the branch of the Lord be beautiful and glorious, and the fruit of the land shall be excellent and comely for them that are escaped of Israel.
> And it shall come to pass, that he that is left in Zion, and he that remaineth in Jerusalem, shall be called holy, even every one that is written among the living in Jerusalem:
> When the Lord shall have washed away the filth of the daughters of Zion, and shall have purged the blood of Jerusalem from the midst thereof, by the spirit of judgment, and by the **spirit of burning.**

Then, in Isaiah 33 verse 14:

> The sinners in Zion are afraid; trembling hath surprised the godless ones. Who among us shall dwell with the devouring fire? who among us shall dwell with **everlasting burnings**?

In other words Israel and, may we say, individual Christians from the Nations, are brands plucked from the burning! All these prophecies refer in the first place to Israel as a nation; but then they overflow to the people of God who are scattered throughout the world.

Now that is glorious; but to hear modern preaching you would think that everybody is safe and happy and does not need to be saved! Yet who will live in the everlasting burnings? Who can stand in the presence of God relying on his own righteousness? Who dare strut before the Almighty? Are we going to say: Well Lord, I went to church and I did this and I did that ... How appalling!

Now see the wonderful way in which Jehovah, surrounded by attendant angels deals with His people in verses 3 and 4:

> Now Joshua was clothed with filthy garments, and stood before the angel.
> And he answered and spake unto those that stood before him, saying, Take the filthy garments from off him. And unto him he said, Behold, I have caused thine iniquity to pass from thee, and I will clothe thee with rich apparel.

The angel of the Lord speaks to Joshua; to the nation itself and says, Not only will I cleanse you and forgive your sins but I will clothe you with rich apparel. Now this is wonderful. Not only are we forgiven and not only will Israel be forgiven; but even more! Our salvation is not a petty, miserable thing such as, 'I will forgive but I will not forget', for this is what men do. No! we are not just forgiven; we are given an impeccable, spotless garment of righteousness; not belonging to ourselves but coming entirely from the mercy and grace and love of Jesus Christ; we are covered with Christ's righteousness. You know, when Paul thought about it his mind absolutely 'blew' and Paul says: I stand before him not in the righteousness which I had by the law (my own efforts, my prayers, my this and my that) but in the righteousness of Christ.

So we are cleansed; we are forgiven; but are also clothed upon with a righteousness, and that brings peace to the Christian and awe too, at the wonder of God's bounty. Though the Christian has peace of mind, the Jew is baffled by this. He is baffled because he still walks around with his suit cut to measure from the Law! I have done this, I have done that, I have given alms of all I possess, he says; I fast, I go to the synagogue, and I keep Yom

Kippur. I am not sneering at them; but they are trying to put on a suit of righteousness, and there are so many holes and so much filth in it that God will not spare it a single glance!

When God forgives, He clothes us (and only in the New Testament can we find the secret of this) with the righteousness of Christ. But He also says to Joshua, the representative of the nation: 'And I will clothe thee with rich apparel'. Now this is a reconsecration of a whole nation, and their calling as a kingdom of priests in the future. Through His prophet God is saying to the little remnant: One day I am going to cleanse you and reclothe you with the clothes of righteousness, and I will reconsecrate you. These are indeed comfortable words, though the metaphors must be interpreted. Can you imagine a man of spirituality like Zechariah listening to all this and understanding and meditating: Forty-eight thousand in Jerusalem; Lord, we must be finished. But God says, No, you are not finished! your enemies will be destroyed; Jerusalem will be filled with people and children and I will dwell in the midst; and I will be a wall of fire round you. And not only so, but I will cleanse you from all iniquity and I will clothe you, reconsecrate you, and once again you will go through the world as kings and priests to the rest of the Nations.

Then the prophet speaks. Remember that he is a priest-prophet and he would have a deeper understanding, this young man, this Na'ar, and he speaks very eagerly in verse 5. (Notice that the 'interpreting angel' has nothing to say in this vision: he has got to be quiet because the angel of the Lord, as it were, is taking the stage:)

> And I said, Let them set a fair mitre upon his head. So they set a fair mitre upon his head, and clothed him with garments; and the angel of the Lord stood by.

Now that does not seem to be very important, but Zechariah's request has great significance to the Jew. You see, when the high priest wore his ceremonial clothes, he was dressed up marvellously. Let us read it in Exodus 28 verses

36 and 37, just to make certain that you realise what the prophet is thinking about, because he was a priest and would know Exodus off by heart:

> And thou shalt make a plate of pure gold, and grave upon it, like the engravings of a signet, HOLY TO THE LORD.
> And thou shalt put it on a lace of blue, and it shall be upon the mitre; upon the forefront of the mitre it shall be.

So Zechariah, being a priest, is saying: O Lord, you are restoring the nation that Joshua is representing; put on him a mitre because on that mitre is the gold plate, and on the gold plate is graven in letters, Holy to the Lord. The mitre was the very crown of all the high priest's dress, and in verses 31 and 32 of the same chapter:

> And thou shalt make the robe of the ephod all of blue.
> And it shall have a hole for the head in the midst thereof: it shall have a binding of woven work round about the hole of it, as it were the hole of a coat of mail, that it be not rent.

Note that the high priest wore a single garment with a hole for the neck. Do you remember Jesus's robe? It is not made much of is it? but it was round; it was bound; and they cast lots for it. Let us not tear it, said the soldiers! Thus we have Jesus the high priest, offering Himself as a victim upon the cross. There is nothing astray in Scripture; it is these little things in Scripture, these incidentals that are so striking. In fact, I have put a line right across my Bible at these verses to say, It is marvellous! Absolutely marvellous! The New Testament does not interpret this, but there is no need if you know your Bible!

Zechariah was thrilled at the thought of the high priest, so wonderfully dressed, being once again allowed into the holy of holies, and he also realised that the whole nation was called to be priests as we find in Exodus 19.

So they set a mitre on his head and clothed him with garments and 'the angel of the Lord stood by'. This is just a reminder I suppose, that no one can enter into the presence of God without a robe of righteousness provided for him. The angels provided this dirty, filthy man with a new garment, with rich apparel, with a mitre having the very name of God on it, so that he could go into the holy of holies. The New Testament says that no one can go into the presence of God except through the blood of Jesus. Recall that telling parable of the wedding feast: when everybody went in and the lord of the manor found a man without a wedding garment and said, Friend, how comest thou here without a wedding garment? and the man was speechless. And the lord said, Bind him and cast him out ... there will be wailing and gnashing of teeth.

Again, it is this congruity, this total identity of Scripture with Scripture that is so wonderful. No one can go into the presence of God without the righteousness provided by someone else - by our Lord Jesus Christ Himself. Men can deceive each other by their dress. You can have a rogue who dresses so well he could pass for an ambassador and you might think you could trust him. Men, by outward appearances, can deceive each other but no one can deceive God.

Verses 6 and 7 deal with the implication of salvation:

> And the angel of the Lord protested unto Joshua, saying,
> Thus saith the Lord of hosts: If thou wilt walk in my ways, and if thou wilt keep my charge, then thou also shalt judge my house, and shalt also keep my courts, and I will give thee a place of access among these that stand by.

Notice the word 'protested'. It is a very strong word. It is like a committee which makes decisions. Note also the interchangeable titles, 'the angel of the Lord', and 'the Lord of Hosts'. Salvation implies new life for the nation now cleansed: it also implies new behaviour, which will be rewarded. But salvation without new behaviour on our part means that we will suffer loss; not eternal loss but loss nevertheless, and that is what St Paul talks about. We will all stand before the judgment seat of Christ and those who have built of gold and silver and so on will be rewarded; and those who have built only of wood, straw, and hay will be saved, but so as by fire.

The phrase 'keep my charge' means to take care of God's house; and 'judge my house' reminds us of what Moses did; and 'keep my courts' is a command to stay free from all idolatry and uncleanness. The reward for changing our behaviour and obeying God's commands is: Then I will give thee places to walk in among these that stand by. Now here indeed is something for us to get hold of! Who are these that stand by? They are the Malachim, the angels of God; the elite angels of God. Here Joshua is being addressed both as a person and as the representative of Israel. God says to him, and God says to us: If you will do these things and show obedience then I will give you places to walk in among these elite angels, these impeccable, glorious Seraphim, these servants of mine who do my will throughout the whole universe. Our reward will be to share their honour and privilege.

You see, as we go along in Scripture we are getting glimpses of what it is going to be like in Heaven. Oh you poor lazy people, who think that you are going to sit down all day with nothing to do but play harps! You will be rejuvenated, indeed more than rejuvenated; you will be regenerated and you will be given places to walk in among the very elite of God's servants, these that stand by; the Seraphim, the Michaels of that other world, the Gabriels of that other world, always doing God's bidding, and mighty in power. To think that God by-passed those great angels and took the form of a simple man! says Psalm 8. But God is going to raise us unto the likeness of His Son, and we are going to have places to walk in; and so is Israel, especially Israel, who will also be a rejuvenated and a regenerated nation.

But now we come to a most important message in verse 8:

> Hear now, O Joshua the high priest, thou and thy fellows that sit before thee; for they are men which are a sign: for, behold, I will bring forth my servant the Branch.

God is now talking to Joshua as the high priest of Israel and included are his 'fellows' with whom he met daily to run the affairs of the whole nation. God is speaking to the Levites, the priests of Israel, and saying, You represent the nation; you are going to be a sign; you are going to be a wonder to other people. In fact Israel was a sign: already the nations were thinking that it was very strange how the Jews had survived their captivity of seventy years in Babylon. Surely the nation should have been completely destroyed, but no! they were back again, and Tobiah and all those who opposed the rebuilding of Jerusalem and the Temple looked with some apprehension on this little seed of Israel. And God is now telling the little despised remnant that they are going to be a wonder and a sign to all nations, and proof of God's continuing mercy and faithfulness and grace.

But there is more! for 'I will bring forth my servant the Branch'. Now this is the great sign, the great secret of God; the secret of God's saving Grace is about to be opened up. How is God going to do all this? that is what the Jews were asking; and the answer is, By my servant the Branch. That is the secret. God is saying, This is why I can be an advocate for Israel; this is why I can put Satan to rout; this is why I can cleanse what is thought to be impossible to cleanse. The term 'my servant' is the major theme in Isaiah chapters 40 to 66, and we must get this in perspective. To get a picture of the Servant, let us read Isaiah 42 verses 1 to 8. God is speaking:

> Behold my servant, whom I uphold; my chosen, in whom my soul delighteth: I have put my spirit upon him; he shall bring forth judgment to the Gentiles.
> He shall not cry, nor lift up, nor cause his voice to be

> heard in the street.
> A bruised reed shall he not break, and the smoking flax shall he not quench: he shall bring forth judgment in truth.
> He shall not fail nor be discouraged, till he have set judgment in the earth; and the isles shall wait for his law.
> Thus saith God the Lord, he that created the heavens, and stretched them forth; he that spread abroad the earth and he that which cometh out of it; he that giveth breath unto the people upon it, and spirit to them that walk therein:
> I the Lord have called thee in righteousness, and will hold thine hand, and will keep thee, and give thee for a covenant of the people, for a light of the Gentiles;
> To open the blind eyes, to bring out the prisoners from the dungeon, and them that sit in darkness out of the prison house.
> I am the Lord; that is my name: and my glory will I not give to another, neither my praise unto graven images.

Now that theme goes on. The whole of the second part of Isaiah is about this mysterious Servant of God and in Isaiah 53, that mysterious chapter to every Jew, He is the Servant of God laying down His life, apparently for Israel; and the Jews are confused! They try to say that 'he' means Israel in, Surely he hath borne our griefs; but verses 4 and 5 say:

> Surely HE hath borne our griefs, and carried our sorrows: yet we did esteem HIM stricken, smitten of God, and afflicted.
> But HE was wounded for our transgressions, HE was bruised for OUR iniquities: the chastisement of OUR peace was upon HIM; and with HIS stripes WE are healed.

You cannot have both pronouns meaning Israel: it is the

Servant of the Lord! What does Isaiah 53 say in verse 11?

> He shall see of the travail of his soul, and shall be satisfied: by his knowledge shall **my righteous servant** justify many: and he shall bear their iniquities.

This great theme of the Servant of the Lord is amplified in Zechariah. Not only are the people of Israel a sign in themselves, but God is going to bring forth 'my servant', now described as someone called **the Branch.**

This is the great messianic title of Christ and I want you to think about this carefully. You get the title first in Isaiah 4 verse 2:

> In that day shall **the branch of the Lord** be beautiful and glorious, and the fruit of the land shall be excellent and comely for them that are escaped of Israel.

And there follows an account of the goodness of God in the days of Israel's return and regeneration, with **the Branch as God Himself.** And then in Jeremiah 23 verse 5, the Branch is seen as **a King** reigning in the days when the seed of Israel has been brought out of the North country, and all the countries 'whither I have driven them':

> Behold, the days come, saith the Lord, that I will raise unto David a righteous Branch, and he shall reign as king and deal wisely, and shall execute judgment and justice in the land.

Then as we have read in Zechariah 3 verse 8, we see the Branch in that day of restitution as **the Servant of God.** And finally in Zechariah 6 verses 12 and 13, we shall see the Branch described as a **Man**, as a **Priest-King.**

This fourfold description of the Branch (as God, as a King, as a Servant, and as a Man, a Priest-King) is paralleled by the four Gospels, which also give four pictures of Jesus Christ. In Jeremiah's prophecy of the Branch, He is going to be the Son of David and to bear the rule. So in Matthew we get Jesus as the King of Israel with His descent traced back only to Abraham. Both sources present Jesus as King. But what do we get in Mark? No genealogy because Jesus here is presented, as in Zechariah 3, as My Servant the Branch, and servants are not given genealogies: they just do their master's will. So Jesus is seen in Mark as doing His Father's will; this is the great theme in Mark's Gospel. In Luke our Lord is presented with a special emphasis on His Humanity. He talks for instance to women and to outsiders, and He tells the parable of the Good Samaritan, with its emphasis on a non-Jew. The picture here, as in Zechariah 6, is that of **the Man** whose name is the Branch (Behold, the man whose name is the Branch); **the Man**, the humanity of Christ! and in Luke His descent is traced right back to Adam, the first man. Then finally, in John's Gospel we go back long before history starts. There is no genealogy but: In the beginning was the Word, and the Word was with God, and the Word was God. So both John's Gospel and Isaiah 4 portray **the Branch as Lord.**

To repeat, the prophets and the Gospels give four pictures of Jesus Christ: the Branch as a King, the Branch as a Servant, the Branch as a Man, and the Branch as God; a fourfold picture of Jesus Christ; the messianic title of a priest upon His Throne.

But let us return to Zechariah 3 verse 9:

> For behold, the stone that I have set before Joshua; upon one stone are seven eyes: behold, I will engrave the graving thereof, saith the Lord of hosts, and I will remove the iniquity of that land in one day.

Here is yet another picture. A stone is laid before Joshua and the angel of the Lord says, Upon one stone are seven eyes. Now seven in Hebrew means completeness and the meaning could be that all eyes in heaven and on earth are upon this stone.

But there could be a secondary meaning. Seven eyes means total vision and the stone before Joshua could have seven eyes belonging to it, or perhaps engraved thereon, and it could mean that they depict Christ; that they depict the seven gifts of the Spirit; the sevenfold characteristics of our Lord, and that the stone is the living stone in 1 Peter 2 verse 4. Now the seven characteristics are: (1) the Spirit of the Lord; (2) the Spirit of Wisdom; (3) the Spirit of Understanding; (4) the Spirit of Counsel; (5) the Spirit of Might; (6) the Spirit of Knowledge; (7) the Spirit of the Fear of the Lord. These are the seven eyes of Christ, and His total omniscience. We read in Revelation 5 verse 6:

> And I saw in the midst of the throne and of the four living creatures, and in the midst of the elders, a Lamb standing, as though it had been slain, having seven horns, and seven eyes, which are the seven Spirits of God, sent forth into all the earth.

Seven horns means total power, so, hundreds of years before Christ came, Zechariah is saying the very same thing as Revelation. How wonderfully consistent Scripture is in all this.

What then is this stone that is before Joshua on which are all the eyes of heaven and earth, or to which belongs total omniscience and total power? You must now look at Isaiah 28 verse 16:

> Therefore thus saith the Lord God, Behold, I lay in Zion for a foundation a stone, a tried stone, a precious corner stone of sure foundation: he that believeth shall not make haste.

And now compare Psalm 118 verses 22 and 23:

> The stone which the builders rejected is become the head of the corner.
> This is the Lord's doing; it is marvellous in our eyes.

Oh, how Israel rejected Christ! The stone is Jesus Christ

and on no other foundation can any man build, says St Paul. And what is the meaning of, 'I will engrave the graving thereof' in Zechariah 3 verse 9? Well, although we are perhaps in the sphere of guessing, it is thought to be the Tetragrammaton. You see, it is a fact that no one today knows how to say the word which means Jehovah: but what we do know, is that on the porch of the Temple were written the four consonants of the name of God in Hebrew. And so I believe that the name of God was 'the graving thereof' on the stone. We can say that, carved or inscribed on the stone or on Jesus Christ, is the name of God, and this of course accords with Exodus 23 verses 20 and 21 in: I will send my angel before you ... see you do not disobey him for MY NAME IS IN HIM, and he will not easily forgive you your sins. Let us compare what Philippians 2 verses 9 and 10 says:

> Wherefore also God highly exalted him, and gave unto him the name which is above every name;
> That in the name of Jesus every knee should bow, of things in heaven and things on earth and things under the earth.

Compare also what Revelation 19 verse 16 says:

> And he hath on his garment and on his thigh a name written, KING OF KINGS, AND LORD OF LORDS.

So it is probably the Tetragrammaton that is carved on the stone. And through this stone, through this Branch of the Lord: I will remove the iniquity of that land in one day! Of course, our minds go straight to Calvary, for Jesus Christ in one day, in one offering made once and for all and forever, removed our sin, and the sin ultimately of Israel.

But I think that the day referred to here is probably the day when Israel turns to Jesus Christ; when He comes on the Mount of Olives; that great day of the Lord which we will be discussing towards the end of the book of

Zechariah. On that day Israel will be full of tears and mourning and will bewail themselves because of their past foolishness. But in that day God will open a fountain for cleansing, and the iniquity of Israel will be forgiven through the precious blood of Calvary.
So then, this fourth vision ends with verse 10:

> In that day, saith the Lord of hosts, shall ye call every man his neighbour under the vine and under the fig tree.

How Jewish this is, how Israelitish all this is! This is Israel - the vine and the fig tree. Christ says, 'I am the true Vine and My Father is the Husbandman'. It is to the whole Jewish nation that God is saying: When the Branch comes, when the stone without which no man can build is made manifest, when you trust Jesus Christ, and when He comes in that day and the iniquity is removed; then there will be such joy in Israel that they will be saying, This is wonderful, this is glorious! Every man in Israel will be a converted new creature in Jesus Christ, and the whole of the nation will rejoice as never before. There is a suggestion too that gone will be those great soulless cities and conurbations of today's world. Rather, 'In That Day', each man will possess his own comfortable plot; his own vine and fig tree to sit beneath and he will be able to call unto his neighbour.

5 VISION 5 THE CANDLESTICK AND OLIVE TREES

We come now to this magnificent and fifth vision in chapter 4 of Zechariah, and we are continuing, in a sense, those comfortable words in the previous visions to the nation of Israel. The angel that 'talked within' the young prophet now reappears and interprets what the young man sees.

If you have been to Jerusalem, you will have seen the great Menorah presented by the British Government standing in front of the Knesset. It was a magnificent gesture by the British Parliament to its Jewish counterpart. It is some fifteen feet high and has seven candlesticks, and on it are engraved scenes from Jewish history, from periods before and after Christ. And what does this candlestick signify? Quite simply, it is a symbol of Israel, and it is an obvious symbol for the whole nation of Israel.

You will recall that in Scripture, the number seven always stands for perfection and salvation: for example, seven days of the week; seven words from the Cross; seven times 'Fear not'; the seven churches, and so on. Note also that Sheva in Hebrew means Oath as well as seven: and that 'God has sworn' stands for our salvation. The candlestick with seven branches speaks therefore of the perfect and complete light that comes from God to His chosen people. So to verse 1:

> And the angel that talked with me (or in me) came again, and waked me, as a man that is wakened out of his sleep.

The angel wakes Zechariah **as** out of sleep! Let me again emphasise a point. Many people suggest that sleep is equated with the natural state of our living. When we are in this natural state our bodies are at work and we feel tired; we do not want to think, and we are not able to understand spiritual things. That sort of state is compared in Scripture with a spiritual sleep. In this state we are obtuse and cannot think properly; whereas 'in the spirit' when the lower life or bodily life is subdued, our mental state is exquisitely 'tuned-in'. Now that is the state of mind of Zechariah in this prophecy. Let us turn to Numbers 24 verses 2 to 4:

> And Balaam lifted up his eyes, and he saw Israel dwelling according to their tribes; and the spirit of God came upon him.
> And he took up his parable, and said, Balaam the son of Beor saith, and the man whose eye was closed saith:
> He saith, which heareth the words of God, which seeth the vision of the Almighty, falling down, and having his eyes open:

Note that! Balaam was caught up and his mind exquisitely tuned to the visions he was receiving under the influence of the spirit of God. I touched on this matter in the first vision and I must insist on this fact of total cognition in the mind of the prophet. As you know, certain sections of the Church say that when you speak in tongues and start to sing in the Spirit, then you abdicate the use of your mind: you are unaware of what you are saying or doing; you are communicating with God but your mind is fallow and you are functioning involuntarily. These views are contrary to the whole of Scripture! And they are contrary to the spirit of prophecy that we are dealing with here. Refer again to Numbers 24 verses 15 and 16:

> And he took up his parable, and said, Balaam the son of Beor saith, and the man whose eye was closed saith:
> He saith, which heareth the words of God, and knoweth the knowledge of the Most High, which seeth the vision

> of the Almighty, falling down, and having his eyes open:

So I say that Zechariah was similarly caught up and his mind was exquisitely tuned to the words of God, and in verses 2 and 3:

> And he said unto me, What seest thou? And I said, I have seen, and behold, a candlestick all of gold, with its bowl upon the top of it, and its seven lamps thereon; there are seven pipes to each of the lamps, which are upon the top thereof:
> And two olive trees by it, one upon the right side of the bowl, and the other upon the left side thereof.

Now this is different to the candlestick in the Temple, for on either side of this candlestick he saw an olive tree. From the main bowl of the candlestick ran seven pipes to each of seven lamps lit by olive oil. The picture Zechariah saw was a seven-branched candlestick with a never-ending supply of olive oil which came from the trees to the main bowl, and from there to the seven lamps. When the prophet asks the angel the meaning of this vision in verse 4, the angel seems to imply, in verse 5, that the meaning should have been clear:

> And I answered and spake to the angel that talked with me, saying, What are these, my lord?
> Then the angel that talked with me answered and said unto me, Knowest thou not what these be? And I said, No, my lord.

Then comes the answer addressed to his contemporary, Zerubbabel, the civil leader of the nation, in verse 6:

> Then he answered and spake unto me, saying, This is the word of the Lord unto Zerubbabel, saying, Not by might, nor by power, but by my spirit, saith the Lord of hosts.

The word 'might' here means 'armies'; Cayal in Hebrew today means 'a soldier' and the plural form of the word appears in the text. Again, these are words of comfort from God, for the prophecy is rooted in the contemporary situation.

Zerubbabel and Joshua were the two leaders of this pathetic remnant of less than fifty thousand Jews back in Jerusalem. They were easily discouraged to the point of despair. They were surrounded by enemies and by the Samaritans who were very powerful at that time. There are today perhaps only three hundred Samaritans in the world, but after Christ they literally overran Jerusalem. They had been brought into the country from the Persian Gulf area by the king of Assyria in 721 BC, and were harassing the remnant as they were trying to rebuild their pathetic little Temple. So the two leaders were bearing the burdens of this small state against apparently hopeless odds, and remember, this is always the history of Israel for 'they have afflicted me from my youth up'. It was the same in Egypt, when two leaders Moses and Aaron had to bring this family of slaves out of Egypt against hopeless odds. Again, it is true of the Great Dispersion: the Jew has lived nearly nineteen hundred years against impossible odds, always subject to annihilation and extermination but always surviving. 'They have afflicted me, yet have not prevailed against me'. But why? because, Not by armies, nor by power, but by my spirit, says God. You see there is always a 'but God' as St Paul so often says, because he was a Jew! ... but God. Things might get rough; you might get right down to the end of your tether and feel absolutely lost ... but God!

If this is true of Israel, it is true of the Cross! On the cross hung the one true Israelite; the one Man who obeyed the Father; the one Man who could claim to be the Elect, for: I have pleased the Father in all things; and, This is my beloved Son, this is my Elect One. The whole salvation of the world and all the promises to Abraham lay on the shoulders of one Man. If He were to fail ... the prospect is unthinkable! everything depended on Christ, on one Man and the Father ... but God!

So we have the candlestick signifying the nation of Israel, a light never to be lost, and also signifying that nation in its relation to other nations. Now there is a doctrine of Scripture which says that no nation occupies its geographical position by accident. Read Deuteronomy 32 verse 8:

> When the Most High gave to the nations their inheritance, when he separated the children of men, he set the bounds of the peoples according to the number of the children of Israel.

Now that is remarkable: the disposition of the peoples of this world is not accidental but providential! They were set around for God's own purposes which were centred on this nation of Israel. Turn to Acts 17 where you get the same thing in the Christian dispensation. Paul is preaching to the men of Athens and he says in verses 26 and 27:

> And he made of one every nation of men for to dwell on all the face of the earth, having determined their appointed seasons, and the bounds of their habitation;
> That they should seek God, if haply they might feel after him, and find him, though he is not far from each one of us:

That surely is a remarkable dimension to the Gospel. God has literally put the nations in such a position as to expedite the Gospel in His own way; a way perhaps beyond our logic. And of course God positioned His own people. Read Ezekiel 5 verses 5 and 6:

> Thus saith the Lord God: This is Jerusalem: I have set her in the midst of the nations, and countries are round about her.
> And she hath rebelled against my judgments in doing wickedness more than the nations, and against my

> statutes more than the countries that are round about her ...

So Israel, the candlestick of Israel, was placed in such a position as to give light to the nations round about; but the sin of Israel was that she failed. Even when the Glory departed, the light was left flickering in this little remnant. They came back; they set up their synagogues; and the Pharisees, the men of the Great Synagogue, arose: there was still a light. They had an enormous effect on the Romans. The Jews, says a famous writer, were the accepted nonconformists of the pagan world, for the pagans were tired of their own religions. The Glory had gone, but God had given them another spell of five hundred years to bring forth the Messiah; another reprieve until the coming of the Light of the world. But when the true Light of the world came - the Branch and the Stone which the builders set at nought - Israel rebelled yet again. She did wickedly and put out the Light of Lights and so lost her glorious mission: 'to give light to them that sit in darkness and in the shadow of death, to guide our feet into the way of peace'. Do you remember (Luke 1 verse 79) Zacharias the father of John the Baptist saying that?

Israel rebelled and put to death the Christ. So what happened to the Light of the world, humanly speaking? Refer to Revelation 1 verses 12 to 14:

> And I turned to see the voice which spake with me.
> And having turned I saw seven golden candlesticks;
> And in the midst of the candlesticks one like unto a son of man ...

In other words, Israel's candlestick was removed and the privilege to become the Light of the world was given to the Church, which in Revelation is portrayed as seven golden candlesticks. Do you notice the difference? Israel is a seven-branched candlestick on a single stem, but the Church has seven separate candlesticks. This is because the

Church is not like Israel: it is not one nation but is made up of people drawn out of all nations. And **seven** churches again reminds us of completeness, perfection, and salvation.

Of course, when you read Revelation, the same thing happens to the Church as happened to Israel. When God speaks first to Ephesus, then Sardis and Pergamos and so on, what does He say? I know thy works; repent or I shall remove thy candlestick! You see, there is never any favouritism with God.

So Israel's privilege of being the Light of the world was taken from her and given to the Church. Then the Church begins to fall away, so that - as St Paul argues in Romans - as the Jew is corrupted, so the Gentile is corrupted; none of us have anything to boast of; we are all under sin. But finally, with an apostate Church and with a hardened Israel, God nevertheless will, right at the end times, restore the Light once again to His ancient people, and the fifth vision is a picture of Israel being so restored. But it is only because of God's grace and His faithfulness to His word to Abraham. You get this spelt out in Isaiah 60 verses 1 to 3:

> Arise, shine; for **thy light** is come, and the glory of the Lord is risen upon thee.
> For, behold, darkness shall cover the earth, and gross darkness the peoples: but the Lord shall arise upon thee, and his glory shall be seen upon thee.
> And nations shall come to **thy light**, and kings to the brightness of thy rising.

See how aptly Scripture fits in? And again in Isaiah 62 verses 1 and 2, if you are not convinced:

> For Zion's sake will I not hold my peace, and for Jerusalem's sake I will not rest, until her righteousness go forth as brightness, and her salvation as a lamp that burneth.
> And the nations shall see thy righteousness, and all

> kings thy glory: and thou shalt be called by a new name, which the mouth of the Lord shall name.

And that of course is when Israel once again becomes the Light of the world; when He comes; when ten men take hold of the skirt of him that is a Jew and say, We will go with you, for God is in your midst.

I defy you to put any other meaning to these Scriptures, except to write them off as the critics do. And not only the critics! One conservative churchman says that the Scriptures are the product of sanctified imagination; a sort of Shakespearian writing. But it is not true. Prophecies which specifically concern Christ's first coming are generally admitted to be literal and true. But I say that **all** prophecies similarly are literal and true and in Zechariah's prophecy the light **is** going to be restored to Israel; Israel's candlestick **will** be restored; the nation **will** be restored as the bearer of good tidings of Him who is the Light of the world.

But it is also important to remember that prophecy is rooted in contemporary events and then stretches out to the future. It goes far beyond the actual historical incident upon which it is based. So in verse 7, the prophecy is addressed in the first place to Zerubbabel who is facing mountains of difficulty:

> Who art thou, O great mountain? before Zerubbabel thou shalt become a plain: and he shall bring forth the head stone with shoutings of Grace, grace, unto it.

So God is telling Zerubbabel that by His Spirit, the great mountain of difficulty facing the leaders and the nation will be smoothed out as a plain. We can apply that to ourselves, for, in a way, this verse is a spiritual talk. Think of the mountains of your difficulties; and then think of God's words. What problems have you on your mind right now? What did God say to Zerubbabel and what does He say to you? He says, You are scheming; you are worried; you are planning (we all do it); but it is not by might nor by power, but by My Spirit!

So verse 7 is, I think, a direct encouragement in the first place to the men of Zechariah's day. However, the words are also addressed to 'O great Mountain', which is the Gentile world, the Nations, the Babylonians, the Medo-Persians, the Greeks, the Romans, and in the Last Day, the Beast! to all the Nations that have opposed and tried to destroy Israel. Did He not say to the Nations: I was but a little displeased, but **you** pressed hard upon My people? So here God is not only speaking to Zerubbabel, but He is looking forward to the last days, when the great mountains in the way of His people's becoming once again the lamp of the Lord will become a plain, absolutely smoothed out. In both cases God is saying that there will be a song of rejoicing, the Temple will finally be completed and the Headstone put in. We know that the Headstone typifies Jesus Christ bringing all men together: it is also a historical fact that this Temple was indeed completed under Ezra. But verse 7 reaches out finally to the Temple of God, to Jew and Gentile when Christ comes the second time to this earth; for then the **spiritual** Temple will be complete, God's family will be complete, and Christ will be the Head Stone and all nations will shout the same cry, Grace, grace! In other words we are saved by Grace alone and God's purposes cannot in any sense be nullified or hindered. So this verse is a wonderful example of prophecy being both contemporary and also stretching out to the future.

I mentioned the little difference between the earthly candlestick in the Tabernacle and the candlestick in this vision. The candlestick you read of in Exodus had seven bowls. The people brought in the oil and the priests poured it into the bowls and trimmed the wicks night and day to keep the lights burning. This happened every day. But in the vision the candlestick is fed with a constant supply of oil from the olive trees on either side. There is no human addition here; the lights never go out. They represent a constant supply of God's works through His Holy Spirit; God's Holy Spirit will never fail and this is brought out in verse 9 which is very important:

> The hands of Zerubbabel have laid the foundation of this house; his hands shall also finish it; and thou shalt know that the Lord of hosts hath sent me unto you.

The angel of the Lord is saying here that, when the Jews see their Temple completed, they will know that all that has been prophesied is true - not only of things contemporary but also of things yet to come; the deliverance from dispersion and return to the land; the peopling of Jerusalem and God's protection as a fire around it; and God's gift of salvation to the whole world.

Remember, this vision was five hundred years before Christ. If Zechariah could come back and we could rehearse the history of the Jew to him, he would be astonished at his own prophecies! So the completion of the Temple was a kind of proof when they saw it, that the rest of the prophecies by Zechariah (which are very deep as we shall see) were true, and that God had indeed spoken to His people through the young prophet. Verse 10 is also quite extraordinary:

> For who hath despised the day of small things? for they shall rejoice, and shall see the plummet in the hand of Zerubbabel, even these seven, which are the eyes of the Lord; they run to and fro through the whole earth.

Many great things were happening in the world at that time. The power of the Medo-Persian empire was very great and Professor Bruce says that the king had his spies in every one of his provinces, which numbered one hundred and twenty-seven in all. These spies were known as the eyes and ears of the king and this fits in with the first vision concerning the riders sent by the Lord to walk to and fro through the earth. The king had his riders too; they were continually on the watch for any sign of rebellion and so you have a topical picture here that the people could well understand.

But God's eyes, the seven eyes, the seven spirits of God, were on that despised little Temple, on that insignificant man Zerubbabel trying to keep the little remnant together; and on this plummet in the hand of Zerubbabel, measuring the Temple, building the walls, but meaning nothing in the eyes of the world! Great empires were there, rising and falling; great men were strutting about; but God was saying that the most significant thing going on in the world that day was Zerubbabel and his plummet! They were far more important than the rise and fall of Babylon, the rise and fall of Medo-Persia or of Alexander the Great. The work by the leader and his remnant was to lead to Herod's Temple, to the Christ, to the rending of the veil from top to bottom, to the destruction of the Temple, to the dispersion, to the apostle of the Gentiles; and it was to lead to Matthew 23 and the last days.

So right in the heart of tremendous happenings in the world, the most significant thing going on was God's care of an insignificant minority. Now apply that to the Church. God's concern in the world today is for His Church; but you will not believe it. You read the newspapers concerning the great things that are going on, the arguments between powers in the various capitals of the world and so on; but God's concern in this world is not for great nations, great culture, and great progress but, beginning with Abraham, always to call out a people unto His name!

A prayer meeting called earnestly and with sincerity is more significant in the eyes of God than all the meetings of government officials or business men that might go on in Moscow, Geneva, Washington or anywhere else. Now that is an incredible truth of Scripture. God is not interested in man building his towers of Babel. Let them go up! and they will crash and go to dust. Where is Nebuchadnezzar today? Where are the kings of the Medes and Persians today? Where is Alexander the Great? Where are the Roman emperors? But where is Jesus Christ and Who is it that is coming? And to Whom is all power on earth and heaven given? and what does Daniel say when the great stone rolled and smashed the image? - 'To the saints of the Most High'; and this identifies us with the Son of Man. Daniel also says (in chapter 7): I saw one like unto the son of man approaching the Ancient of Days. In a parallel passage (verse 22) he says, To the saints of the Most High there was given the kingdom.

Now that is very thrilling. I sometimes think of the Church, so weak and so insignificant. This is a day of small things! but do not despise it; we are waiting and praying for a revival, but do not despise the day of small things, the small groups of people, God's people; for God is intimately concerned in preserving His people and we will see the whole truth of it one day. And I especially think of the Cross on a lonely hill in Palestine as THE day of small things. In those days of the Roman Empire, no one knew the Man Christ Jesus, did they? The Romans were full of their intrigues; Britain had been taken; the Romans were pushing north; Augustus turned the Republic into an Empire and became the first Emperor. No doubt 'the papers' were thrilled with all this going on and ... there was a Man on a Cross! that Man was going to conquer the world but no one thought about Him or even knew Him. Only Pliny and Tacitus wrote about it; there are perhaps only three secular references to Jesus Christ.

I believe that the Cross is THE tremendous example of small things. Though hard to believe, it is the true philosophy of history that God is not interested in the 'great progress' of the nations, or in the wars of the nations, or in the peoples of the nations, or in the empires of the nations: He is concerned only with the Saints of the Most High, His people. This should not make us silly or puffed with spiritual pride. But when you read the newspapers and when you consider life in general, it is a great thrill to feel and to know that God is at work. So to verses 11 to 14 which end the fifth vision:

> Then answered I, and said unto him, What are these two olive trees upon the right side of the candlestick

> and upon the left side thereof?
> And I answered the second time, and said unto him, What be these two olive branches, which are beside the two golden spouts, that empty the golden oil out of themselves?
> And he answered me and said, Knowest thou not what these be? And I said, No, my lord.
> Then said he, These are the two sons of oil, that stand by the Lord of the whole earth.

Zechariah anxiously questions the angel that talked with him, and at first no answer is given. Then comes the answer, and what a text to preach on! It seems an enigmatic answer, and let me say immediately that there is no certain interpretation of it. But let us turn to Daniel 12 verses 8 and 9:

> And I heard, but I understood not: then said I, O my lord, what shall be the issue of these things?
> And he said, Go thy way, Daniel: for the words are shut up and sealed till the time of the end.

So who are these two sons of oil who stand by the Lord of the whole earth? Let me provoke your biblical thinking with several answers.

Some suggest that they are men of Zechariah's day, and are in fact Zerubbabel and Joshua; the former being the civic head and the latter the great high priest. They are an inspiration to the nation and are the two sons of oil. Others say that they are the priest and the king. Refer to Zechariah 6 verses 12 and 13. We will deal again with these verses, but here the thinking is that the sons of oil standing by the candlestick of Israel are the King and the Priest but combined in one Man, Jesus Christ. Another interpretation is that the two sons of oil are Christ and the Holy Spirit. But others say, with probably more acumen, I think, that they are the two witnesses of Revelation. So look at Revelation 11 verses 1 to 4:

And there was given me a reed like unto a rod: and

> one said, Rise, and measure the temple of God, and the altar, and them that worship therein.
> And the court which is without the temple leave without, and measure it not; for it hath been given unto the nations: and the holy city shall they tread under foot forty and two months.
> And I will give unto my two witnesses, and they shall prophesy a thousand two hundred and threescore days, clothed in sackcloth.
> These are the two olive trees and the two candlesticks, standing before the Lord of the earth.

Now that is almost word for word plucked out of Zechariah! If you continue on to verse 12 you will see the wrath of the world in the killing of these two witnesses and God taking them into heaven in the sight of their enemies.

So who are these two sons of oil? Is it Zerubbabel and Joshua as a limited application to their day and generation? Is it the priest and the king in one Person? Is it Christ and the Holy Spirit? or is it these two witnesses? Remember that in Revelation we are reading of the very last days when there will be tremendous apostasy. There will be the Beast, the Dictator, the Man of Sin; the mystery of iniquity will be uncovered and this brilliant personage, this Antichrist, will rule. And these two witnesses will resist him and will have great power. Who are they?

Well, if you are very 'churchy', you will say that the two sons of oil stand for the Word and Sacrament, which will witness and resist and testify right to the end, and will be overcome but will be resurrected. That is the Church explanation, though personally I am not impressed by it. Some say that it means the Church in general: Christ sent them out two by two; the Church is made up of ministers and missionaries; and perhaps both answers might have a partial insight.

But these two witnesses in Revelation are associated in Zechariah's prophecy with Israel's restoration; with the last throes of the earth! so I do not think that it is the Church they are talking about. So a second answer might be Enoch and Elijah because neither of them saw physical death. Both were translated so they should not see death; and were they preserved unto this particular day when they shall serve God again upon earth? to withstand the Beast, the Antichrist, and to be killed and then taken up into heaven once again? Others contend that the two sons of oil are Moses and Elijah because in Revelation the earth will be afflicted with plagues, and boils, and so on. Moses brought such afflictions upon Egypt in his day and both men had the power to shut up the heavens so that it would not rain. That was Elijah's first prophecy to Israel.

Await the unveiling! Shut up the books, says God. There is a great mystery here. It is nice to be able to speculate but we must never let our speculation develop into a hard doctrine. We simply do not know. God's words to Daniel were, Go thy way Daniel, for the words are shut up and sealed till the time of the end! Only to those living 'in that day' will all these things be apparent and evident; only then will we know who are the two sons of oil who stand by the Lord of the whole earth.

But we must not miss the point of this great vision. The candlestick of Israel shall yet blaze forth; the candlestick is the Light of the world, 'the true Light that lighteth every man that cometh into the world', says St John. 'And we beheld His Glory; full of Grace and Truth'.

So although there are mysteries, all the Scriptures brought together nevertheless assure us that our God is coming, that Israel will be restored, and that all Jews will say, This is our God. And the Jews will be a blaze of light, a whole nation of St Pauls, carrying the Light of Christ to the uttermost parts of the earth. Remember too that God is not interested in the great nations of the world, their histories, their cultures, but in the small despised things. Do not despise the day of small things!

6 VISION 6 THE FLYING SCROLL

The central theme of the sixth vision is the removal of all wickedness. This is essential for our forgiveness and restoration whether in prophecy or in the Gospel. There cannot be a sort of bland 'I forgive you' for that would be the worst form of liberalism and contrary to God's nature. We cannot remain morally in the same state as before, with God waving His hand and saying that we are forgiven. That is nonsense! Where do you get that in Scripture? It absolutely defies everything that runs through the Bible.

No! through Scripture is always the offer of grace and its acceptance or refusal. If there is an acceptance like Nineveh, then Nineveh is forgiven for a hundred years or more. If it is refused like Sodom and Gomorrah there is judgment. God will not stand wickedness for one moment, whether you are a Jew or a Gentile. The removal of wickedness is emphasised particularly in Revelation 21 verse 27 which talks about the new Jerusalem:

> And there shall in no wise enter into it anything unclean, or he that maketh an abomination and a lie: but only they which are written in the Lamb's book of life.

And chapter 22 is even more emphatic about the removal of all wickedness. So let us continue with chapter 5 of Zechariah where the sixth vision begins at verse 1:

> Then again I lifted up mine eyes, and saw, and behold, a flying roll.
> And he said unto me, What seest thou? And I answered, I see a flying roll; the length thereof is twenty cubits,

and the breadth thereof ten cubits.

A flying scroll means a roll of the Bible. The Hebrews did not not have books; they had parchments, or scrolls, or rolls, or a Scroll Book as it is called elsewhere. But this scroll is not rolled up, but opened and flying and it measures roughly thirty foot long by fifteen foot wide. The scroll has writing on both sides. Now this is interesting because the Law was written on both sides. Refer to Exodus 32 verse 15, and note that none of the so-called 'incidentals' in the Bible are in fact incidental:

> And Moses turned, and went down from the mount, with the two tables of the testimony in his hand; tables that were written on both their sides; on the one side and on the other were they written.

So the Law handed by God to Moses was written on both sides, and an even more emphatic insistence occurs in Ezekiel 2 verses 9 and 10:

> And when I looked, behold, an hand was put forth unto me; and, lo, a roll of a book was therein;
> And he spread it before me; and it was written within and without: and there was written therein lamentations, and mourning, and woe.

Now what is this scroll that Zechariah sees? It is the same as that in Ezekiel's vision; it is the Ha Ala, the curse! the great flying curse covering all the land, or perhaps the whole earth in its flight. The Hebrew word used is Eretz, and this means land or earth. It is not a new curse but that which is from the beginning, and written on this scroll is the sentence of God against all unrighteousness.

It is not vindictive; not just anger at this particular time; it is the steady attitude of God against all wickedness. Read Deuteronomy 28 starting at verse 15 and going on right through the next chapter and what do you get? curses, and curses, and curses! What terrifying verses and what intensity, yet what God is saying to Moses is: There is an alternative to Blessing. Notice that God does not say that to this young prophet. But God said to Moses: If you obey Me, if you live by faith in Me (God expected faith and trust, not perfection), you will be blessed in every possible way; but if you defy Me, go away from Me, renounce Me, leave Me and fall into apostasy; then you will be cursed. And then come verses 15 to 68, and if you follow history you will see how those curses have been applied to the Jewish nation down the years. So what is happening in vision 6 is nothing new, but the old curse summed up in Deuteronomy 30 verse 1:

> And it shall come to pass, when all these things are come upon thee, the blessing and the curse (this sums up all the curses listed in chapter 28), which I have set before thee, and thou shalt call them to mind among all the nations, whither the Lord thy God hath driven thee ...

Every Jew knows this awful alternative to blessing. What was the first thing that they had to do when entering the promised land? God said that the twelve tribes were to be divided into two groups, six tribes on Mount Ebal and six on Mount Gerizim. The six on Gerizim were to call out the blessings that God will pour upon His people if they trust Him, and those on Ebal were to call out the curses that will follow if they defy and renounce the God of Israel and follow other gods. And as I say, every Jew who reads the Torah, those first five books of the Bible, knows of the Blessings and the Cursings that God has already declared.

Now on the flying scroll are written two specific offences only, and these are indicated in verse 3:

> Then said he unto me, This is the curse that goeth forth over the face of the whole land: for every one that stealeth shall be purged out on the one side

according to it; and every one that sweareth shall be purged out on the other side according to it.

Written on the first side of the scroll is the offence of stealing. Now this offence is in the second part of the Decalogue (the ten commandments), and out of the offences listed there, one is picked to represent the whole. This is because the second part of the Decalogue deals with offences against one's neighbour, and stealing epitomises the thief, whether you take a man's life or his wife or any of his property. So this single offence written on the scroll sums up the curse of God for offences against one's neighbour.

On the other side of the scroll is the second offence of swearing falsely, and this offence is in the first part of the Decalogue. As I have previously said, if you used the name of Jehovah falsely and swore corruptly by The Name, then you incurred the death penalty. Do you remember how Jezebel had Naboth put to death for that very offence? She procured two false witnesses to stand up and say that Naboth had blasphemed the Name of God, the Holy Name of God. And of course our Lord too was put to death for using that Name.

So what the prophet is being told is: The flying scroll is the whole Law and cursed is he that breaks the great commandment of the Lord. When they went to Christ and asked Him what were the chief commandments in the Law, He answered, Thou shalt love the Lord thy God with all thy heart and with all thy soul and with all thy strength and with all thy mind: this is the first and great commandment and the second is like unto it; thou shalt love thy neighbour as thyself. In these two commandments are all the law and the prophets.

You see, this vision is in accordance with the whole of Scripture. The curse over the whole land is on those who have so frequently committed offences against their neighbour, and on those who blaspheme the name of God in so many, many ways; whether by false religion, or apostasy, or hypocrisy, or in other ways. But note also the significance of the measurements of the flying scroll. Let us read 1 Kings 6 verse 3:

> And the porch before the temple of the house, twenty cubits was the length thereof, according to the breadth of the house; and ten cubits was the breadth thereof before the house.

So, the flying scroll had the exact dimensions of the porch of the Temple. Now read 1 Kings 7 verses 6 and 7, and note verse 7 particularly, which reads:

> And he made the porch of the throne where he might judge, even the porch of judgment: and it was covered with cedar from floor to floor.

In other words, the flying curse had the same dimensions as the porch of the Temple where God met with His people. More importantly, it was the place of judgment by God; for if you read Joel, you will see that the priests laid themselves down on their faces in the porch to make repentance to God.

The dimensions were also the same as the holy place of the Tabernacle that you get in Exodus. Quite clearly, the meaning of this is that men's actions are not to be judged by their own standards, but by the measure of The Sanctuary. Do you get the point? God has **His** holy standards for us to live up to. We excuse ourselves and give all sorts of reasons why we do this, and why we do that, but God speaks to us from an eternal standard! The dimensions of the Curse on the face of the earth, are the dimensions of the Porch and not the vain imaginings of men; and our actions therefore are judged by the measure of the Sanctuary of God.

Now that is a very solemn thought. It hits very hard at liberalism. God is a Holy God; He tells us what He requires of us and will only accept what comes out of His Sanctuary. He will not accept what comes out of our little minds or out of our specious reasonings. The meaning and the import of the dimensions of the scroll is that God abides by His declared Will alone, and this is Holy.

I began by stating that the removal of iniquity is the essential prerequisite for the establishment of God's kingdom, and verse 4 is a most solemn warning:

> I will cause it to go forth, saith the Lord of hosts, and it shall enter into the house of the thief, and into the house of him that sweareth falsely by my name: and it shall abide in the midst of his house, and shall consume it with the timber thereof and the stones thereof.

The house of anyone who breaks God's commandment is entered by the scroll which will **abide** in it! This is an awesome warning; this is not just a passing visit, as some commentator has said. In the day of judgment, the curse will abide and consume the timber and stones of that house. Now look very carefully at Leviticus 15 and recall what happened if a house was infected with leprosy. The priest came to inspect the house; he saw the blemishes and rot going through the wood and formally declared it to be leprosy of the house. And what did they do? They pulled it right down and cleared even the dust away! See how totally consistent Scripture is. When God removes iniquity He does not just pardon it; He will abide in the house of the offender. There will be the just examination and in the day of judgment everything, but everything, will be removed! This is brought out particularly in Revelation 22 verse 11 where God is going to remove all iniquity from His presence. That is going to be true of Israel and of all redeemed people. We will not only be forgiven but we will be delivered from the very presence of sin.

But there is only one escape from sin and this is the awful thought; who will abide the day of His coming? If you feel afraid, then I feel more afraid! Who will escape the judgment of the Sanctuary? And the answer is the Gospel, but first of all let me look forward for a moment to Zechariah 13 verse 1:

> In that day there shall be a fountain opened to the house of David and to the inhabitants of Jerusalem, for sin and for uncleanness.

Now that is lovely; but that is all the Jew could hope for and he did not know what the fountain was. Look now at Galatians 3 verses 10 to 13, because it is here we get the full light of the Gospel. Notice how integrated are the apostles and the prophets and how the Word of God stands or falls by itself:

> For as many as are of the works of the law are under a curse: for it is written, Cursed is everyone which continueth not in all things that are written in the book of the law, to do them.
> Now that no man is justified by the law in the sight of God, is evident: for, The righteous shall live by faith;
> And the law is not of faith; but, He that doeth them shall live in them.
> Christ redeemed us from the curse of the law, having become a curse for us: for it is written, Cursed is every one that hangeth on a tree:

So the gloom of the sixth vision of Zechariah is only finally answered by Galatians! Although this vision is covered by only four verses, there is much to ponder over. There is a flying scroll which covers the earth, and which indicts you and me; but it accuses especially the Jewish nation, because we are dealing here with prophecy. The flying scroll is an indictment against all men who have offended against their neighbours and against God. They are under the curse and they shall die; but - and this is the glad tidings of the Gospel - Christ was made a curse for us!

How could these prophets give these minor details if they were not inspired of God? Paul was a rabbi; he was well versed in the Old Testament, but he could see it all working out in Jesus Christ. He says: I am a cursed man, I accept the Law as a way of life but I have not walked therein; I have never really kept it; I pretend to keep it; I am under the Curse. But then in Galatians 3 verses 13 and 14 he says: Christ was made a curse so that we might become the blessing of God in Abraham. Iniquity must be removed, abolished, exterminated before the Kingdom of God is established; for then there will be no curse, no sin, no wickedness whatsoever, says Revelation. And the Lord God Himself has provided the escape from the Curse.

7 VISION 7 THE WOMAN IN A TUB

The seventh vision is also interpreted by this very nice angel. Dr Pusey says that the angel keeps retiring to the choir of angels and then comes out to talk to Zechariah! However, here is the angel again and we start the vision in chapter 5 and verses 5 to 7:

> Then the angel that talked with me went forth, and said unto me, Lift up now thine eyes, and see what is this that goeth forth.
> And I said, What is it? And he said, This is the ephah that goeth forth. He said moreover, This is their resemblance in all the land:
> (And behold, there was lifted up a talent of lead:) and this is a woman sitting in the midst of the ephah.

This may seem enigmatic; but first of all what is an ephah? It was a bath or container; it was a tub for storing dry goods and it was the common measure of Israel. Ten ephahs of goods equalled one homer, and although in those days they did not appear to use an actual homer, it was nevertheless the standard - rather like our measure of a ton today, since we do not normally have a container which holds one ton. Now the tub or ephah was large enough to hold a person and in the vision, Zechariah saw a woman sitting inside the tub. To stop her escaping (which is implied), a sort of lid is thrown on top of the ephah, a lid made of lead. And then in verse 8:

> And he said, This is Wickedness; and he cast her down into the midst of the ephah: and he cast the weight of lead upon the mouth thereof.

So, the woman inside the tub represents wickedness. And then two other 'unsavoury' women appear in verse 9:

> Then lifted I up mine eyes, and saw, and behold, there came forth two women, and the wind was in their wings; now they had wings like the wings of a stork: and they lifted up the ephah between the earth and the heaven.

These women must clearly be unsavoury because the stork was an unclean bird. You will remember that the Old Testament gives a list of birds that you can eat and those that you cannot eat; and similarly for animals, those clean and unclean from a ritualistic point of view. The two women pick up this tub with their companion in the middle of it and the heavy lead weight on top so she cannot get out, and fly off with it. And then follows Zechariah's question and the answer in verses 10 and 11:

> Then said I to the angel that talked with me, Whither do these bear the ephah?
> And he said unto me, To build her an house in the land of Shinar: and when it is prepared, she shall be set there in her own place.

Now what does all this mean? There are three explanations and there is a lot of truth in the first explanation which is favoured by many people. This claims that the ephah is an example of Jewish history filled up to the brim with all the wickedness of the people throughout the ages; their wickedness heaped together and absolutely measured. You know, God never deals precipitately with any of His people. He said to Abraham: I am going to send your descendants down into Egypt and they will there for four hundred years, because the iniquity of the Amorites is not yet full. You see, God lets us go on and on until we have fulfilled our evil ways.

Martin Luther puts forward an interesting exposition on this point in his book, The Bondage of the Will. Luther says that God, in a sense, is the Author of wickedness, or that He raises up wickedness simply by showing mercy to the utmost possible extent; He holds back as long as He possibly can and so men think that He is not going to judge them! Do you see what I mean? We do something; God takes no notice. We do something worse; God apparently still takes no notice. Men go on doing evil and God still seems to take no notice. So Wickedness stands up and then, when it is full to the brim, when the ephah is exactly one tenth of a homer and full of wickedness as it were, then God will judge. But He waits until the last moment, until the last grain of our iniquity goes into this tub. It is very frightening, and Pharaoh is the supreme example of God's method. So in this first explanation the wickedness of the nation of Israel has now reached a perfect measure; it is filled to the brim. Look at Matthew 23 verses 29 to 33, for these are most important verses:

> Woe unto you, scribes and Pharisees, hypocrites! for ye build the sepulchres of the prophets, and garnish the tombs of the righteous,
> And say, If we had been in the days of our fathers, we should not have been partakers with them in the blood of the prophets.
> Wherefore ye witness to yourselves, that ye are sons of them that slew the prophets.
> **Fill ye up then the measure** of your fathers.
> Ye serpents, ye offspring of vipers, how shall ye escape the judgment of hell?

The brim of wickedness occurred when the Jews crucified the Messiah, for then Jerusalem was destroyed with immense slaughter and the Jews were dispersed world-wide. All these judgments of God are prophetic of the way He acts in perfect justice. Wickedness is heaped together and measured and then removed; it is taken away, it is removed absolutely!

A second explanation is given by Jerome. He thinks that the woman inside the ephah is Israel herself being removed in the Great Dispersion, to show everybody how wicked she really is. When Israel was in her land, says Jerome, we did not know how wicked she was, but now that she is dispersed we can all see what a wicked lot those Jews are! We should of course remember that some of the early Fathers were very anti-semitic. However, these two explanations do not really go far enough. So here is a third explanation.

What does an ephah really stand for? It stands for the new idolatry of Israel, and this explains the position today. It represents the new idolatry that ensnared Israel when they came back from Babylon. Before banishment they were always engaged in idolatry, but on returning from Babylon the Jews would never even look at another idol! The change, though slow at first, was extraordinary: they became absolutely monotheistic; they had been taught a severe lesson in seventy years of exile and never again went after strange gods. But a new idolatry came in, the idolatry of **commerce** and this affected the Jew especially!

An ephah, a container of goods, stands for possession or commerce, with all the lying, the stealing, the thieving, and the unethical traits that can so closely attend commerce. Since the exile, the Jew has become particularly adept at sharp practice; he has become notorious in his commercial methods. Indeed, the Pharisees themselves were notorious for saying long prayers in the market place but then robbing the widow, and selling houses over the ophans' heads, and lining their pockets. Read the woes of Christ; for He makes it quite clear that these religious men thought that it was quite in order to use sharp practice in commercial transactions.

Read the history of the Jew in commerce and ponder on the hatred they engendered in every country. Even in our Lord's day, in the days of Philo the great Jewish philosopher, the Jewish court in Alexandria was so rich and so marvellous that the Jews were hated. They were detested for their brilliance in business, whether at Rome or at Alexandria or elsewhere. They were hated for their buildings, their organisation, their fellowship, their riches. They were notorious throughout the Middle East for their commercial ability; and has that hate grown less?

It has come down through the ages to us today. The Jew! He is a Jew, we say. And we talk of anyone indulging in sharp practice in these contemptuous terms. The idolatry of the Jew is Commerce! Money! and this view is supported by the talent of lead that is thrown on the ephah because that was the round weight by which gold and silver were measured.

The vision is now beginning to open up. So the woman in the tub is the personification of this great system of commerce which is to rule and pervert Israel from those days forward. But the Nations also! and this is certainly supported by Amos 8 verses 4 to 7:

> Hear this, O ye that would swallow up the needy, and cause the poor of the land to fail,
> Saying, When will the new moon be gone, that we may sell corn? and the sabbath, that we may set forth wheat? making the ephah small, and the shekel great, and dealing falsely with balances of deceit;
> That we may buy the poor for silver, and the needy for a pair of shoes, and sell the refuse of the wheat.
> The Lord hath sworn by the excellency of Jacob, Surely I will never forget any of their works.

You know, these verses spell it out better than anyone else could. I want you to follow this very carefully because this is so important in the last days. We are living in times when this sort of interpretation has a particular relevance. Notice 'making the ephah small' meaning short weight; and 'the shekel (money) great'. In other words, short delivery and a huge profit! and this is what the Jews were guilty of; dealing falsely and harshly. So you see, we are not being anti-semitic, we are just repeating what is spoken by their own prophet who says, All you look for is to make a profit and your methods are deceitful.

So the vision is anticipating the new force coming into

the world on the return of the Jew from exile, the power of Commerce represented by a woman. And why a woman? Because she is a temptress; she is enticing, she is seducing, she has a seducing influence over the souls of men and over the Jew in particular. Commerce is a woman tempting men, and tempting this former agricultural and tribal people, to become a nation of 'sharks' with great business acumen. This is their resemblance or aspect or 'eye' (the word in Hebrew is Eye) in all the earth. And this has spread all over the world: the one thing that matters today is money!

You could certainly say that this is not confined to the Jews, but they are particularly prone to worship the Mammon of unrighteousness (as Luke calls it). The worship of wealth, the worship of money and of the power that it gives: you know, the ramifications of this are enormous, as we will see shortly in the Scripture. Tawney in his book, Religion and the Rise of Capitalism, writes bitingly of the commercial system of England a hundred years ago; but what would Tawney have written today? with the oil empires, and the multinationals and the control exerted world-wide by these vast commercial groups; to say nothing of the exploitation ation of the emergent countries that often occurs today. And do monarchies have any say in the matter? Does the Church have any effective say? No, they just try to jump on the bandwaggon. The Vatican is well known for its great bank balances and its dealings in high finance; and it is the same with the Church of England, for money buys everything today.

And it is all here in Zechariah: the evil that commerce can lead to once it gets a grip of the soul; the ruthless exploitation of the weak. This caused the rise of Karl Marx and if you read him you will see that it is all this put in secular terms; the cursing of the bourgeoisie, the exploitation of money, the problem of the true value of the labour cost of production, and so on. Some might say that he is too simplistic in his solutions, but nevertheless, Karl Marx has made an appeal to the whole world which is responding today and saying that the system must be wrong! Why should we be in the grip of international financiers or under the influence of multinationals? Why should we not control our own destiny? Why should money be the be-all and end-all of life and why should people have to sweat and sell their labour? Why should children die in Africa (and elsewhere) and the advanced nations keep their sales and profits rising?

I am not justifying Karl Marx: I am justifying Zechariah who says that this ephah (with its talent of lead on top) which stands for **Materialism**, is the final great system which will militate against God and His Gospel.

But you do not automatically turn to communism: their answer is simplistic and ludicrous and takes no account of human sin. The communists do the same thing under a different set of equations. I am not justifying anything: I am simply saying that what is written in Scripture is absolutely relevant to the situation we have today. Has not the whole system got out of hand, and is not money our god? and is not the Jewish involvement in it enormous? The fact is that the Jew is a genius in financial matters; but where is God in all this? Oh, B'ruch Ha Shem, they say and put on their hats! and that is how God is excluded. They make their money all over the world and when they think they are going to die they transfer huge sums to Israel to atone for their sins, and they think they will get away with it! The Jew is totally involved in commercialism and we are equally as involved, but to the Jew big business is his god and the Mammon of unrighteouness. Our Lord says, You cannot serve God and Mammon: you either love one or the other.

Towards the last days it will become a systematised transgression, says Zechariah. We are now in, I think, or at least we are beginning the last days, and already it has become a systematised transgression, and to underline this read Revelation 18 (the whole chapter please). This is a picture of the last day when commerce, money, and the like are wrapped up with the system of apostasy against God; when the chief people on the face of the earth are the merchants! In Revelation 18, wickedness is portrayed as a woman and men lust after her; men indulge their souls in wickedness. This is metaphor, but it portrays the way men go lusting after this systematised tyranny of profit; money, money ...

But when God judges it - how are the mighty fallen! for: Fallen, fallen is Babylon the great ... the merchants of these things, who were made rich by her, shall stand afar off for the fear of her torment, weeping and mourning. Read the whole chapter.

So Zechariah does not stand alone with his vision of the woman in the tub, for there you have in Revelation what must be the quintessence of idolatry. The early peoples worshipped idols, crude-looking images; but idolatry still goes on, says Malcolm Muggeridge. But what is idolatry, what is imagery? It is imagination. And sophisticated idolatry is the worship of trade, of things, of materialism, and not the worship of God; it is not the worship of the Maker.

You get this in the incident of the rich young ruler. That is why our Lord spoke to him and we can understand His severity. It was not so much severity but rather His love: He wanted so much to drag this young man away from the false god of materialism which is going to be damned in one hour and be put to death; be carried out of the land. And so Jesus said, Give away all that you have and follow me. But the young ruler went away because he was very rich. Do you see the point of the incident? Many people feel sorry for the rich young ruler but that man's end, say fifty years later if he lived to be seventy, must have been very miserable. He would have been full of empty materialism but with no hope of God; with no hope of eternity. You should read Alexander Whyte; how he looks at the man going down to Hell with the Devil mocking him and shouting down to him, Kept the commandments, Aha! kept the commandments! You see, no one can really keep the commandments, and as the man had rejected the Christ of God and His free grace, in the end he possessed nothing.

So, the love of money is the root of all evil, as St

Paul says, and the Jew has been almost totally seduced. So we come back to Zechariah and 'make small the ephah and make large the shekel'. But of course we are not speaking of every Jew, and we must not be silly when we make these general statements. The word 'all' in Scripture must always be carefully monitored and it does not mean every single individual. But we are certainly talking about the characteristic, and that is what is being condemned here.

But let us now consider the two women who are spiritually unclean. What can they be and whom do they represent? Well, if we are to be consistent we must keep in mind that in the book of Zechariah there are always the two powers; Zerubbabel representing the civil power, and Joshua the ecclesiastical power. If we follow that (which is good exegesis) then the two women represent these powers, both of which had gone corrupt; indeed totally corrupt in the case of the ecclesiastical power; and they are associated with the woman in the ephah as we know from Scripture.

So there will be an apostate Christianity. The love of many shall wax cold, says Christ, and the Church will go the same way that Israel went. In the last days, says Revelation, the Jews will even make a pact with the Antichrist for their own commercial and survival reasons. But, corruption is to be expelled; iniquity is going to be removed in one day and, says verse 11, taken to the land of Shinar.

Why Shinar? Because it was the plain on which Babylon was built. It was where the tower of Babel was built. It was the scene of the first United Nations when all the nations got together and rebelled against God saying, Come let us build a tower unto heaven that we may no longer fear disaster, famine, or want of any kind. They talked among themselves and they started to build, but God looked upon them and said, Let us go down ... You know what happened!

And so Shinar, later to be known as Babylon, is the classical first instance of a united rebellion against God; a rebellion in its civic and religious guise; a united rebellion in any guise. It was the United Nations marshalling themselves against God, the first instance of sinning in a corporate way. Does the vision mean that Babylon (which is modern Iraq) will have a great part in the final drama? Or is it simply the spirit of Babylon that is being referred to here? We cannot answer that.

Is Mesopotamia to be revived as modern Iraq? Who knows; stranger things have happened. Israel did not exist fifty years ago! Iraq today with her oil could again become the commercial centre of the Middle East; could again become the centre of an anti-God, an anti-Christ movement. We do not know; but we do know that it is the spirit of Babylon that is condemned, for it is always opposed to Christ. That is why the name of Babylon is used so much in the last book of the Bible, and that is why this woman is called Babylon and why the city is called Babylon. Some say that it is just another name for Rome; if so, then Rome is in the spirit of Babylon; Rome is in the spirit of anti-Christ and building her own empires.

But we know that by the judgment of God all wickedness is going to be totally removed; all will cease and the details will emerge later as history goes on. But remember also that this prophecy of Zechariah - rooted in the past and relevant today - is moving towards **That Day,** the day of the total victory of God. We are very close to That Day and we live in a world where all these things are not only feasible, but evident and obvious before our eyes.

So underneath these clashes of nations in the Middle East and all over the world is the spirit of Babylon, warring against the spirit of Christ, and the Jews are involved! They are involved in their unbelief and in their hardness of heart and in their commercial activities, trying, as it were, to buy their future and their destiny. What a drama is going on all around us. You think that you live in a dull world, but you do not!

8 VISION 8 FOUR CHARIOTS FOUR WINDS

The eighth vision in chapter 6 of Zechariah ends his night of visions. What marvellous visions we have had in the previous chapters: visions to restore the Jewish nation and to repopulate Israel and Jerusalem especially; visions to rededicate Israel to God's service, and to cleanse Israel so that she repented and converted, so that Jerusalem becomes the centre of world worship. We are moving on to a great climax of history and these visions are all pointing that way; to Jerusalem as a centre of world worship of Jehovah, the redemptive name of God, and of His Christ, the Messiah. Remember, all these visions came upon Zechariah in one night; to that young priest-prophet prophesying in Jerusalem on return from exile; to a young man surrounded by a remnant of discouraged and dispirited people to whom these prophecies must have appeared absolutely impossible, at least to the more cynical among them.

Yet, some two thousand five hundred years after these events, we are living to see these words come about, and that is the great challenge of the Word of God. It is easy to sit in one's day and generation and judge God's Word, but the Word remains; it never moves; it stands for ever. Men come, and they are like the grass of the field. Scholars come, and they pass away. But the Word of our God has this habit of standing and being justified and being endorsed by the events of history; and it is very much so here in this eighth and last vision. We should note at this point, that eight is the number in Scripture for Resurrection.

Think back to the first vision. There we were in the depths; we were among the myrtle trees in the bottom, in the hollow. I said that the myrtle trees represented Israel, and the bottom represented their sadness and dispersion and destruction almost to the point of elimination. But here, in the eighth vision on the day of Resurrection, they are coming out! they are rising from the dead. And so to verse 1:

> And again I lifted up mine eyes, and saw, and behold, there came four chariots out from between two mountains; and the mountains were mountains of brass.

The chariots come out of THE two mountains. The Hebrew is Ha Harim; the definite article is used and that makes all the difference. They are strong mountains, impenetrable mountains, and in verses 2 and 3:

> In the first chariot were red horses; and in the second chariot black horses;
> And in the third chariot white horses; and in the fourth chariot grisled bay horses.

'Grisled' is a difficult word in Hebrew and might mean 'speckled' horses: but the Hebrew word for 'bay' used here is Amuzin and it means 'strong' horses. So we have red, black, white, and strong grisled horses. The rabbis say that they were chariots with four horses each, but the rabbis so love the Word of God that they often make fantastic exegeses of that Word! Their view however, is derived from 1 Kings 10 verse 29:

> And a chariot came up and went out of Egypt for six hundred shekels of silver, and an horse for an hundred and fifty: and so for all the kings of the Hittites, and for the kings of Syria, did they bring them out by their means.

Their reasoning is that since a chariot costs six hundred shekels, and a horse one hundred and fifty, and since one figure divided by the other is four, therefore there must be four horses to a chariot! Rabbis love obscure texts and they love building exegesis on them. However, in verses 4 and 5 Zechariah questions the angel 'in me' and receives his answer:

> Then I answered and said unto the angel that talked with me, What are these, my lord?
> And the angel answered and said unto me, These are the four winds of heaven, which go forth from standing before the Lord of all the earth.

The Hebrew word Ruach for 'wind' also means 'spirit', as in: And the spirit of God moved upon the face of the waters. So these four winds or four spirits come out from standing before the Lord's chosen earthly dwelling place, which is THE two mountains, meaning Jerusalem. But it is not just from Jerusalem, but from the two mountains of Jerusalem that the His judgments go forth; and with a bit of thought they can be identified.

One is the Mount of Olives on the east side of Jerusalem just across the valley of Kidron; the Mount where our Lord ascended into heaven and from where the Glory departed and to which Christ will come again (in chapters 12, 13, and 14 of Zechariah). The other mountain is Mount Zion because that is David's city; it was specifically built by David. Now if you have been to Jerusalem you will know that between the Mount of Olives and Mount Zion is a valley called the Valley of Jehoshaphat, the Valley of the Kings. Absalom's tomb is there; so is that of Zechariah and also of James, for example. So what I am emphasising is that on the east side of Jerusalem is the Mount of Olives, and on the west side is Mount Zion (the distance between them is probably a couple of miles) but between them is the valley of Jehoshaphat and this is very specific. Let us read Joel 3 verses 1 to 3:

> For, behold, in those days, and in that time, when I shall bring again the captivity of Judah and Jerusalem,
> I will gather all nations, and will bring them down into the valley of Jehoshaphat; and I will plead with them

> there for my people and for my heritage Israel, whom they have scattered among the nations, and parted my land.
> And they have cast lots for my people: and have given a boy for an harlot, and sold a girl for wine, that they might drink.

So you see, the valley of Jehoshaphat is the valley of decision; and it is believed by Moslem, Jew, and Christian to be the valley of Judgment! Our Lord will return to the Mount of Olives on one side of this valley. In the very last day, when the great Armageddon spreads and bursts on the Middle East and when great armies are concentrated with all their weapons of war on that land; **In That Day**, when the Lord comes in His glory, there will be a judgment of the nations; and that judgment will be from the valley of Jehoshaphat. The very name means, Jehovah will judge!

Now coming from between these two mountains and going north, or looking north, are the four winds, the four chariots. And what does 'four' remind us of in these studies? We are reminded of the four empires in Daniel 2, the empires of gold, silver, brass, and legs of iron; of the whole history of the world in that great image! Prophecy must be linked up and we think of those four great empires that have pushed forward the affliction of Israel; Babylon, Medo-Persia, Greece, and the last unnamed empire which has suspicious links with Rome. Refer to Daniel 7 verses 2 and 3:

> Daniel spake and said, I saw in my vision by night, and, behold, the four winds of the heaven brake forth upon the great sea (the Mediterranean).
> And four great beasts came up from the sea, diverse one from another.

Notice that the four winds from heaven, God's winds, God's spirits, made this sea into a turmoil and caused four great beasts to come up from the sea. Again, these four beasts are synonymous with the four great empires brought about by the action of God. God provokes people into rebelling against Him - in His mercy oddly enough! So we have the four great empires, the four great beasts; and in Zechariah 1 verses 18 to 21 we discussed the four great horns and the four smiths. In other words, four chariots are now coming from between the mountains of judgment, and they take us back to the whole sphere of judgment: they bring us back to the four empires, the four beasts rising out of the sea, the four great horns that have persecuted Israel; they are all connected with God's judgment, as are these winds, these spirits. Look at Psalm 103 verses 20 and 21:

> Bless the Lord, ye angels of his: ye mighty in strength, that fulfil his word, hearkening unto the voice of his word.
> Bless the Lord, all ye his hosts (armies); ye ministers of his, that do his pleasure.

That is what we are looking at now. We are looking at the secret agents of God, and in Psalm 104 verses 3 and 4:

> Who layeth the beams of his chambers in the waters; who maketh the clouds his chariot; who walketh upon the wings of the wind:
> **Who maketh winds** (or spirits) **his messengers**; **his ministers a flaming fire**:

Notice that verse 4 is quoted in Hebrews 1 verse 7. What we have in vision 8 is a picture of the divine chariots of God that are always at work behind the human agencies. We said that the four smiths were each empire destroying the empire before it. But behind these human activities, and initiating the flow of history, is God - the divine chariots of God, judging the nations. Now read Psalm 68 verse 17:

> The chariots of God are twenty thousand, even thousands upon thousands: **the Lord is among them,**

as in Sinai, in the sanctuary.

Again in this poetical language, we are talking about the total sovereignty of God. Behind all human history and all human action and all human wars and destruction, are the chariots of God. Our God is at work and His spirits, His chariots, are coming forth from the two mountains of judgment and the valley of Jehoshaphat.

This is of particular encouragement to the Jew, to that beleaguered race. Israel is standing absolutely alone in the world, and you might say, justifiably so, for look what she has done. But that is not the point; God is going to judge her for the things she has done. Nevertheless she stands today as always, outside the Nations and absolutely bereft, so what a picture this vision is for the Jew! the chariots of God are streaming out from the valley of judgment against those who have afflicted Israel over and above what God has ordained.

Recall in chapter 1 the red riders, 'the eyes and ears of the king', finding the whole earth at peace; all except the chosen people who are in turmoil, in sadness, and in distress. The red riders are on reconnaissance, seeing the great empires and the great cultures flourishing; but in the midst of them is this despised and hated nation, suffering and going through the anguish of the night. That was chapter 1, but now there is a difference! Now you have chariots of judgment because we are moving towards the last days; we are at the end of the visions. And in verses 6 and 7:

> The chariot wherein are the black horses goeth forth toward the north country; and the white went forth after them; and the grisled went forth toward the south country.
> And the bay went forth, and sought to go that they might walk to and fro through the earth: and he said, Get you hence, walk to and fro through the earth. So they walked to and fro through the earth.

Note that nothing is said of the chariot with red horses. However, the north is the danger spot for Israel: the uttermost parts of the north is where all the attacks on Israel come from. In Ezekiel chapters 38 and 39, in these great Gog and Magog chapters which paint a tremendous picture of Armageddon, it is from 'out of the north' that all the great armies come. The red horses apparently do not go anywhere (we will see why in a moment), but the black-horsed chariot goes north and the white-horsed chariot follows, while the grisled bay horses, 'the strong horses', go south. These chariots are God's great winds, they are God's great spirits, they are God's great chariots of fire, and they are on the move! We are in the last days!

Why do we not hear something about the red horses, and why are we not told where they went? Well, simply because they have already done their work. They have executed judgment on Babylon, the first great Antichrist, and first great persecutor of Israel, and Babylon has fallen. Four chariots are spoken of for the sake of the completeness of God's judgments, but the first chariot, the red-horsed chariot, has already done its work and Babylon has been conquered by the Medes and Persians. The people of that fallen empire have suffered terribly and you read all about that in Jeremiah and Isaiah. The Babylonian empire had fallen nearly a hundred years earlier and Zechariah was living in the days of the Medo-Persian empire; so the prophet was not interested in telling us about the red horses; we can find that out for ourselves.

But the black horses: what does black stand for? It stands for mourning; it stands for sorrow; it stands for distress. They are going north from out of the mountains of God and they bear His judgments. They are going to destroy the Medo-Persian empire and the Greek empire which was to follow it. The white horses follow them and the white horses stand for victory. The black horses carry their sorrow to those empires that have persecuted Israel, and to those who will persecute Israel; and they are followed by white horses who establish a victory over the enemies of God and over the enemies of God's people. Then you get the grisled horses, the strong horses going to the south. They seem to be specially strong. Those going north are of course strong, for they are God's judgments; but those going south appear to be particularly strong because of the Hebrew word used. But why are the grisled horses going to the south and what lies south of Israel? Egypt! and this is very significant. You see, this was where Rome, that final and most powerful nation (read Daniel 7 verse 7), first came into contact with Israel. We must remember that the last empire to try to destroy the people of God is notable for its tremendous strength; it is made of iron and it is worse than all the other beasts.

When Rome grew in power, her first great conquest, apart from Carthage, was Egypt, and it was through Egypt that Rome, this terrible beast, this fourth empire (a strong assumption), this mighty Antichrist, first met the people of God. So these very strong horses, these strong winds of God go south; and not only so but they seek an extension to their work. They plead with the Lord that they might walk to and fro through the earth and execute God's judgment; and the answer is, Go and walk to and fro through the whole earth! And why? because this last empire, this mighty anti-Christian, anti-God, anti-God's people empire which was stronger than all the others, was to dominate the world. It was to last longer than any other enpire, indeed, in its essence, to last right up to the very last days. In the last days we shall see a worldwide resurgence of the spirit of the Roman empire; so the strong grisled horses walk everywhere, doing God's work in judgment over the whole earth; and they do so until now.

The Jews have been kept alive simply because the winds of judgment from between the two mountains have protected them. And here we are today: it is still going on; we are living in the days of the strong grisled horses combating the anti-Christian and anti-God forces of this world in judgment and it is all building up. And then we read in verse 8:

> Then cried he upon me, and spake unto me, saying, Behold, they that go toward the north country have quieted my spirit in the north country.

The meaning of this is not the obvious one. It means that the chariots that have gone north will destroy Medo-Persia and Greece, and thus relieve God's spirit in judgment upon these two nations. But we are in the last vision and that is going to happen again; God's judgments are going to be placed upon the nations, and God's spirit is going to be quieted only when He passes judgment upon **all** the nations of this world who are against the Lord and against His Christ.

I do not think that this is at all fantastic. As you look at the world today and take note of the terrible turmoil, the evil, the blasphemous philosophies, you can see that this spiritual warfare is going on all the time and that we are moving steadily towards a day of colossal judgment. The troubles that we read about today, such as in Afghanistan, Nicaragua, Africa, and so on; what is it all leading to? It is leading to this mysterious culmination of history; and at the heart of it all is Israel! and behind all the evil forces that are at work is the Antichrist who one day will become personified. He will persecute the Church; he will persecute the Jew; he will do his utmost to destroy the very covenants of God. This battle is going on all the time, and it is the cause of all the turmoil in the world today.

You know, when we talk in modern theology of 'winning the world for Christ' and the 'setting up of Christian culture everywhere', and 'extending our borders and making everyone civilised' and other such cliches, I am tempted to say, Brothers, you are in a dream world! You are not only going against the appalling events of history that we read about daily, but you are going against the Word of God. Where does the Word of God say that the whole world is going to be gradually civilised and christianised and made amenable to the will of Christ? Nowhere does it say that. In fact it says the very opposite. The world is still in rebellion today as it was from the beginning: Nimrod the mighty hunter before the Lord was the founder of Babylon; the whole spirit of this earth is anti-God! Our world is becoming more distinctly and more overtly anti-God every day in its methods of business, its methods of war, its ethics, and in almost every other facet of life.

I say that this is where the dividing line comes in the various wings of the Church. I refer to the division between Biblical believers and liberal believers. I am bound to say that the liberal stands on the most shaky ground; it is just wishful thinking to believe that the world is getting morally and spiritually better all the time. This does not mean that we must cease our efforts to stand for Christ; of course it does not; nor should we stop trying to be full of good works or patient in well-doing. But it does mean that Biblical believers look once again for a cataclysmic event that will put the world right; an event such as the first coming of our Lord, only this time He will come in majesty.

Today, as we think back, we have already witnessed much of what was portrayed in the eighth vision: God sending His secret agents, His winds, His chariots of fire to conquer and subdue the four afflictors of Israel; Babylon, Medo-Persia, Greece, and the Rome of two thousand years ago; but Rome will again be conquered and subdued in her revived and in her last great manifestation, as many of our prophetic students believe. We stand at an astonishing point in history; less than fifty thousand Jews to listen to Zechariah in his day, and now the regathering of three and a half million Jews in Israel! How amazing to look back on eighteen hundred years of dispersion, of being in the hollow, of being in the depths of despair, and then to see modern Israel today. How amazing that students of the Bible do not realise the significance of the regathering or take any notice of it. But it is all there in Scripture and it is there to alert us to the fact that God is on the move; the chariots of God are speeding out; the chariots are coming from the valley of judgment, and our Lord says, When ye see these things begin to come to pass, lift up your heads.

I have mentioned a renewal of the spirit of Babylon and a resurgence of the Beast. Consider Revelation 13 verses 1 to 4:

> And he stood upon the sand of the sea. And I saw a beast coming up out of the sea, having ten horns and seven heads, and on his horns ten diadems, and upon his heads names of blasphemy.
> And the beast which I saw was like unto a leopard, and his feet were as the feet of a bear, and his mouth as the mouth of a lion: and the dragon (Satan) gave him his power, and his throne, and great authority.
> And I saw one of his heads as though it had been smitten unto death; and his death-stroke was healed: and the whole earth wondered after the beast;
> And they worshipped the dragon, because he gave his authority unto the beast; and they worshipped the beast, saying, Who is like unto the beast? and who is able to war with him?

And in verses 11 and 12:

> And I saw another beast coming up out of the earth; and he had two horns like unto a lamb, and he spake as a dragon.
> And he exerciseth all the authority of the first beast in his sight. And he maketh the earth and them that dwell therein to worship the first beast, whose death-stroke was healed.

In other words, we are looking at the last days and we are possibly seeing the resurgence of the Roman empire. We are seeing a counterfeit Trinity: instead of the Father, Son, and Holy Ghost, we are seeing the Dragon (Satan) producing the Beast (the Antichrist); and the False Prophet imitating the Holy Spirit, but in fact urging all the people of the world to worship the Antichrist! You see, this is how Satan always tries to imitate God. This Beast, this incarnate Evil Man rising up has a death wound; he has risen from the dead and in the last days we will see all this. We shall see the evil force which sought to crush Christ in His first coming - that great Roman empire with all its evil ways which seemed to have been smitten down to death - healed, and rising up again.

I say that we are working towards all this; it is not fantasy. We are in a world today where evil is not only increasing but is becoming more and more sophisticated, and the Beast of course is a description of the man's nature. As C. S. Lewis says, if you cannot understand metaphor then do not read Revelation. The meaning is that a sophisticated man **like** unto Christ will demand the worship of the nations; and he will get it readily! You know, we are very ready to give worship to men, whether they be a Stalin, a Hitler, or anybody else. Such a man has an enormous fascination, but behind the Beast will be the False Prophet and, hidden as it were from view, will be the Dragon, Satan himself. So underlying the superficial events that go on, or the human events that go on, is the real history of the world: that great spiritual struggle which began at Eden when 'the seed of the woman shall bruise his head' and 'thou shalt bruise his heel'.

So I would say again, Lift up your heads; when we know these things we are not so mystified at the awful events that go on in the world, and we need not ask that silly though natural question that we hear so often, Why does God allow ... Why does God allow? - as if only God were involved in the whole of the history of this world!

God is being opposed by the man He made; man's opposition is inspired by Satan and the effects of that are enormous. The ramifications of a man's siding with Satan mean trouble, pain, and mystery; yet all we can say is, Why does God allow? Well my friends, God is patient; God will not allow for ever; but the outworking **will** take place, and in that outworking we are being tested. Put your faith in Him, the Christ who died. God has entered into this turmoil; Christ has been the subject of attack from Satan; Christ has hung on a Cross and God has been rubbed out as every other good thing has been rubbed out. But God lives! It is not therefore just a question of, Why does God allow? rather it is an admission that we are in the midst of a great spiritual conflict. How sad that this is so seldom preached today.

Remember however, that the prophet is always speaking about the destiny of Israel and that we, the Goyim, come in only incidentally. We stand today when Israel is back in the land, isolated, hated, and hateful; we are making no excuses for her. But the judgments are going out; the spirit of anti-God and anti-Christ is still at work until God vindicates his covenant with Abraham, and redeems His people Israel.

9 THE NEXT MORNING

The last vision now gives way to prophetic action. We get no more angels 'talking within me'. From now on we get the usual prophetic statement: The word of the Lord came unto me ... and Zechariah sums up the significance of all the visions. This man had had one wonderful night of eight visions, and in one night he had seen, in a sense, a panoramic view of the history of his people; he had heard the good and comfortable words to cheer them and to say, Brother, at the end, you will reign with God; keep trusting, keep believing! And we are in the position today to say that those words were true. But now he speaks just as a prophet and not as a visionary.

The picture from verse 9 of chapter 6 onwards is this: he had had the eight visions in the night and the next morning three men from the dispersion had arrived in Jerusalem. You will remember that there were many thousands of Jews left behind in Babylon and that this little group who were building a temple in Jerusalem were very isolated; three of their brethren had now come from Babylon with offerings of silver and gold for the new but very small Temple and Joshua the high priest was giving hospitality to these distinguished guests from the dispersion. And God said to this young man after he had had all his visions: Now you go along immediately to Joshua's house by the Temple and take their offerings and make crowns of them and put them on the head of Joshua the high priest. The Hebrew words are 'two crowns into one', meaning, make a crown of gold and interweave it with the silver symbolically. Or to put it another way: Go along to the priest's house, take their offerings and crown Joshua with many crowns. Now of course, 'Crown Him with many crowns' comes from a hymn, but it also comes from Revelation. Christ is going to be crowned with many crowns; with a magnificent mixture; it will be one crown but it will be symbolic of every possible diadem in the world: And He shall be crowned with many crowns! So this young man is told to make a crown; to make two in one so we can describe the crown in the plural and crown the high priest with gold and silver.

It is the sight of strangers coming from afar (eight hundred miles or more) to the Temple, that inspires this prophecy. In the spiritually-enlightened mind of Zechariah, he sees strangers coming from the East and from the West; strangers to Jerusalem; and they are going to sit down with Abraham and Isaac and Jacob. One day, strangers shall all flock to the Temple of God in Jerusalem! You see, prophecy comes out of contemporary events. They will flock to the Temple of God for there will be no prohibition when those days come; there will be no wall of separation! But there was such a wall between Jew and Gentile in Herod's Temple, and on the wall in the Court of the Gentiles was a plaque which read: No Goy (no Stranger) may enter here on the pain of death. The Temple was destroyed in AD 70 but the plaque is still in Istanbul for all to see. The threat was a stark one: any stranger who gets in here will be killed! Remember, the Romans permitted the Jews to pass the death sentence in one instance only, and that was for defiling the Temple. That was why the Jews wanted to put Paul to death; they accused him of bringing strangers into the Temple. But these strangers ARE going to come. Look at Malachi 1 verse 11:

> For from the rising of the sun even unto the going down of the same my name is great among the Gentiles; and in every place incense is offered unto my name, and a pure offering: for my name is great among the Gentiles, saith the Lord of hosts.

But as I say, the news of these three strangers staying

with Joshua just makes this young man, by the spirit of God, declare that strangers shall all flock, they will all come and bring their gifts to Jerusalem, to the mighty God; and God's name will be great among the Gentiles, says Malachi.

But why put the crown on Joshua's head? Well, this is a theological question. Normally it is a king who is crowned: surely then the crown should not go to Joshua, a son of the priestly tribe of Levi, but to a son of the royal tribe of Judah! In fact, Joshua's companion Zerubbabel was not only the civic leader, he was also of the tribe of Judah and of the royal seed. He actually went back to Babylon when he had finished his work. Nevertheless, the prophecy is quite clear on the point: it is the high priest who is to receive from Zechariah this symbolic crowning, and it is only in the light of Hebrews and Psalm 110 that we can understand this.

With the above in mind, let us now read verses 9 to 12 of chapter 6 of Zechariah:

> And the word of the Lord came unto me, saying,
> Take of them of the capitivity, even of Heldai, of Tobijah, and of Jedaiah; and come thou the same day, and go into the house of Josiah the son of Zephaniah, whither they are come from Babylon;
> Yea, take of them silver and gold, and make crowns, and set them upon the head of Joshua the son of Jehozadak, the high priest;
> And speak unto him, saying, Thus speaketh the Lord of hosts, saying, Behold, the man whose name is the Branch; and he shall grow up out of his place, and he shall build the temple of the Lord.

Behold the man! You get this great 'Behold!' from God four times in the Old Testament and it is always referring to the Messiah. You have: Behold the man, in the above verse; Behold my servant, in Isaiah 42; Behold your king, in Zechariah 9; and, Behold your God, in Isaiah 40, and they convey four aspects of God's King and God's Christ. I discussed in the fourth vision how these four aspects are also related to the four Gospels: Matthew, King; Mark, Servant; Luke, Man; and John, God. You could not get a more agreeable relation of Scripture than in this instance. Did not Pilate use two of them? they were inspired by the Holy Ghost. He used Zechariah's words when he brought Christ out on the Via Dolorosa and said, Behold the man! And later when he judged Christ, put a crown of thorns on His head, dressed Him in a purple robe and brought Him out to the people, he said: Behold your king! Of course neither he nor Caiaphas knew what they were saying but, as we have said before, even wicked men pronounce the truth of God.

Joshua knew that it could not refer to himself; he knew that only a son of David would be crowned; that is Scripture through and through, so this high priest knew that what was happening to him was purely symbolic. He knew also that One would come who would combine priesthood with royalty. Refer to Psalm 110 verses 1 and 2:

> The Lord saith unto my lord, Sit thou at my right hand, until I make thine enemies thy footstool.
> The Lord shall send forth the rod of thy strength out of Zion: rule thou in the midst of thine enemies.

This is a mysterious psalm. Our Lord used it against the Pharisees when He said: David spake by the Holy Ghost ... so you have the highest imprimatur upon this psalm. Note also the words 'out of Zion' which is the Mountain, the Valley of Judgment that I discussed in the eighth vision. And in verses 4 and 5 of Psalm 110:

> The Lord hath sworn, and will not repent, Thou art a priest for ever after the order of Melchizedek.
> The Lord at thy right hand shall strike through kings in the day of his wrath.

Now that is tremendous! and that is why in one person, priesthood and royalty were going to be combined. He was a priest for ever after the order of Melchizedek, which means King of Righteousness in Hebrew. Joshua knew the Scripture and that he was being used symbolically. He knew too, (read it in Zechariah 3), that he and his fellow priests were only types of what was to happen in the glorious days of the Messiah that were to come. And so the high priest is crowned with these words, Behold, the man whose name is the Branch.

Now let me say again, the Branch is mentioned in Jeremiah 23 as My King, in Zechariah 3 as My Servant, in Zechariah 6 as The Man, and in Isaiah 4 as The Branch of Jehovah; again a fourfold picture which concords with the four Gospels. The Branch is the great Messianic term for Christ in those four aspects. The verse emphasises both the uniqueness and the greatness of Christ: He shall grow up out of Himself; out of His own roots; in humility; but He shall build the Temple of the Lord! Again, we have prophecy rooted in contemporary events, for the remnant were building a Temple.

Here we are moving towards a picture of communion with God: the Temple of the Lord where we can walk with God. God has always had a place where we can walk with Him, worship Him, and feel at home with Him. Firstly it was in the tabernacle, then in the first Temple, then in the second Temple, poor place though it was and the rabbis weep about it. Five things were missing from the second Temple, they say: the Ark was not there; the fire that consumed the sacrifices was not there; the Shekinah Glory that came down in a great cloud, God's presence, was not there; the gift of prophecy of the Holy Ghost was not there; and the Urim and Thummim, the lights and perfections by which they received the Word of God, were not there. That is why there was much non-conformity at the time of Christ.

But God has always had a Temple for His people, even when there is no physical Temple (God is not worshipped in Temples made with hands, says Stephen). Christ Himself was the Temple of God, for He said, Destroy this temple and in three days I will raise it up. And then our Lord talks to Peter of another Temple of God: On this rock I will build my Church and the gates of Hell will not prevail against it. Peter and Paul, taking this up say, Ye also as living stones are built into a spiritual house for God to meet in. Ye are the temple of the Holy Ghost.

The Messiah Himself shall build the Temple of Jehovah; we hear of these great things in verse 13:

> Even he shall build the temple of the Lord; and he shall bear the glory, and shall sit and rule upon his throne; and he shall be a priest upon his throne: and the counsel of peace shall be between them both.

Christ shall bear the glory and it will be a theocratic rule, an autocratic rule. Read the whole of Psalm 72 for a wonderful picture of Christ's reign. This is the reign of this Christ; this is the reign of our priest-king. And note what sort of king He is; we said autocratic! if only we had someone like this ruling over us. It is a glorious picture. Did you know that it applied to Christ? He shall bear the glory, and He shall rule on His throne: who would object to an autocratic rule of that nature!

'And he shall be a priest upon his throne'. Read Hebrews 5 verses 1 to 6, which talks about the great high priesthood of Christ. You see, only Christ is the answer to this: Christ is our great High Priest who humbled Himself, bore our sins, and was obedient unto death; that is the priesthood element. He came first as a Priest to carry away our sins; to make reconciliation with the Father. Christ humbled Himself even unto death, Wherefore, says Philippians, God also has highly exalted Him and given Him a Name which is above every name. Do you see the sequence? The Son of God humbles Himself and becomes the Priest for us; and bears our sins in His own Body on the Tree. And God highly exalts Him: He shall rule, He shall bear the glory; a King, yet an Intercessor; our Lord Jesus Christ the great High Priest. Without the New Testament, you see, the Jew is mystified by all this. In his targums he applies it to the Messiah but he cannot work it out.

According to all the pundits, the text 'and the counsel of peace shall be between them both' is a mysterious one. What does it mean? Is it between our Lord and the people? is it peace on earth and goodwill to all men? Yes, perhaps. But most commentators believe that it is the peace between Christ and the Father. Here is a fulfilling of Psalm 110 in, The Lord saith unto my lord, Sit thou at my right hand, until I make thine enemies thy footstool. Here is the counsel of peace between God and His Son working out the salvation of the earth, subduing the earth, and Both absolutely as One in Their purposes for us. Here is the counsel of peace, the eternal peace between Father and Son, because Christ has offered Himself once and for all, well pleasing to the Father.

And this will be perfected especially in the millenium period on the face of the earth. Now many people do not believe in the millenium period; many evangelicals do not believe in it. But when F. F. Bruce was asked if he beiieved in it he replied, If you mean a reign of Christ upon the earth and the establishment of righteousness according to the prophets and so on, yes, I do believe in the millenium. I say then, that this counsel of peace between Father and Son will be especially visible, overt, seen, and experienced, in the millenium reign.
And in verse 14:

> And the crowns shall be to Helem, and to Tobijah, and to Jedaiah, (and to Hen) the son of Zephaniah, for a memorial in the temple of the Lord.

This verse refers to the three men from Babylon whom we discussed in verse 10. The word Hen is not a person; it means grace. Their gifts are put in the Temple as a memorial for the grace and kindness of the high priest who lodged the strangers in his house and treated them with great affection. The gifts of gold and silver are laid up as a memorial in the Temple of the Lord; but they are also a pledge, for in verse 15:

> And they that are far off shall come and build in the temple of the Lord, and ye shall know that the Lord of hosts hath sent me unto you. And this shall come to pass, if ye will diligently obey the voice of the Lord your God.

The gifts are a pledge that many afar off are going to come and build the Temple of the Lord. It is looking to the last days. What does Peter preach in his sermon on the day of Pentecost? He says, For to you is the promise, and to your children, and to all that are afar off ... And does not Paul say the same thing in Ephesians: Ye were afar off but now ye have been drawn nigh by the blood of Christ. Yes, the middle wall of partition has been broken down, and we are one Temple of God. Perhaps Paul was reading this book of Zechariah or had it in mind when he said those words. So the gifts of the three strangers and the kindness of the high priest are referred to, not only as a memorial, but as a pledge that the day is coming when Jew and Gentile shall come together and build the Temple of the Lord in Jerusalem, and shall enjoy the communion of God and His Christ in Jerusalem.

This is the end of the rainbow. After the storm and rain the sunshine; the victory of Christ, the victory of God, the reconciling of God's promises to Abraham, and the calling in of the fulness of the Gentiles. We will all be made one in Jesus Christ, and the whole meaning of this world is moving to that end. As I have said, cultures, governments, and armies are of little importance on a secular level. God is moving, and this great river of grace from God is bringing all the nations of the world back to Himself. It will be paradise regained. And in the last sentence, God is saying to His people through Zechariah: If you are obedient you will participate in this great movement and in this great climax, this great finale, this glory.

10 JUSTICE AND MERCY

Chapter 7 marks a division in the book of Zechariah. Some time had passed since Zechariah had had those eight visions all in one night. They were different from ordinary prophecies. God had laid down before him all these great visions and now the prophet was older and it is reasonable to suppose that from chapter 9 onwards he was older still. God was still teaching him: a prophet is a prophet if he is obedient to the Lord. So you do get changes of style in the prophets. As we grow older we also alter our style of writing.

The Temple had been built. You remember that the prophet Haggai exhorted the people not just to be looking after themselves and their houses, but to do something about the house of the Lord. Go to the mountain, he said, and bring wood and build the house of the Lord and I will bless thee. Consider! (that was the great word of Haggai) Consider in your hearts: you are looking after yourselves and ignoring the work of God. Haggai prophesied almost in the same month as Zechariah but whereas Haggai was a practical prophet, urging the people to come out of their depression and slumbers and build this little Temple, Zechariah was given the further vision of the final Temple of the Lord. So that is the background to chapters 7 and 8. And there was, in a sense, relative prosperity: the city was being improved and cedar was being used in the houses that were going up in Jerusalem. Perhaps hope was returning. And then we find that the men of Beth-el sent a deputation to Jerusalem.

Now Beth-el is only about twenty miles away on the north road towards Samaria. In the last chapter Babylon had also sent a deputation, and Zechariah had used the occasion to make a prophetic action and had crowned Joshua as the king-priest. Life was returning to Jerusalem: the fame of these prophets had spread and Beth-el, which had been the centre of apostasy in Jeroboam's kingdom and was a rival to Jerusalem, now sent a deputation. It is perhaps important to recall those earlier events. In the division of the land Beth-el ought to have belonged to Benjamin, but when Jeroboam broke off from Solomon he sought to discourage the people from going up to Jerusalem by promoting Beth-el. He built a temple at Beth-el and put in priests and calves and all Israel went a-whoring after Beth-el. The 'disobedient prophet' went to Beth-el and said, Listen, you are defying the Lord of hosts and a man named Josiah will come one day and burn bones on this altar of yours! (1 Kings 13 verse 2). I mention this because some people say that when you read Isaiah, and Cyrus is mentioned by name, though still far in the future, one could not possibly know the name of a king a hundred years ahead of time! But Isaiah was right and this is not an isolated case of the critics' being wrong: Josiah too was mentioned by name long before he appeared - by the disobedient prophet.

So Beth-el was the centre of apostasy, a centre of unbelief, a centre which in itself had compared with Jerusalem and had rivalled Jerusalem. But it is obvious that these men of Beth-el had lost all such pretension in their souls and were no longer trying to carry on this status of Beth-el or to make it a rival to Jerusalem. In fact the little deputation came to ask questions, and to pray and to entreat God and to enquire of the priests and of the prophets. Verses 1 to 3 tell us this:

> And it came to pass in the fourth year of king Darius, that the word of the Lord came unto Zechariah in the fourth day of the ninth month, even in Chislev.
> Now they of Beth-el had sent Sharezer and Regem-melech, and their men, to entreat the favour of the Lord,
> And to speak unto the priests of the house of the Lord

> of hosts, and to the prophets, saying, Should I weep in the fifth month, separating myself, as I have done these so many years?

Now the fifth month is an extraordinary month for the Jews. The ninth of Ab is one of the most solemn days in the year for them. It is February and on the ninth day of February (Ab) all the Jews go to the Wailing Wall in Jerusalem and weep. That is why it is called the Wailing Wall although modern Jews call it the Western Wall. They weep on the ninth day of the fifth month because the rabbis say that **that** was the day when God said to the Israelites: Because of your lack of faith you will not go in to the Promised Land. How the rabbis decided on that date I cannot imagine! Where they conjure these facts from nobody knows; in some ways the rabbis resemble the Plymouth Brethren with their typological treatment of Scripture! The rabbis can find esoteric secrets everywhere. However, you remember that God was angry when the spies came back and gave a bad report to Moses about the Promised Land, and God would not let the unbelieving Israelites enter, apart from Joshua the son of Nun and Caleb the son of Jephunneh (Numbers 14 verses 22 to 25).

The rabbis also say that it was on the ninth day of the fifth month that Solomon's Temple was destroyed by Nebuchadnezzar's general. And on the same day of the same month, according to the great Jewish philosopher and rabbi Maimonides, Herod's Temple - Our Lord's Temple - was destroyed. So there we have three great tragedies which all took place on the same day.

But there is more! It was on this ninth day of the fifth month that the town of Bethar was taken, when Bar Kokhba, the false messiah, led the Jews after the fall of Jerusalem in a second revolt against the Romans. Bethar fell into Gentile hands and many myriad Jews, say the rabbis, died along with their great leader Bar Kokhba.

And it did not stop even there, say the rabbis; for it was also on the ninth day of the fifth month that the wicked Turnus Rufus, a Roman devoted to punishment, ploughed up the hill of the sanctuary and the parts around it and so fulfilled the prophecy of Micah (Micah 3 verse 12). It literally came true after the Bar Kokhba rebellion when the Romans said: Right, we have finished with this recalcitrant, stubborn, stiff-necked people! They then killed as many of them as they could, sent the rest into exile, and ploughed Jerusalem over and salted it with salt, and all this is historical fact. It is interesting that the rabbis have connected this one day of judgment, as it were, with sorrow and wailing and weeping; with not going into the land; with the first Temple; the second Temple; the death of the false messiah Bar Kokhba in AD 135; and then the ploughing up of Jerusalem.

So the Jews, reflecting back, can truly say what a sad day this is, and on this particular day they go to the Wailing Wall. If they are in England, for example, they observe it as a holy day, a day of fast, this ninth day of the fifth month. It was, and still is, a national day of mourning.

You can tell from the text that the Jews at the time of Zechariah did not know all that was going to happen and could not add on all these other events. They were mourning specifically the fall of the first Temple, so probably there is no question that the first Temple did indeed fall on the ninth day of the fifth month: there would be people still alive who remembered it. It is subsequent rabbis and subsequent sorrows in the Jewish race which have added all these other things that followed after.

Then, they had been mourning for seventy years. That glorious Temple had fallen; they had been taken away and now they were back; and so this little group of prominent men from Beth-el had come up to Jerusalem and asked, Shall we go on mourning? Shall we go on fasting? But the interesting thing is that what was on their minds was the question of the Jewish restoration. Would **that** take place now that the Temple was rebuilt? Did it mean that all the promises of the prophets - about the restoration and future greatness of the Jew and the coming of the Peace of God and the knowledge of the Lord covering the earth as the waters cover the sea - were now to come about?

You know this is always at the back of Jewish minds. There is an enormous division between us half-believing Christians and the Jews. What did the Jews ask Jesus when before He ascended into Heaven? What was the one last question that they asked Him before Pentecost? It was, (Acts 1 verse 6) Lord, dost thou at this time restore the kingdom to Israel? The question is trembling on every Jewish lip, and I say to unbelieving 'believing Christians': You are out of tune with the expectation of the Jewish race. They are in darkness, but **they** do not disbelieve the prophets as we disbelieve them! **They** do not write off all the prophets and say that it is airy-fairy utopianism! After our Lord had taught these men for three years and even after our Lord rose from the dead, they still asked the question; and if there had been any serious change in the prophetic vision, surely our Lord would have told them. Yet what are people saying today? Oh, there is nothing to Judaism; they are a spent force; but, in so saying, they miss the heartbeat; they miss the throb not only of the ancient people of God, but of the ancient Book of God! Do you see what I am saying? And so these men of Beth-el came, almost trembling in excitement in a way, wondering whether, now that the Temple was rebuilt, now that there was a relative prosperity and Jerusalem was being rebuilt, this could be the beginning of some glorious future now that they had learned their lesson!

You know, the Jews did indeed learn a great lesson in the exile. The change in the Jews before and after the exile is remarkable. They wanted, before the exile, to be like every nation on the face of the earth; they wanted other gods, idols, images, sun-worship, prostitution, and all the wickedness of the Gentile nations around about them - in a religious sense. The Jew was intoxicated by it all. Even when Ezekiel was taken in a vision from the river in Babylon to the Temple in Jerusalem it was so. Son of man, says God, What do you see? And he saw the Jews worshipping the sun; women weeping for Tammuz, the false

Syrian god; all mixed up with base sexuality and false spirituality, and just longing to be like the rest of the nations. Then came the exile! Seventy years and back they came. One lesson that they did learn was: No false gods. No false gods! and from then on they became madly strict monotheists. They would not even look in the direction of another god. In fact they became too strict; they turned in on themselves and kept so far away from what they wanted to be formerly that they termed the Gentiles 'the dogs of the Gentiles'. They were not even to help a woman in labour if she was a Gentile; not even to lift a finger to help. They thought that all Gentiles were predestined for Hell; no one was to lend a hand to them; no one was to enter a Gentile house. The apostle Peter would not enter a Gentile house, so when God was trying to get him to go to the house of Cornelius, Peter was in danger of refusing on the grounds of uncleanness. So you see that there had been a big change in attitude after the exile. Even today they are totally unlike the other nations, and this annoys people. The Jew keeps to himself. He builds around him certain of his race who are permitted by rabbinical law to keep outer relationships happy, so that he can remain safe in his cocoon. Now God did not intend this attitude either! So you see, sin takes many forms, exclusion as well as inclusion.

Would the restoration as promised take place? Wilt thou at this time restore the kingdom to Israel? The answer comes in two parts of which chapter 7 of Zechariah is the first part. This chapter is very consistent and goes over the same grounds as the visions. There are again good and comfortable words in vision form coming to this remnant, to show them that they will go on to the end of days and that God will never desert them; that though God will take them through the fires and purify them, He will establish Jerusalem as the beauty of the whole earth. Good and comfortable words. But you will also remember that in chapter 1 the good and comfortable words were introduced by a call to repentance. You know, God is no man's debtor! He does not favour the Jew. If the Jew is to take any part in God's plans he has to repent, to trust and to be sorry for his sins. And so just as chapter 1 of Zechariah begins as a call to repentance, so does chapter 7 in verses 4 and 5:

> Then came the word of the Lord of hosts unto me, saying,
> Speak unto all the people of the land, and to the priests, saying, When ye fasted and mourned in the fifth and in the seventh month, even these seventy years, did ye at all fast unto me, even to me?

Notice the order to speak to all the people, not just to these men of Beth-el, and importantly, to speak to the priests. The priests had sunk as low as the people. Note also the division between the prophetic and the priestly. This division is always in the Church. I preach the Gospel and hold forth from the pulpit: but you can go to many churches where the man is nothing but a priest. He stands at the altar and offers communions and communions and communions, whereas I stand in the pulpit and preach and preach and preach. Both have their place, but the prophetic ministry was taken by Christ Himself. He was not in His life on earth primarily a Priest; He was a Preacher and held forth the Kingdom of God in parables. You always get this division, yet priests seem to feel that they have the best of it, because there is a certain honour in dressing up and standing as a mediator between the people and God, and doing something on behalf of the people. There is a certain pride engendered in that, but it is a very dangerous situation. If I may say so, it has no place in the New Testament. There is no such thing as a priest in the old sense of the word in the New Testament. Make a note of that! Study as many men as you like on this point, but there is no individual sacrificing priest in the New Testament except Jesus Christ and the whole body of believers in Revelation. When Rome tells me that they have sacrificing priests, then I say, Well you might have, but it is not New Testament. Christ, our great High

Priest, offered one sacrifice, once and for all, for sins. There is no need for men to stand at a thousand altars daily offering a thousand sacrifices.

Now **that**, in a sense, is the basis of evangelical truth. It is a tremendous truth. We do not need to offer sacrifices; we do not say that Communion is an extended Incarnation, or a repeated Calvary, and that by virtue of its being done on a Sunday morning things happen! That is denied by the New Testament, which says that when Christ died, on that day, the veil of the Temple was split and the way to God was opened wide from henceforth and forever, and that He ascended and sat down. The writer rubs it in! Priests **stand** daily, offering, don't they? But this Man, when He had offered one sacrifice for sins for ever, **sat down**! It is an enormous truth that even evangelicals forget or do not know, and if you do not know it, then the natural tendency of the heart is to have a priest of your own who will offer something for you and propitiate the face of God. Until we get back to Bible truths like this, there will be a constant movement towards priestcraft in our churches.

So both the people and the priests were spiritually poor. And here, you see, the prophet's office is exalted; and our Lord's office was exalted. He was both Prophet and Priest in His lifetime: as a Prophet, preaching, preaching, preaching and offering the Kingdom of God; and then in His sacrificial death on Calvary He became both the Priest and the Victim, the Lamb of God that takes away the sin of the world. Remember too that God, through Zechariah, is addressing the whole race and He is addressing, in a sense, us. We must not stand aside from Scripture and say, Well, that is for Jews! Of course it is, in the first place; but it is also for all spiritual people of God.

Now verse 5 includes fasting and mourning in the seventh month and the seventh month is a bit different. That was a recent fast that had been put on. Do you remember when Jeremiah was left behind in Jerusalem by the Babylonians? The poor of the land were also left behind and a man named Gedaliah had been left in charge of them. People went to Gedaliah to warn him of the king of Ammon's plan to kill him but the warning was disregarded and a refugee officer named Ishmael assassinated Gedaliah. So the remnant left behind by Nebuchadnezzar were leaderless and they came to Jeremiah for advice. Were they to stay or go into Egypt? Jeremiah told them to stay in the land and that God would build them up. But they disobeyed him, and went into Egypt taking Jeremiah with them. However, they had instituted a fast in the seventh month commemorating the death of Gedaliah.

And so God's question in verse 5 to all the people: there had been great mourning and fasting for seventy years for the fall of Jerusalem and the Temple especially, and for the death of Gedaliah but, 'did ye at all fast unto me, even to me?'

Now this is where it comes home to us! We do not fast today, but are our religious exercises centred on ourselves or centred on God? Although the Jews had fasted for seventy years and there had been great mourning and great care and a thorough to-do about those tragedies, nevertheless, it was centred entirely on themselves. Their sorrow was for their calamities and not for their sin. Now this is said of Esau. You can be terribly sorry for the results of sin, and weep and wail, but not be sorry for the sin itself! You can be sorry that certain things have happened because you have been foolish, and weep, and so on, but that is not repentance. That is regret! And this is what these people were doing. So in verse 6:

> And when ye eat, and when ye drink, do not ye eat for yourselves, and drink for yourselves?

For seventy years they had been fasting; it was a strict fast from sunset to sunset and it was a continuous fast. But they fasted as an end in itself and as an act of righteousness. They thought they had achieved something simply because of not eating and of course, this goes on among the Moslems at Ramadan. They fast all day and it is an act of righteousness and one of the five pillars of Islam: if you can keep Ramadan and the prayers and alms and other requirements, then you are counted righteous. Thus, by virtue of the work done, I become a Christian! If I fulfil this and do that and the other, I am therefore right in God's eyes. But what does God say? That is utterly wrong: you have fasted entirely to gain merit for yourselves; your sorrow was for your calamities and not for your sin at all; you were trying to build up a sort of righteousness and it was not at all unto Me! you were not repenting in the true sense of that word, you were not turning your back on wrong-doing! And it is the same, says God, in your feasts; even the happy times were all man-centred.

You know, this disturbed me as I wrote it. We ourselves can fall into this trap. We have been to church and to communion, and though evangelicals do not quite say this like the anglo-catholics, but rather say, Well, have you had your quiet time? read your portion? and so on and so forth, it is as though by virtue of these things in themselves that we will be justified. But these are not enough! Whether ye eat, says St Paul, or whether ye drink, eat and drink unto the Lord - for only that keeps the question virile and makes a Christian stand out among other men because people realise that he is true, and not a man who just follows a list of rules of self-righteousness.

People resent this; but it is the whole message of the Bible. God will not let you rely on a list of rules. There is nothing wrong with the rules, but if you are going to keep the rules you must keep them from the spirit, from inside, and not just say: I have kept the rules therefore, ipso facto, I am justified. And in verse 7 God goes further:

> Should ye not hear the words which the Lord hath cried by the former prophets, when Jerusalem was inhabited and in prosperity, and the cities thereof round about her, and the South and the lowland were inhabited?

He is saying: Are these not the same things, these fastings and these feastings that went on in the former days when

Jerusalem was inhabited and when the Negev was inhabited (that means the district of Beersheba) and the Shephelah was inhabited (that means the plain) when all the people were there? You had fasts, you had feastdays, you had sacrifices, you had ceremonies in those days before the fall of Jerusalem when the land was reasonably prosperous; you were meticulous! But what does God say in Isaiah 1? I am sick of your sacrifices, I am sick of your feasts; you are an absolute running sore, all of you, and yet you bring to me your new moons, your feasts, your lambs, and all the rest of it; you keep the ritual going and live in total disobedience!

That is the whole burden of Isaiah 1: in other words, ritual is a moral opiate. Take note of that. I say that to myself. It is so easy to fall into the trap of 'I have done the ritual' (whatever it might be - Evangelical, Anglo-Catholic, Roman Catholic or any other religious sect), 'I have done it, therefore I can separate the rest of my life from it, I can act independently, I can please myself'. Ritual is a moral opiate indeed, and that is the message of all the prophets. It should be repeated frequently in the Church because we all have hearts that go that way; we love to rely on what we have done! But the principle (1 Samuel 15 verse 22) always emerges: To obey is better than sacrifice; to hearken better than the fat of rams.

Perhaps the best chapter in the Bible on this theme is Isaiah 58. This goes back to the former prophets, and Zechariah is giving the essence more or less of the former prophets rather than quoting any particular one. Isaiah 58 verses 1 to 9 is a marvellous summary of **why** God will not listen to His people and **what** they must do to please Him: Then shall thy light break forth as the morning, and thy healing shall spring forth speedily. They are wonderful verses and God says much the same to Zechariah in more humble language in verses 8 to 10:

> And the word of the Lord came unto Zechariah, saying, Thus hath the Lord of hosts spoken, saying, Execute true judgment, and shew mercy and compassion every

> man to his brother:
> And oppress not the widow, nor the fatherless, the stranger, nor the poor; and let none of you imagine evil against his brother in your heart.

This is a resume of Isaiah 58. But they refused to hearken ... So you see we have religious practices which people delight to do, yet keep separate from their own personal, private lives. It is a great sin at all times, among all people, and it is in our midst now, and what does God say? We are not to worry ourselves with fastings; we are not to build up our own little sphere of holiness; true and undefiled religion is this: that we show mercy and compassion to our brother! We are sometimes so concerned about our own holiness that we forget that there is someone in great need; that he is our brother. So forget yourself, and your own little practices, giving yourself credit before God. In other words, be hard on yourself and soft on others! Think of the other person and think too of the widow, the fatherless, the stranger, and the poor. Think of defenceless folk; think of the folk of no-account!

You know, it is terrible to find in fashionable churches (and I would hate this to happen in my church) that the so-called 'no-account folk' are not taken account of! That is damnable in the eyes of God; the poor, the not-so-great, someone who does not have a car. What sort of person do you take notice of in the church of God? Is it just the great, the mighty, the acceptable, the educated, the monied? What about the others who perhaps have not had any such things? And all the time, if we will examine our hearts, the tendency of our hearts is to err in this way. Show mercy to those who are defenceless, to those who cannot pay you back - Our Lord said that. Do not invite only those who can invite you back; invite someone for a meal who cannot invite you back because they do not have the means, or the money, or the facilities; it will give them, and God, tremendous pleasure and you are showing them something of the Love of Christ.

Thus the phrase in verse 10, 'imagine evil against his

brother' means: Do not despise people in your hearts; do not condescend to people; do not patronise people. Now that is not to deny your own gifts, your powers, your gift of articulation; there is nothing wrong with that. But do not divide people into categories and treat some with contempt or condescension, for God looks upon your heart!

So at first sight chapter 7 may not appear to be important, but it is indeed important because of what I have said previously. The exaltation of Israel, as the exaltation of an individual Christian, is not just a matter of automatic right from God; it is all linked with true spirituality, true repentance, and right in the heart of it all is the Cross of Christ. So you must never conclude from my discussion simply that Israel is going to be regathered! There must also be a spiritual regeneration and a cleansing of Israel: cleansing must go along with restoration; repentance with restoration. The kingdom of God is not just going to be chosen from a few elitists; it is going to be of those who repent and believe in Christ and we must never get that out of perspective, as some people do when we talk about prophecy.

Let us read what many men (they tend to be religious humanists!) say is the most classic passage in Scripture - Micah 6 verses 6 to 8:

> Wherewith shall I come before the Lord, and bow myself before the high God? (El Elyon) shall I come before him with burnt offerings, with calves of a year old?
> Will the Lord be pleased with thousands of rams, or with ten thousands of rivers of oil? shall I give my firstborn for my transgression, the fruit of my body for the sin of my soul? (Child sacrifice was practised in the old days)
> He hath shewed thee, O man, what is good; and what doth the Lord require of thee, but to do justly, and to love mercy, and to walk humbly with thy God?

You cannot truly make that passage humanistic! Some

people say that all religion is wrapped up in doing good: but the humanist does not walk humbly with his God; he walks with his fellow man; he does not worship, he does not draw his inspiration for service from God.

So in verses 11 and 12 God, through Zechariah, reminds the Jews what caused the judgment and sent their fathers to Babylon:

> But they refused to hearken, and pulled away the shoulder, and stopped their ears, that they should not hear.
> Yea, they made their hearts as an adamant stone, lest they should hear the law, and the words which the Lord of hosts had sent by his spirit by the hand of the former prophets: therefore came there great wrath from the Lord of hosts.

Yes indeed! They refused to hearken to the greatest prophet in the world, Isaiah. They shrugged their shoulder! Now that is marvellous. If you know Jewish people at all it is a favourite gesture. You talk to a Jew (especially in Palestine) and he frequently uses a disdainful shrug. I have often watched them in Jerusalem; they shrug the shoulder; they must always have done that. They stopped their ears! This is what we refer to as judicial blindness or judicial deafness. If you stop your ears or close your eyes to God when He speaks to you, and goes on speaking to you, and showing you things, but you close your eyes deliberately because you do not want to know His truths, and you stop your ears because you do not want to hear, He gives judicial blindness and judicial deafness. He will close your eyes Himself, and you are caught in the snare of your own sin: That seeing, they may not see, says Christ, And hearing, they may not hear lest they be converted.

People complain: What a terrible thing to say! but of course it is **not** a terrible thing to say; it is the natural outcome of a man's reaction to God. If you go on closing your eyes and your ears to God, He will confirm you in your blindness and in your deafness. It is pure justice and it is not selective. Do you see that? People accuse God of being harsh, but He is simply confirming a man in the state the man wants to be in. Hell will be like that. If you want to be without God, then God says, Fair enough! Be without Me! Hell will be a God-less place and that means a sun-less place and a pleasure-less place, and every other-less place, but you have put yourself there, says God.

The Hebrew word for 'adamant' in verse 12 is Shamir, which is a difficult word. It means something that cannot be written on, even by a diamond; not even the name of God can be carved on this particular stone, it is so hard. And we can make our hearts so hard that neither God's law, nor the words sent by His spirit by the hand of the prophets can touch us.

Now my dear friends, make a note of this very important phrase, 'the words which the Lord of hosts had sent by his spirit by the hand of the former prophets'. Here is the claim to inspiration in the Old Testament. Our Lord says: David, by the spirit ... and in our verse it says, 'the words which the Lord of hosts had sent **by his spirit ...** Now refer to Nehemiah 9 verse 30 and put a cross reference in your Bible:

> Yet many years didst thou bear with them, and testifiedst against them **by thy spirit through thy prophets**: yet would they not give ear: therefore gavest thou them into the hand of the peoples of the lands.

Note the words 'by thy spirit through thy prophets'. You get it in Peter; you get it in Paul; it is the eternal testimony of Scripture to inspiration, and that is the point that I am making here. We are often asked to defend inspiration; but one of the evidences of inspiration is Scripture's **own testimony** to inspiration: 'Thus saith the Lord', 'By the spirit', 'David spake by the spirit'- holy men of old moved by the Spirit. So those two texts are important in relation to the subject of inspiration.

So they stopped their ears and made their hearts an

adamant stone; they were blind, deaf, and defiant, and they excluded the spirit from the Word of God. The outcome of this is that a man can hear the Word of God, but it can have no effect upon him if he excludes the Holy Spirit, and that is terrible. The word 'God' becomes indeed a dead word; he can hang on to a dead word. Or a man can hang on to a dead doctrine, and this is our danger as evangelicals; we hear the Gospel preached so much that our hearts can be hardened to it. Although the wonderful truths of grace and forgiveness through the Blood are preached, we know it so well that we can fall into that trap. We can hang on to the dead word 'God', go to the ceremonies, go to services, and yet let it have no impression on us, and we can commit every sin in the book in consequence. It was Pascal who said that 'God' can be a dead word!

The priests and the Pharisees in our Lord's day did just that. They were well read in the word of God; they were 'evangelicals' and they worshipped the word of God; but they did not worship God! I recall talking to a person who attended the church of Dr Martin Lloyd-Jones and I remarked how fortunate he was. The reply was to the effect that 'the Doctor does not really teach me much, you know' and I was astounded. How pretentious and how arrogant! and how easy to fall into such a state of deadness. We must always keep these two things linked: that we are not just in love with this Bible, without also being in love with the Spirit that dictated the Book, and the God who is speaking to us through the Book, and the Lord Jesus who is portrayed on every page of the Book.

So they crucified the Lord of Glory: it was men of the Bible that crucified the Lord of Glory, not outsiders. This is one of the dangers worth bringing home to us all. We see the behaviour of the men before the destruction of the Temple, and we see great wrath from God fall upon them. And now this sad verse 13:

> And it came to pass that, as he cried, and they would not hear; so they shall cry, and I will not hear, said

the Lord of hosts;

You see, if we defy God long enough (and I say '**we**', not the world) and God keeps sending messengers and preachers, and all sorts of tokens of His love and He cries to us to return, to come back and repent and believe, there will come a day when He will stop crying to us, and our calamities will come, says the Bible; we will cry to Him, but He will not hear us! Again, this is strict justice ... 'My spirit shall not always strive with man'. Again, how telling is this verse.

Our attitudes reflect our characters: each person's life is a multitude of simple reactions and decisions, and this frightens me too. It is a probation - how we hear, how we see, how we shrug our shoulders at things and at people, how we think, and what we do. The Christian life is not coming to church or to Thursday Fellowship: it is a series of little tests. We are converted once and for all and thank God for that; but all throughout life our reactions to other people reflect our characters, so that life itself is a kind of probation, and 'hearing' is reciprocal. As God cried and they would not hear, so they will cry one day, and God will not hear. We not only pray to God: He speaks to **us** and we have got to listen to Him. And the nature of God's wrath is revealed through Zechariah in verse 14:

> But I will scatter them with a whirlwind **among all the nations whom they have not known.** Thus the land was desolate after them, that no man passed through nor returned: for they laid the pleasant land desolate.

Thus were the men from Beth-el and all the people and the priests reminded of the wrath that fell upon their fathers. God is long-suffering: He does not want to condemn anybody, but in the end His righteousness must be revealed. He will not fail in the end to execute judgment, although He keeps it away as long as He can from people and this sometimes deceives us into thinking that He is not there, says Peter.

I will toss them with a whirlwind among all the nations where no pity can be expected; I will shake you out like a sieve, says Amos, and all this began indeed at the fall of Jerusalem. The Jews defied God and they were sent into exile; only the little remnant came back and Zechariah is talking to them now. But it all began again! They hardened their hearts; they would not receive the word of Christ; and no impression could be made upon them. Our Lord's prophecy concerning the Jews of His day, the descendants of Zechariah's remnant five hundred years on, as it were, is in Luke 21 verse 24:

> And they shall fall by the edge of the sword, and shall be led captive into all the nations: and Jerusalem shall be trodden down of the Gentiles, until the times of the Gentiles be fulfilled.

This time the prophecy is a dispersion **to all the nations** and not just into Babylon, until ... Thank God there is always an 'until' in God's planning. Zechariah's prophecy is for the Beth-elites, the people of the land, the priests, and it is for us too. The land will be desolate, and you know it **was** desolate for some eighteen centuries. There was no scurrying to and fro; it was absolutely empty - people without a land, without a pleasant land.

This is the basis of all true repentance. The Jew has come back to the land now; he has been whirled among the nations for eighteen hundred years; the land has been lying desolate but now he is coming back. Yet God is still saying the same sort of thing: You are not coming back because you are special in yourselves; you still need repentance, forgiveness - a change of heart. Nevertheless, God will work all these things out Himself, and we will see later how God will fulfil this to the end. God is determined to have a people for Himself you know. How encouraging all this is. So as the Calvinists say, Grace, grace, grace, irresistible grace!

11 THE PROMISE TO BLESS

Chapter 8 of the book of Zechariah is a summary of the first seven chapters. We can divide the chapter into two parts, the first part being verses 1 to 17 and we begin with the statement in verse 1:

> And the word of the Lord of hosts came to me, saying,

Now this statement, or the variant, Thus saith the Lord of hosts, appears eleven times in this chapter and we may wonder why is it said so many times? It is to impress the reader with the power and authority that lie behind what may seem to be an impossible prediction. People say, These things are not going to happen are they? aren't you living in 'cloud cuckoo' land? Why do you talk like this, saying that Christ is coming and **that** is why this people are being regathered? But God says, Listen! it is not incredible; it is not impossible. What God is going to do is going to be true absolutely. So, eleven times you get, Thus saith the Lord, or, The word of Jehovah came unto me. Then in verse 2 God repeats what was said in chapter 1:

> Thus saith the Lord of hosts: I am jealous for Zion with great jealousy, and I am jealous for her with great fury.

In chapter 1 we saw that God was furious with the nations for afflicting Israel far beyond the punishment He intended, and that the nations would themselves be severely punished. Israel is still the apple of His eye; although they have fallen away from Him, they are still loved for their fathers' sakes, for the sake of Abraham, Isaac, and Jacob.

If you backslide from God and pursue your own desires, God does not like it and will chastise you, but He will never cease to love you. So, because He had chosen this race to bring His gospel to the world, then despite their backsliding, He loved them still and was furious with the nations all round Israel for the abominable treatment they meted out to them. We have already pondered the question as to the fate of those nations - Babylonia, Medo-Persia, Greece, and the Roman empire, all in the dust: I will bless them that bless thee, and him that curseth thee will I curse, was the promise of God to Abraham in Genesis 12 verse 3. And continuing with verses 3 to 5:

> Thus saith the Lord: I am returned unto Zion, and will dwell in the midst of Jerusalem: and Jerusalem will be called The city of truth; and the mountain of the Lord of hosts The holy mountain.
> Thus saith the Lord of hosts: There shall yet old men and old women dwell in the streets of Jerusalem, every man with his staff in his hand for very age.
> And the streets of the city shall be full of boys and girls playing in the streets thereof.

God had sent the Jews into exile for seventy years, but now He is saying that He will dwell among them. This broken-down city that alien armies had walked over will become the Mountain of the Lord. It will become a holy mountain, but only when God returns to it. He had left Jerusalem seventy years before, when the Glory had departed, but now He is saying: I am going to return to this city and make it into a marvellous example of a city where God Himself dwells, the Holy One of Israel, but only when the people acknowledge their sins and come back to Me! Let us read Hosea 5 verse 15:

> I will go and return to my place, till they acknowledge their offence, and seek my face: in their affliction they will seek me earnestly.

But when God returns to Jerusalem, then something else will happen, something very pleasant: Jerusalem will be full of old men who are so old that they must walk aided by a staff. You know, today, many people die at fifty and sixty years of age which is not really old. But not in this day, when God returns to Jerusalem, for then the city is going to be full of old men and old women. I read in the papers recently of a woman in Jordan aged one hundred and thirty-five (although the Arabs do not keep records, and can exaggerate terribly, you know!) And not only this, but Jerusalem is going to be full of boys and girls. It is an ideal picture you see, and very difficult for the little remnant of Zechariah's day to believe; streets full of men living to a ripe old age, and boys and girls laughing and playing without any danger of being killed. And in verse 6:

> Thus saith the Lord of hosts: If it be marvellous in the eyes of the remnant of this people in those days, should it also be marvellous in mine eyes? saith the Lord of hosts.

God is able to do what He promised; He is a God of miracles and will bring it to pass. We are living in days where we are beginning to see this coming to pass. Although Jerusalem is normally called the City of Peace, it has always been a city of war; there has always been slaughter, misery, and uncertainty in Jerusalem; but when God returns to it - when Christ returns - it will be transformed. The evidence of that transformation will be old men living in peace and young children filling the streets with happy laughter. If that is impossible with men, and you can imagine the people with Zechariah listening with great scepticism, then keep hold of the truth that with God nothing is impossible.

Now take this not only in a historical sense, but take it to yourself: nothing is too marvellous or too hard with God. The first time that those words 'too marvellous' or 'too hard' were used is with Sarah in the Old Testament. Do you recall (Genesis 18 verses 9 to 15) when Sarah was told that she was going to have a child? She was past child-bearing age and laughed, and God said to Abraham: Why did your wife laugh? and Sarah denied that she had. And then God says in verse 14: Is anything too hard (too marvellous) for the Lord? She had her child - Isaac, a child of promise, and a nation was built on a miracle, in a sense: the Jewish nation was built on a miracle from start to finish through that child of promise. God is saying this: You do not think that I can bring this nation back; you are only fifty thousand strong; you think that you are going to be decimated; you do not think that I can bring you right through and fill the streets of Jerusalem with young and old, and let very old men live in peace? Is anything too hard for the Lord?

So He was rebuking their little faith and we can learn from this also. We can have faith in God's power; God does not need any assistance from us, but He loves to see faith in our hearts - faith that believes His promises. If you have anything on your mind and you are saying, Well, that could never happen, then pray to God; pray to God; there is nothing too hard or too marvellous for the Lord to do. Read Jeremiah 32 verse 17:

> Ah Lord God! behold, thou hast made the heaven and the earth by thy great power and by thy stretched out arm; there is nothing too hard for thee:

And in verses 7 and 8:

> Thus saith the Lord of hosts: Behold, I will save my people from the east country, and from the west country:
> And I will bring them, and they shall dwell in the midst of Jerusalem; and they shall be my people, and I will be their God, in truth and in righteousness.

The verses show that this prophecy is not only to encourage the people of Zechariah's day, but that the prophecy looks forward to the distant future. God says that He will save His people from the east and from the west countries, and then four things will happen: He will bring them; they will dwell in Jerusalem; they will be His people; and He will be their God. Notice also, that the Hebrew says that He will bring His people 'from the land of the rising of the sun to the land of the going down of the sun'. Now you know the Jews had never been in the land of the going down of the sun: they had been sent to Babylon and had never gone westward. Yet here you get a distinct prophecy from God that He is going to bring back His people from the East (true of the first exile and partially fulfilled) and from the West; from all the earth in other words. He is bringing His people back not just from Babylon, but from the whole Dispersion of the Jews; and that had not taken place at the time of the prophecy.

Thus the Bible consistently shows us what would happen to the Jews: that they would be dispersed all over the world and not only to Babylon and Egypt; that God would, in His own time and in the last days, bring this people back from every nook and cranny of the earth. When you go to Israel and meet Jews as I have done over these many years, you will learn that they have come from every nation in the world. The streets of Israel to this very day have little notices in them reading, 'Not seventy nations, one nation'. This is because the Jews believe that the world is divided into seventy nations, and they are trying to tell their people not to regard themselves as still linked to those seventy nations from which they have returned, but to look on themselves as one nation! and this is the whole message of the Bible. Look at Isaiah 43 verses 5 and 6:

> Fear not; for I am with thee: I will bring thy seed from the east, and gather thee from the west;
> I will say to the north, Give up; and to the south, Keep not back; bring my sons from far, and my daughters from the end of the earth;

What I am trying to show you now is that the Bible prophesies that the Jews will come back to their own land from every part of the world, and not just from the East. Again, read Isaiah 11 verses 11 and 12:

> And it shall come to pass in that day, that the Lord shall set his hand again the second time to recover the remnant of his people, which shall remain, from Assyria, and from Egypt, and from Pathros, and from Cush, and from Elam, and from Shinar, and from Hamath, and from the islands of the sea.
> And he shall set up an ensign for the nations, and shall assemble the outcasts of Israel, and gather together the dispersed of Judah from the four corners of the earth.

Note the phrase, 'in that day'. That is a favourite expression in the Old Testament; it is always pointing to a specially appointed time in the future, That Day! When we come to the last chapter of Zechariah those words are used time and time again: That Day, That Day, That Day! in other words the world is moving on to the Day of Christ. I believe the world will not be blown to pieces by a hydrogen bomb; but that the world is in the hands of Christ, and we are moving forward slowly but surely to That Day when Christ is going to take complete control. He will come and the whole of history will be summed up in Him.

God is saying in this prophecy: I will not only bring you back as I have brought the fifty thousand from the East, but the day is coming when I am going to bring you from every corner, and you are going to repopulate Jerusalem and Palestine, and you are moving towards that day. I will bring Jews back, not because of their believing in Me, but because they will be moved by a hidden mysterious power! And that is what is happening today. Jews are going back to Israel **not** through personal faith in prophecy, but nevertheless they are going back because God is at work. They are coming back from every part of the earth to settle down in this land to be ready, or to be brought face to face with Christ, In That Day.

The statement in verse 8 'they shall be my people' is very important. When the Jews crucified Christ, God gave them a title in Hebrew when He said: I will call you from henceforth Lo-Ammi! which means 'NOT my people' (refer to Hosea chapters 1 and 2). But God also said: I will keep you, you will survive; but because you have rebelled against Me, I am going to write Lo-Ammi across the heading of your book; but when I bring you back from the four corners of the earth and when I prepare you for That Day, that Great Day of Christ, that Great Day of God's Triumph, you shall once again be called Ammi, MY people, and not Lo-Ammi.

And then God states in verse 8 that He will be their God, but only in truth and righteousness. Every unrighteous Jew will be judged as every other man will be judged; God is not favouring the Jews; He deals only in truth and righteousness. But as all these people come back they are going to be converted in the end; converted through suffering and all sorts of things; and chiefly by the coming of Christ. God is going to dwell in the midst of a converted and repentant people who deal only in truth and righteousness.

But we can only get to truth and righteousness by faith in Jesus Christ, for none of us possess it ourselves. This situation has not as yet been fulfilled, but I think that it is becoming very close to being fulfilled and of course, this will only be so when He comes again. Now look at Jeremiah 32 verses 37 to 40:

> Behold, I will gather them out of all the countries, whither I have driven them in mine anger, and in my fury, and in great wrath; and I will bring them again unto this place, and I will cause them to dwell safely:
> And they shall be my people (Ammi), and I will be their God:
> And I will give them one heart and one way, that they may fear me for ever; for the good of them, and of their children after them:
> And I will make an everlasting covenant with them,

> that I will not turn away from them, to do them good; and I will put my fear in their hearts, that they shall not depart from me.

Here is another prophet saying the same thing. Here is the promise of God to this little people, and what is He saying? just this: You look ahead and you think that you have no chance; but I am faithful to my promises to Abraham, Isaac, and Jacob, so, although you are going to be dispersed; and although you are going to do dreadful things to the One who is called the Messiah and will put Him to death; and although you are going to be severely punished; yet! I will bring you back and I will dwell in the midst of you; I will give you a heart of flesh instead of a heart of stone and I will be your God, and Jerusalem will become the joy and the centre of the whole earth! And in verse 9:

> Thus saith the Lord of hosts: Let your hands be strong, ye that hear in these days these words from the mouth of the prophets, which were in the day that the foundation of the house of the Lord of hosts was laid, even the temple, that it might be built.

Let the glorious future that I have shown you, God says, fill you with faith and works. Build the Temple; come out of your spiritual depression. Look at my promises; look at the things that I have told you and say to yourselves, My Goodness! I have found the greatest thing this world can offer me; I am on God's side.

These things are taking place: it is not our subjective feelings that matter - how we feel today. We too are part of God's great triumphal march which is taking place in the midst of this struggle going on between America and Russia and amidst all the rest of the world's confusion. But God is on the march; God is doing His thing! If we get spiritually depressed, let us look upon the promises of God and let us work today, not because we feel like it, but because we know that God is faithful to His word; He is doing His will and we can look on the happenings outside ourselves and say: My word, it is true, it is all true! And in verses 10 and 11:

> For before those days there was no hire for man, nor any hire for beast; neither was there any peace to him that went out or came in because of the adversary: for I set all men every one against his neighbour.
> But now I will not be unto the remnant of this people as in the former days, saith the Lord of hosts.

So God exhorts the people of Zechariah's day: Look at the glorious future and start building and living faithfully. Before these days you had dissension, no wages, hardship and no peace at all; bad relationships everywhere; surrounded by your enemies and selfishness among yourselves. But from this day, if you believe My word, if you trust Me and take these promises, and see that the future is secure, and that My word **can** be trusted, then, I will bless you.

Now let that go home to you. Do not be slack; do not be depressed; do not be affected by spiritual ups and downs. Look at the promises of God, for we have seen so many of them fulfilled, If we say: Lord, thank you very much; it is not how I **feel**, it is the faithfulness of your Word that I trust, then God begins to bless. Just believe. You do not **feel** you believe? you lack a sort of psychological feeling of 'isn't it nice to be a Christian'? But in fact you do not need to have these feelings. Who is there among you, says God, who walks in darkness and has no light? Now many of us are like that: we walk in darkness and we have no light, yet what does God say? Let him trust in the Lord! Yes indeed, let him trust because, although you do not actually feel anything, God is at work. He is faithful; He will not let you down; He is the strong member of the partnership; and if on any day you are walking in darkness and have no light, but trust Him, then He is pleased with you. And it is not a sign of His displeasure if you are having to hang on to Him saying: Lord, I do not feel anything, and I do not feel particularly like a

Christian, but I am still trusting you! Then, says God, I will bless you. This was the message meant for the little remnant with Zechariah, and the blessing that the small flock of God will inherit is spoken of in verse 12:

> For there shall be the seed of peace; the vine shall give her fruit, and the ground shall give her increase, and the heavens shall give their dew; and I will cause the remnant of this people to inherit all these things.

This applies not only in the day that this Book was written but in the Last Day too. And then in verse 13 God reminds the people that, though they were a curse, all that is to be changed:

> And it shall come to pass that, as ye were a curse among the nations, O house of Judah and house of Israel, so will I save you, and ye shall be a blessing: fear not, but let your hands be strong.

We have already said that the Jew has always been hated; he has always been cursed and he is cursed today. In every nation of the world there is tremendous anti-semitism. It was so strong in the 1930s that Hitler talked about 'a final solution' and some six million Jews were eliminated in gas chambers. The feeling against Jews is going on all the time and why? Part of the reason (and only part) is the way they themselves often act, because they are without Christ. God is not sympathising with them when He declares that they were a curse among the nations. You have acted in such a way, says God, that you have blasphemed My Name in the world; men hate you because you are hateful; you are a curse, hated and hateful! It is sadly true that they have been bitter enemies of the Gospel of Christ; look at 1 Thessalonians 2 verses 14 to 16:

> For ye, brethren, became imitators of the churches of God which are in Judaea in Christ Jesus: for ye also suffered the same things of your own countrymen, even

> as they did of the Jews;
> Who both killed the Lord Jesus and the prophets, and drave out us, and please not God, and are contrary to all men;
> Forbidding us to speak to the Gentiles that they may be saved; to fill up their sins alway: but the wrath is come upon them to the uttermost.

So the people are a curse, partly because of their own ungodly blasphemous ways. They are a stiff-necked and self-righteous people; and when Jesus came they put Him to death, and were dispersed for it and punished for it and hated of all men. But nevertheless God says: I am not going to leave you; I am going to save you and I am going to make you a blessing. What a transformation this will be for a people currently hated by most nations.

Today, Israel has no friends apart from America and Zaire. No other nation in this world likes Israel, and why? it is in fulfilment of this Book. Israel is still in unbelief; she is still acting in a haughty, self-righteous, and very abrasive way; all the nations of the world have turned their faces against Israel, partly for what she has done in Palestine and Lebanon. She is a kind of grit in the eye of the nations, but God is going to bring the Jews through and purify them. Let us read Ezekiel 34 verses 22 to 26 and note what is going to happen:

> Therefore will I save my flock, and they shall no more be a prey; and I will judge between cattle and cattle.
> And I will set up one shepherd over them, and he shall feed them, even my servant David (this is a prophecy that the great son of David will reign); he shall feed them, and he shall be their shepherd.
> And I the Lord will be their God, and my servant David prince among them; I the Lord have spoken it.
> And I will make with them a covenant of peace, and will cause evil beasts to cease out of the land: and they shall dwell securely in the wilderness, and sleep in the woods.

> And I will **make them** and the places round about my hill **a blessing**; and I will cause the shower to come down in its season; **there shall be showers of blessing.**

Even the popular hymn refers back to God's relationship with Israel. What I am trying to do is to relate Scripture to Scripture, and to say that the pattern that I am expounding from Zechariah is to be found in all the prophets, but that you have to search! But the same message is in all the prophets: God chose this people to bring forth the Christ; they turned their back on Him; He dispersed them; He punished them; but because He is faithful to Abraham He is going to bring them back; although the Jews have been hated and cursed and still are accursed, He is going to make them a blessing when Christ comes the second time.

In Romans 9, 10, and 11 St Paul takes up the theme and says: Do not hate the Jews; I know they are nasty (and Paul was of course a Jew) but love them for the Father's sake, for the sake of Abraham, Isaac, and Jacob. Paul says: I tell you this, when the Jews are converted to Christ, it will be as though life has come from the dead. They will change suddenly and in such a wonderful way that they will be unrecognizable! they will be like a nation of St Pauls, all glorious Christians. And we are waiting for that day when the Jew will indeed become a blessing. So God recalls the past and states the future in verses 14 and 15:

> For thus saith the Lord of hosts: As I thought to do evil unto you, when your fathers provoked me to wrath, saith the Lord of hosts, and I repented not;
> So again have I thought in these days to do good unto Jerusalem and to the house of Judah: fear ye not.

God said that He would send the Jews into exile in Babylon, and He did just that; He did not relent; He punished, for He always keeps His word. So, says God, when I promise to come and dwell with you one day, I will keep My word also.

Has any of this been fulfilled as yet in this marvellous way? No! but I believe that we are seeing it about to be fulfilled. But in verses 16 and 17 God reiterates that He will not do all this simply because they are Jews: He will only have people that are justified by faith and are righteous; He hates the things the Jews have done, so His word is:

> These are the things that ye shall do; Speak ye every man the truth with his neighbour; execute the judgment of truth and peace in your gates:
> And let none of you imagine evil in your hearts against his neighbour; and love no false oath: for all these are things that I hate, saith the Lord.

We can now deal with verses 18 to 23, which form the second part of chapter 8. Now Jews love fasting from sunset to sunset; they regard it as a kind of credit mark against their name, a religious credit in their favour; and in verses 18 and 19 the prophet tells the people what God says about the main fasts:

> And the word of the Lord of hosts came unto me, saying,
> Thus saith the Lord of hosts: The fast of the fourth month, and the fast of the fifth, and the fast of the seventh, and the fast of the tenth, shall be to the house of Judah joy and gladness, and cheerful feasts; therefore love truth and peace.

May I recall the reason for these fasts: the fast of the fourth month was to mourn the day that Nebuchadnezzar took the city, and the fast of the fifth month was to mark the day the Temple and the city were absolutely destroyed; the fast of the seventh month was to commemorate the death of Gedaliah and this we discussed in the previous chapter; and the fast of the tenth month marked the beginning of the siege of Jerusalem. In fact the Jews mark every little thing with a fast day and then they go about claiming to be righteous, and in this way they think they might twist God's arm!

We can think that way too, but God is never moved by such behaviour. You can never work out your own righteousness; you must trust Christ for righteousness. Let us take that home to ourselves; and let us not think that anything we do adds to our righteousness. We are saved by Christ and we are saved unto good works, but, it is not our good works that save us!

What God is saying here is this: In those days when I come again, when I gather you back in Jerusalem, and when I defend you against the nations, all these fast days are going to become feasts. Away with your miserable fasts! sitting in sackcloth and ashes and looking religious and miserable; for then there will be great gladness, joy, and cheerfulness; and therefore love, truth, and peace! Then verses 20 to 22 reveal the extent of the reaction of the world to That Day when Christ comes again:

> Thus saith the Lord of hosts: It shall yet come to pass, that there shall come peoples, and the inhabitants of many cities:
> And the inhabitants of one city shall go to another, saying, Let us go speedily to entreat the favour of the Lord, and to seek the Lord of hosts: I will go also.
> Yea, many peoples and strong nations shall come to seek the Lord of hosts in Jerusalem, and to entreat the favour of the Lord.

In the Last Day peoples of many cities, of cities of the great Gentile nations, will come and seek God's face; the whole world is going to be affected. People in the cities of every nation in the world are going to be agitated in their minds, and be stirred to go and seek the true God. In a sense, through the preaching of the Gospel, this has already been partly fulfilled; but in the Last Day there is going to be a marvellous outspreading of the Gospel. Men are going to go from city to city it says (in verse 21), and they will go in companies to encourage each other and to evangelise each other; and they will go individually. People from every part of the world are going to be drawn in to this great manifestation of God's love in Christ to us; and the restoration of the Jewish nation, now repentant and now recovered. And then this wonderful last verse 23:

> Thus saith the Lord of hosts: In those days it shall come to pass, that ten men shall take hold, out of all the languages of the nations, shall even take hold of the skirt of him that is a Jew, saying, We will go with you, for we have heard that God is with you.

The number ten, in the Old Testament particularly, often means an indefinite number. Ten men are going to take hold of the skirt of a converted Jew! The Jew wears white garments with blue tassels, and the picture is the Jew and the Gentile coming together; the Gentile with a great hunger for God, and the Jew radiant with faith in Christ! People are going to gather around the Jew and say: It has happened! Christ has come! You are converted; take us and let us share in the blessing that God has promised you. Yes, Jew and Gentile are going to be together; ten men will take hold of the tassels of a Jew and say, We have heard that God is with you.

And all this is a summary of the first seven chapters of Zechariah and we are living in the beginning of it. The Jew is still in unbelief; he is still hated; but the Jew since the turn of the century has started to go back to Palestine. The world is getting darker and darker: we all wonder what is going to happen; but Zechariah tells us what is going to happen! It will get worse and there will be a manifestation of even greater evil; sophisticated evil; and in the end the Nations will turn their fury upon this nation of Israel, the Jew, in a more intense way than ever before. But in the midst of that fury of attack Christ will descend, and ... we will deal with the traumas of those Last Days in chapters 9 to 14.

PART B THE END OF THE AGE

12 ALEXANDER THE GREAT: A CHRIST-TYPE CONQUEROR

Chapters 9 to 14 form the second part of the book of Zechariah. The critics say that these chapters are a post-exilic production, and may not have been written by Zechariah but by one or more great anonymous writers. This is a rationalistic and (if I may say so) ungodly way of looking at the book of Zechariah. There is much evidence linguistic and otherwise to say, as the Jews always believed, that the Book is indeed the work of the prophet. What the critics object to is that the Bible foresees anything in the future: in other words they say to God, You are not able to do it! When they come to the Messianic prophecies they strive desperately to keep them solely within the context of contemporary history, no matter how difficult that may be.

All conservative Bible students from Bible days to Anstruc, to the middle of the last century, never doubted the Bible. But then came the rationalistic schools which do not believe Scripture, and treat it as an old document, looking for evidence as to who wrote this and who wrote that. They go so far even as to divide a verse and allocate authorship to anonymous writers based on stylistic and other analysis.

But now let us consider these last six chapters of Zechariah. We could, if we wish, divide them into three aspects. Firstly, we have in chapters 9 to 11 a general view of the destruction of the enemies of Israel; then in chapters 12 to 14, the events towards the end are presented in sharp focus and we come to the actual turmoil of the Last Days; and thirdly, arising from these chapters, you see Israel herself being chastised, purged, and restored, because repentance and faith are an essential part of the salvation of God. Israel is going to be saved **not** because she is simply Israel, but because she is to be purged and restored by the Coming of Christ. I reiterate this to show that there is never any inequality or lack of balance in sections of Scripture; there is none whatsoever.

Now when I say 'a general view of the destruction of the enemies of Israel', you must not think in political terms and you must not think of **all Israel** as if there were something special about them. You must think of the **remnant** of Israel that God is going to bring through to honour His holy Name. God said to Abraham that in him every nation would be blessed. He said to the Jew: Though you have left Me, I will nevertheless bring Glory unto my Name and a remnant will come through. This nation will never disappear and a remnant of believing Jews will indeed come through.

We are getting a general view of the destruction of the enemies of Israel, but the immediate events in chapters 9 to 11 point to the great final events. Remember that there is no perspective in prophecy. It is rather like standing at a view-point and looking at mountain peaks in the distance: you can identify the peaks although they all look within touching distance of each other; and you could imagine standing on one of the peaks and striding, as it were, to the next! but you know that you cannot do so and that probably valleys of twenty or more miles separate peak from peak. Nevertheless, from the view-point you have no perception of those valleys. It is the same in prophecy; there is no perspective and in the Old Testament you get the first and second Coming of Christ absolutely in juxtaposition. This occurs even in one verse. For example, 'Unto to us a son is born, unto us a child is given; and the government shall be laid upon his shoulder'. Here we have the Incarnation and the second Coming referred to in one verse, a difference **you** can see and a jump from one aspect of the Messiah to another. But the prophet did not see what God had hidden from him: the mystery of the Church which was revealed to Paul; the prophet did not see the valley in between the two peaks of the Incarnation and the second Coming, and this principle in prophecy must be appreciated in order to understand the New Testament.

So to continue; every delivery of Israel anticipates the great and final delivery. They were delivered from Sennacherib in a small way in Hezekiah's day, but that is only a picture of what is going to happen when Christ comes. Every delivery points to the Great Deliverance and that is one of the emphases of this first aspect. I now turn to chapter 9 of Zechariah and the first three verses are very specific:

> The burden of the word of the Lord upon the land of Hadrach, and Damascus shall be its resting place: for the eye of man and of all the tribes of Israel is toward the Lord:
> And Hamath also which bordereth thereon: Tyre and Zidon, because she is very wise.
> And Tyre did build herself a strong hold, and heaped up silver as the dust, and fine gold as the mire of the streets.

The 'burden' in Hebrew means something very heavy, something very serious and something talking about trouble. It is not an oracle. Until a few years ago Hadrach was thought not to have existed and to have been a kind of fanciful guess on the part of Zechariah; but now evidence has been found that Hadrach did exist after all. You know Scripture has this habit of justifying itself in the end!

In this vision Damascus will be the centre of confusion and turmoil; the prophet is looking forward to a special event and saying: The burden is going to come in Hadrach and in Damascus, and everyone is going to be very troubled; people are going to turn away from their superstitions and stupidities and look to the Lord. One could pose the question as to what would happen today if the hydrogen bomb were about to be dropped? You would stop fiddling about with trivialities; you would be so alarmed by impending events that 'the eye of man' would indeed be turned to the Lord. And so fear, consternation, trouble, and the coming of a conqueror strike fear in every heart. Somone is coming who is going to destroy all the nations round Israel and sit in judgment on them, and on Israel itself. A conqueror is coming! and that took place. The earthly conqueror in view here is Alexander the Great. He swept like a leopard against the Persian empire; he circled round the Holy Land without hurting it; he went to Damascus and that city opened its gates to his general. Now Darius of Persia kept all his treasure in Damascus, but such was the fear of this leopard-like army of the Greeks that the city surrendered and was totally plundered. Everyone trembled.

The great Phoenician cities of Tyre and Sidon trembled at what was going on in the north. They were not twin cities and to this very day it is Tyre that takes the preeminence, but both were tremendously rich. The prophet underlines the vast wealth of Tyre with his description of silver as common as dust, and gold abounding as mud in the streets! Tyre was famous and her fleets sailed as far as Carthage; the Phoenicians controlled all the trade of the Mediterranean and were immensely strong; yet they heard and saw and noted what was happening to Damascus and the surrounding cities and they trembled! the great Persian empire, The Bear, was being shattered by this new Western power. The frightening question for Tyre was, What do we do? do we defy this man and his armies? To safeguard their wealth they had fortified an island lying about seven hundred paces off the mainland, and had built a wall one hundred and fifty feet high all around it; so the city of Tyre was a sea port with the island as its fortress. In earlier days Shalmaneser had tried to take the fortress island but had given up after five years. It is said that Nebuchadnezzar attacked the island for thirteen years without success, although he took the city port. So they decided to defy Alexander the Great, who sent a message saying, You despise this land-army of mine, but I will make you as though you are part of a continent! In the space of seven months this brilliant and charismatic man had a huge dam built across the waters, and it is there to this very day. He took the fortress and put the defenders to death, some ten thousand in all.

Now, we live far removed from those days, but read Ezekiel 28 for an astonishing and frightening allusion to Tyre as the Antichrist. You were, says the prophet, in Eden; you were perfect and covered with jewels and gold; there was no fault until the day sin was found in you. And the prophet likens this powerful, arrogant, and wealthy city so full of earthly pride to Satan, the enemy of God, who shall be brought down! This goes on all the way through Scripture: Babylon the Great is fallen; Rome is fallen; we can almost personalise cities and empires in Scripture. You have got to see what the Spirit is saying to man in this way and say to ourselves, Are we so different to Tyre in our day? Are we so different today from that proud and powerful city? And continuing in verse 4:

> Behold, the Lord will dispossess her, and he will smite her power in the sea; and she shall be devoured with fire.

Now recall the four smiths and the four horns in the second vision. Behind all the movements in all the world is the Lord. That is what God is continually saying. He is working His purposes out; they are strange; we do not understand why a nation which is wicked is allowed to dominate the world. The answer is that God, in a world of sin (our virtues are relative in any case), in His awesome sovereignty, will use His enemies; for example, 'I raised up Pharaoh', said God. And God raised up Alexander the Great: the Lord is behind this; the Lord will dispossess Tyre and His servant in this is Alexander the Great. Again, Sargon the Great was the Lord's rod, and you get this truth repeated time after time. In other words, the sovereignty of God covers evil as well as good; so we might also say that communist Russia today is not there by historical accident, nor is capitalistic America.

The comforting thing to the Christian is that, behind

all the events on the face of the earth, the rebellions of the third world, the atheistic might of Russia, and the capitalistic might of America, God is at work. His ways are past finding out and He will bring about His solutions. Of course we must do our little political bit and try to keep peace: but God is at work and He was at work in the times we are speaking of. The great dam was built; the defenders were destroyed; and all the prophecies of Ezekiel were fulfilled absolutely. Alexander scraped the dust off this island: later on it was repeopled and regained modest prosperity; but never again was Tyre the Tyre of Old. You cannot keep the Lord out; you cannot keep the conqueror out.

In verses 5 and 6 he swept on to the four cities of the Philistines on the coast, Ashkelon, Gaza, Ekron, and Ashdod:

> Ashkelon shall see it, and fear; Gaza also, and shall be sore pained; and Ekron, for her expectation shall be ashamed: and the king shall perish from Gaza, and Ashkelon shall not be inhabited.
> And a bastard shall dwell in Ashdod, and I will cut off the pride of the Philistines.

Note that Gath, the fifth city of the Philistines, is not mentioned: this is because it had been taken by Judah. I know these coastal towns very well and used to travel by rail right up the coast as far as Lebanon when I lived in the Middle East. The railroad from Gaza to Beirut was built by British engineers, but now it is destroyed, though there are remnants of the line at Rosh Hanikra.

So the Philistines also saw what was happening and feared greatly. They were a powerful and proud people coming originally from Cyprus and Crete; they worshipped the fish god Dagon and they were very proud of their blood and heritage. They were Philistine and Palestine was called after them; but they were also part of the Persian empire and they resisted Alexander the Great. It took him five months to take the city of Gaza. The Persian ruler was bound to the wheel of a chariot through holes in his feet and dragged through the streets, and the city was made desolate. That was how Alexander treated anybody who got in his way; he was totally ruthless. So the prophecy states that Gaza was going to be taken, and that the ruler would perish; their pride would be crushed and a rabble of half-breeds would dwell in Philistine lands. Now that means nothing to us but to the Philistines it was an awful fate: from a pure and noble race of 'Caphtorim', the land from now on would be inhabited by a mixed race of nobodies!

And then we come to the flowery language of verse 7:

> And I will take away his blood out of his mouth, and his abominations from between his teeth; and he also shall be a remnant for our God: and he shall be as a chieftain in Judah, and Ekron as a Jebusite.

This means that, not only will the people be crushed and become a rabble of half-breeds, but all their superstitions, their blood-offerings and sacrifices, and their abominations to their gods will be taken away from them. They will be absorbed into Judah and become like Araunah the Jebusite. Do you recall the incident of Araunah who owned the Temple site? David had committed the sin of numbering the people and the angel of God stood over the city and was destroying the people. David wanted to offer sacrifices to God, so God gave him a choice of three things, then David went to Araunah and asked for the piece of land to raise up a tent for sacrifices. Now Araunah was a Jebusite, and he offered the land and also ploughs for the burnt offering: so why does he appear in this verse? Let me summarise it for you. Alexander the Great has taken Tyre: he now comes and captures the land of the Philistines and reduces them from being a proud people to a rabble. He destroys their religion, and they become like Araunah the Jebusite, absorbed into the faith of the God of Israel; and this is exactly what had happened to Araunah, and to the old Jebusites who owned Jerusalem when David took their city.

Again I ask, did not all these things happen to the Philistines exactly as prophesied? And again I say that all these events are only precursors of the Great Event. Everything that happens is a precursor of what God is going to do finally; and similarly, all the antichrists that come into the world are all precursors of the great Antichrist. We get Attila the Hun, we get Napoleon, we get Hitler; people look at them and say, Who is this man? and according to the doctrine of Scripture, they are only precursors. One day a man will come to this earth who will be greater than past antichrists; who will be THE Antichrist and who will persecute the saints of God. He will raise tremendous rebellion and things will be seen such as have never been seen before; but all these other men on the road, so to speak, are a prelude to the Great Event. So, the taking over of the land of the Philistines, and their becoming believers (as a Jebusite chieftain), is a prophetic insight into what is going to happen when the Lord of Glory comes, and that is rather wonderful is it not?

And now Alexander marched on Jerusalem. He was furious with Jerusalem, because he had sent a note to the high priest before starting his campaign demanding the payment of taxes; Jerusalem was still under the sovereignty of Persia and they had refused to pay. So there was great terror in Jerusalem and it was there that the eyes of men, and especially of Israel, turned to God. Would He let them be consumed by this antichrist? and long before all these events took place what does verse 8 say:

> And I will encamp about mine house against the army, that none pass through or return: and no oppressor shall pass through them any more: for now have I seen with mine eyes.

God is looking upon this earth: He is observing every move of every man and of every nation. He makes a distinction between people. I will put a difference between the

Egyptians and My people, says God in Exodus! And you must also take that to yourselves. God puts a difference between Christians and non-Christians. God is watching everything; but especially He watches the land of Palestine. Mine eyes, He says in the Old Testament, are always upon that land. He knows what is going on in Beirut and in the West Bank and in Gaza, which has again raised its head in commotions.

So the prophecy is that all Jerusalem is in terror at the coming of the conqueror: no army has ever resisted this man. But Jehoah the high priest had a dream in which he had a vision from God, and Jehoah said to the people: We will not resist, but we will go out to meet Alexander dressed in our robes. This they did, choosing a vantage point where you can see both the city and the Temple; and Josephus tells us what happened. Alexander came up and saw the white robes of peaceful people; he saw the priests dressed in their marvellous attire, all shimmering in the sunshine; and when the conqueror approached the high priest (whom he had intended to kill along with everyone else), he worshipped in the human sense and showed him great reverence. His general Parmenio, who had sacked Damascus said: You have been worshipped in every land in Asia; why are you worshipping this unknown person? and the reply was that before starting the campaign Alexander had, in a dream in Macedonia, himself looked upon this very scene of a man dressed like the high priest with his priests round him, standing before him.

So instead of ravaging Palestine, Alexander skirted the land and gave great concessions to the Jews. This is quite astonishing and it is all so clearly prophesied by Zechariah in verse 8. We know that Alexander permitted the Jews to go into Alexandria and to Ephesus and to other places; and as a special concession to the high priest, Alexander excused the payment of taxes every seventh year. Here surely, is an extraordinary incident: the ruthless invader destroying all before him; coming to Jerusalem with a special hatred; and then suddenly changing overnight - the conqueror being conquered as it were. But God was defending the Jews as the prophecy had foretold. It would all come to pass.

A Remarkable Prophecy

The above incident was history and only concerned a human conqueror; but in verse 9 the prophet looks forward to a much greater event:

> Rejoice greatly, O daughter of Zion; shout, O daughter of Jerusalem: behold, thy king cometh unto thee: he is just, and having salvation; lowly, and riding upon an ass, even upon a colt the foal of an ass.

Note the words, **thy king** cometh unto thee, and not, **another king** cometh unto thee. You know, many preachers on Palm Sunday miss the tremendous force of THY KING! The hinge of history hangs upon this text: it is not simply that Christ came into Jerusalem on a donkey and fulfilled the prophecy of Zechariah, as though that were some incidental occurrence! such an approach is entirely inadequate. Here is Alexander, a great conqueror, overcome by God in His own way; God was using this great conqueror; God was turning the whole of Alexander's might to defend His people in distress. Now, says the Holy Spirit through the prophet, Rejoice, Israel; you may think that this was a wonderful deliverance, but think also of the Last Days; think of this deliverance in terms of the whole of your own destiny and not just of one event; think of the day Thy King cometh unto thee!

This text of Zechariah bursts so richly on us. He is just, He is saved, He is lowly - lowly because He rides on an ass, for even in those days people did not ride on asses. From the time of Solomon men rode on horses. The judges used to ride on asses in the old days but not after David and Solomon, and the ass was the royal beast of burden only in the very early days. So the prophet is saying: You are going to see, worked out in history, the coming of a ruthless conqueror; but you are also going to see your own King come; He too will be an irresistible

Conqueror but He will come at first in justice, and mercy, and humility, and with salvation. And so the prophet shows the contrast between the Messiah and Alexander the Great.

This is marvellous, absolutely marvellous! and Christ did come: He came unto His own; but His own, who received Alexander the Great with humility, did not receive Christ. We see in the New Testament, in a sense, the terrible failure of Christ in the Scriptures. He was crucified under Pontius Pilate; He, the King of Kings, the Lord of Lords, the Prince of Peace; yet He was saved and ever lives to make intercession for us, and now He is the King in spirit of millions and millions. But what happenned then is again only a precursor of **what is going to happen** when He comes the second time, for then He will come in great judgment, in great power, in great majesty, and in great glory.

So these words of verse 9 are not just isolated words: they are all from the Old Testament; they are all from historical incidents; and we will never be strong Christians if we just think of the words of this text as bits of poetry. The words all spring out of history, divine revelation, actual suffering, and actual people! If you want a picture of Christ coming in glory, look, in a sense, at Alexander the Great; what happened then will happen again; but first He is to come to the Jews as their own King, in lowliness and humility, and to save those who want to be saved. At the same time this first appearance is a prediction of His second and final Coming, when He will come with great power and glory, and when all the people will acclaim Him: This is our God; we have waited long.

Verse 10 changes abruptly from the first Coming in humility, lowliness, justice, grace and mercy, and leaps to the End Days (remember, there is no perspective in prophecy) when He will come in majesty:

> And I will cut off the chariot from Ephraim, and the horse from Jerusalem, and the battle bow shall be cut off; and he shall speak peace unto the nations: and his

> dominion shall be from sea to sea, and from the River to the ends of the earth.

So the Divine King, the Great Conqueror that is to come a second time, is going to do something special. First of all He is going to take weapons out of the people's hands. He is not, so to speak, going to let them have tanks, rockets, guns, and bombs; He is going to save them without any weapons at all, 'Not by might or power but by My Spirit', for when Christ comes the people will not need weapons. Read Hosea 1 verse 7:

> But I will have mercy upon the house of Judah, and will save them by the Lord their God, and will not save them by bow, nor by sword, nor by battle, by horses, nor by horsemen.

This is just one reference. When the Divine King comes in the end He will not rely on armaments; He will cut them off from His own people, and He will cut them off from other people. And secondly, He will publish peace to the nations in a universal and in a personal way. Has Christ spoken peace to you? peace from sins forgiven? peace and reconciliation to God from His death on Calvary? When He comes He will speak peace, and justice, and mercy, and grace to the nations.

He is also going to set up His kingdom: the verse says 'from the Nahar' (the River), and in the Old Testament this always means the Euphrates, the furthest border of the Promised Land which God promised to Abraham. In a sense this means that the Messianic kingdom will have the Euphrates as its border and the whole of the Middle East will have become one undivided kingdom. Let us read Psalm 72 verses 7 and 8, just to relate scripture to scripture:

> In his days shall the righteous flourish; and abundance of peace, till the moon be no more.
> He shall have dominion also from sea to sea, and from

the River unto the ends of the earth.

The days referred to are the days of the Messiah, so we could say that Zechariah had indeed read his Bible. This Zechariah quoted his Bible and he breathed out what he had read! it is a repetition of God's eternal truth, and of what is going to happen when the Lord Jesus comes. And who is this Man who is going to have such dominion? Well, you get it in Micah 5 verse 2:

> But thou, Beth-lehem Ephrathah, which art little to be among the thousands of Judah, out of thee shall one come forth unto me that is to be ruler in Israel; whose goings forth are from old, from everlasting.

And again in Micah 5 verses 4 and 5 (part):

> And he shall stand, and shall feed his flock in the strength of the Lord, in the majesty of the name of the Lord his God: and they shall abide; for now shall he be great unto the ends of the earth.
> And **this man** shall be our peace ...

Is it not futile how the world sees peace, when we read the Scriptures? We should not resist any movement that seeks peace; we should not criticise the United Nations and its efforts for world peace; but when you look into the secrets **behind** the secret of peace, is it not rather futile? When I read my papers I say: God bless you, you are doing your best to stop wars and so you should! but in the end it will not depend on political activity. 'This man shall be our peace'; there is no hope for this world, for Jew or Gentile, until This Man, whose goings forth are from everlasting to everlasting, the eternal God - until This Man comes and is our great peace.

Well, that day is coming, when men shall beat their swords into ploughshares, and their spears into pruning hooks, and learn war no more. All that I can say here in Zechariah is that this is the precursor, through a local event, through a small weak event, of what is going to happen at the End of Days. Someone has said that God never loses His thread in history: two thousand five hundred years have elapsed since Zechariah spoke and God has never lost the thread! Today, we are almost in a similar position: through modern technology we are hearing about Lebanon, and about Israel actually back in the land; about the confusion in Gaza; about the trouble between Arab and Jew; God has not lost the thread! If I had said this one hundred years ago I would have been stoned as a lunatic, because Israel was not back in the land and there was no hope of seeing this despised people anywhere near Palestine, but today! ... God never loses His thread.

Release

In verses 11 and 12 is the promise of release from the pit:

> As for thee also, because of the blood of thy covenant I have sent forth thy prisoners out of the pit wherein is no water.
>
> Turn you to the strong hold, ye prisoners of hope: even to-day do I declare that I will render double unto thee.

This is addressed specifically to the Jew. Why is God doing this? because He made a promise to Moses when Moses shed the blood of the covenant, saying: I will never desert you, I will never leave you, you will never ultimately fail. Now that is the blood of the covenant. God is faithful to His own oath; not because people are good or because the Israelites obeyed Him; but because He made the oath, the blood of the covenant, and He made it with Abraham. You remember when Abraham prepared his sacrifices and cut them in two and a flaming torch passed in between them; do you remember that in Genesis 15? That was the blood of the covenant.

Now the Sinai covenant has been broken by the Jew. He still stands on trying to keep that covenant by obedience to the law: that is why he has failed; that is why he is persecuted; that is why he is embittered. He still insists that he is able to do it, but he cannot. He will not accept the grace of God; he persists in justifying himself; he has broken the covenant but, because of the blood of the covenant, God will not desert him. The new covenant is in My Blood, says Christ, and I will never leave you nor forsake you. All the promises of the New Testament are not because of our goodness; it is because Christ has made a covenant with the Father by His blood; all the power of heaven and of earth is His. It is a sworn oath in the Godhead and does not depend on your or my fidelity, thank God! He will see His purposes worked right through.

And, still talking to the Jew, the state of being in a pit, or in the deeps, is again referred to - as happened in the first vision. He has been in darkness for over two thousand years; he has been in a pit as Joseph was in a pit, but it is a pit without water and so the Jew has not been submerged and drowned. But he is a prisoner: he is a prisoner of his own blindness amd obduracy, and God says: I am going to do this; I am going to send you out in the Last Days.

The Hebrew for 'prisoners of hope' is better rendered as 'prisoners of THE hope'. The Jews have lived in hope, and hope is an enormous doctrine in the New Testament: when related to the whole of the Bible the words 'the hope' in the New Testament always mean the Coming of Christ, the victory of God, and not just 'hope' as a virtue. The Jew has always lived in the hope of what God is going to do one day. We live in the joy of The Hope that Christ is going to come one day. Paul takes this theme up when he says: What is The Hope of the Christian? what is The Hope of the Jew? it is that God will reign; that we will be delivered; that Christ will come; that Evil will be overcome; that there will be a cataclysmic event in which the kingdoms of this world will be shattered and God will take up His residence. That is The Hope; never think of it as anything less. You get it in Acts 26 verses 5 and 6 when Paul is defending himself to Agrippa:

Having knowledge of me from the first, if they be

> willing to testify, how that after the straitest sect of our religion I lived a Pharisee.
> And now I stand here to be judged for **the hope** of the promise made of God unto our fathers;

Paul as a Jew is standing before Agrippa, and it was his defence that 'the hope' was the Coming of the Messiah. Paul knew that, as a Jew, King Agrippa knew all about This Hope. Refer to Romans 8 verses 22 to 25:

> For we know that the whole creation groaneth and travaileth in pain together until now.
> And not only so, but ourselves also, which have the firstfruits of the Spirit, even we ourselves groan within ourselves, waiting for our adoption, to wit, the redemption of our body.
> For by hope were we saved: but hope that is seen is not hope: for who hopeth for that which he seeth?
> But if we hope for that which we see not, then do we with patience wait for it.

Now that is The Hope of the Christian. It is referred to again in Titus 2 verses 11 to 13, where Paul is so explicit:

> For the grace of God hath appeared, bringing salvation to all men,
> Instructing us, to the intent that, denying ungodliness and worldy lusts, we should live soberly and righteously and godly in this present world;
> Looking for the blessed hope and appearing of the glory of our great God and Saviour Jesus Christ;

So you see what The Hope means. It is not a passive virtue in the sense of 'I hope that this will happen'; it is The Hope; it is The Great Dawn; and it springs particularly out of Zechariah when he talks of 'rendering double'. You know, when a man in Israel had, say, five sons, he always divided his patrimony into six parts and gave a double portion to the firstborn. God always said this to Israel, and this is what happened to Joseph. He went down into Egypt: Reuben was the eldest son, the firstborn, but he committed immorality and was ruled out; so God looked on the suffering Joseph who had been put into the pit; and Joseph was a picture of Israel. He was in a pit with no water and so he lived, and was taken by traders to Egypt; and what happened? Joseph had two sons and they were both named in the tribes of Israel; Joseph had a double portion for his suffering! instead of the tribe of Joseph we have the two tribes of Manasseh and Ephraim. Do you see how it all fits in? God always rewards His people with double, or indeed punishes them with double. And thinking again of The Hope, it is indeed interesting to note that the National Anthem of modern Israel is actually called Ha Tiqva - 'The Hope'.

Then the prophet, still looking at the Last Days, says in verse 13:

> For I have bent Judah for me, I have filled the bow with Ephraim; and I will stir up thy sons, O Zion, against thy sons, O Greece, and I will make thee as the sword of a mighty man.

Now we are thinking in the context of Alexander, but the prophet takes us forward to the Last Days; yet he uses the contemporary events and says: I am going to use Judah and Ephraim as a bow! This means that the **whole** nation is going to be used, Judah and Ephraim being the classical divisions of Israel. You are going to fight, says Zechariah, against the world power. And the prophet names the world power as Greece, and this actually took place under Judas Maccabaeus when Jews led by him defeated the Greek forces of Antiochus Epiphanes whose officials had defiled the Temple. So out of contemporary events God is saying: This is a picture of what is going to happen in the Last Days; My people are going to stand against world powers, and I will be with them; I will be with them in this way.

Then follows in verses 14 to 16 the promise of what the Lord will do for His people:

> And the Lord shall be seen over them, and his arrow shall go forth as the lightning: and the Lord God shall blow the trumpet, and shall go with whirlwinds of the south.
> The Lord of hosts shall defend them; and they shall devour, and shall tread down the sling stones; and they shall drink, and make a noise as through wine: and they shall be filled like bowls, like the corners of the altar.
> And the Lord their God shall save them in that day as the flock of his people: for they shall be as the stones of a crown, lifted on high over his land.

The statement that the Lord shall be seen over them is not just a vision; it will actually take place one day when Christ comes in His glory; when the trumpet shall sound, and the dead in Christ shall rise first. There is going to be wonder and confusion altogether: 'whirlwinds of the south' means violence; 'tread down the sling stones' means that the Jews will overcome all their adversaries; and the remnant, the elect that come through, will believe in Christ in the Last Day. The Lord of hosts will defend them when Jerusalem is surrounded by armies. The Jews will die in their thousands, even millions, but one third will come through, says Zechariah in a later chapter, and be saved; God will defend them; Christ's feet shall stand on the Mount of Olives!

'Drink', 'noise as through wine', 'filled like bowls', 'corners of the altar': these are all metaphors. The picture of God as the Shepherd, the Great Shepherd, the Shepherd of Israel, and Christ as the Good Shepherd, is brought in with the words 'the Lord their God shall save them in that day as the flock of his people'. All the imagery in Scripture is totally consistent; it is all related. And whereas they tread down the enemies of God as sling stones they, and all believing people, shall be lifted up as the stones of a crown, high over His land; **His land.** Surely, we are living in days approaching that! Then, rather like St Paul (in Romans 11 verse 22), the prophet says in verse 17:

> For how great is his goodness, and how great is his beauty! Corn shall make the young men flourish, and new wine the maids.

What a fascinating chapter this is. The Lord's eyes are upon that land, His land; in Isaiah 8 verse 8 it is known as Emmanuel's Land; and that is what Israel is, Emmanuel's Land.

But let me come back to it again: it is all through grace and mercy; the unbelieving Jew will lose out; it is the remnant, the little flock, the true believer, who is typified here. Let me repeat: the contemporary events of Zechariah; the events of Alexander the Great; the defeat of the Greeks by the Maccabees; these events foreshadow what is going to happen in the Last Day, when Christ Himself shall defend His people and set up His kingdom.

One last word about Alexander the Great's visit to Jerusalem. According to Josephus the historian, the high priest showed Alexander the book of Daniel in which he, the conqueror Alexander, was prophesied. Josephus says that Alexander was rather pleased! Notice that the critics tell us that the book of Daniel was not even written in those days, but Josephus, who lived at the time of Christ, has no doubt when it was written! You can imagine the high priest talking of his dream about Alexander, and the latter speaking of his dream about the high priest; and then the high priest saying: In Daniel, it is written about you! and then actually showing the Book to the conqueror. No wonder Alexander showed favour to the Jews! But the great thing for us all is the mystery and the magnificence of Scripture.

13 CHRIST THE CORNERSTONE, NAIL, BATTLEBOW, AND ABSOLUTE MONARCH

The theme of chapter 10 of Zechariah is deliverance and mercy to a repentant and a restored people who have been regathered. It starts with something very topical in verse 1:

> Ask ye of the Lord rain in the time of the latter rain, even of the Lord that maketh lightnings; and he shall give them showers of rain, to every one grass in the field.

Note the direction to ask of the Lord. This is literal: Palestine under the Turks became a desert, and today deserts are increasing in the world at a tremendous rate. If men are not there; if trees (such as the eucalyptus in Israel) are not there to combat it, the desert rapidly spreads and the whole area soon succumbs. The rainfall is all-important, so we are talking about the latter days and asking for rain of the Lord.

The latter rain! In Israel it rains in October and in February and the rain in February is known as the latter rain, and it is very vital. It is then that the crops depend totally on this short period of rain (about six weks). Rain is essential to this land of milk and honey if it is to have milk and honey; it is also a sign of God's power. Let us read Jeremiah 14 verse 22:

> Are there any among the vanities of the heathen that can cause rain? or can the heavens give showers? art not thou he, O Lord our God? therefore we will wait upon thee; for thou hast made all these things.

Rain is not to be taken for granted: it is a sign of God's power; it is also a sign of mercy. Refer to Deuteronomy 11 verses 11 to 15:

> But the land, whither ye go over to possess it, is a land of hills and valleys, and drinketh water of the rain of heaven:
> A land which the Lord thy God careth for; **the eyes of the Lord thy God are always upon it**, from the beginning of the year even unto the end of the year.
> And it shall come to pass, if ye shall hearken diligently unto my commandments which I command you this day, to love the Lord your God, and to serve him with all your heart and with all your soul,
> That I will give **the rain of your land** in its season, the **former** rain and the **latter** rain, that thou mayest gather in thy corn, and thy wine, and thine oil.
> And I will give grass in thy fields for thy cattle, and thou shalt eat and be full.

Note the distinction between the land of Palestine and Egypt; in Egypt there is total dependence on a single river. Note also that the eyes of the Lord are always on Israel. It is true that the eyes of the Lord are on the whole world: He searches the hearts of men. But, because of His covenants and because Israel is the centre of events; because His Son was to be born in Israel and is to return to Israel; because the whole climax of history is taking place in Israel and it is at the centre of the world; then even Moses, speaking fifteen hundred years before Christ, makes this statement that the Lord's eyes are constantly on Israel!

And note the words: I will give you the rain ... So it is power and it is mercy and without rain it is desolation and desert. Now if that is true, then this also is true: read Isaiah 44 verses 2 and 3:

> ... Fear not, O Jacob my servant; and thou, Jeshurun, whom I have chosen.

> For I will pour water upon him that is thirsty, and streams upon the dry ground: I will pour my spirit upon thy seed, and my blessing upon thine offspring:

In other words, the prophets never talk about purely physical things; the physical simply reflects what God really wants to do to us in our hearts; and Isaiah is speaking about the rain of the Spirit upon God's people.

Not only does He give us good things, a land renewed, as it were, but there has got to be a people renewed; a people whom God has blessed with His Spirit; and that was manifest at Pentecost and, say the Apostles, it is in Jesus Christ that the rain of the Spirit comes upon us. So our Lord says: Ask, and it shall be given unto you; seek, and ye shall find (that is, both good things, and the Holy Spirit). Our Lord here is using the Old Testament imagery. As for 'pour water upon him that is thirsty', this can literally occur, as I recall in Jaffa on one occasion when these rains came: the whole of Jaffa was under water; I have never seen such heavy rain; it was a veritable flood!

As regards the words of Zechariah in verse 1, 'to every one grass in the field'; well, God is not only dealing with nations, He is dealing with every blade of grass, you and me, every single individual; God never forgets the individual. When He blesses a nation it is made up of 'blades of grass', just as a field is made up, and every blade, every person is blessed. This is very wonderful, and this asking is in complete contrast to the former behaviour of the Jews, as depicted in verse 2:

> For the teraphim have spoken vanity, and the diviners have seen a lie; and they have told false dreams, they comfort in vain: therefore they go their way like sheep, they are afflicted, because there is no shepherd.

The teraphim were speaking idols; they were necromancers; you have it at Delphi in Greece, where people asked the oracles and the oracles spoke back; of course there was much deception in all these practices. The verse is referring to people turning away to spiritism, and going round graves and indulging in spiritism. So the teraphim are talking idols, and the pagan world is full of this sort of thing, with much fraud present, and also an element of demon worship. Now the Jews followed these practices before they were exiled to Babylon. They asked of gods: What is going to happen to us? They did not ask of the Lord; they did not go to the Urim and Thummim which were kept by the high priest to ask guidance of God; they turned to spiritists and rejected God's word; they turned to false gods; to a false science practised by diviners. In Ezekiel 21 verses 21 to 23 you get a marvellous picture of the king of Babylon divining, Shall I take Jerusalem? which way shall I go?'

All this goes on today: it occurs in astrology and in many other ways, but where is the word of God? Many people in this country do nothing without consulting their horoscope in the papers! If you go to a spiritist he will put on a sort of show; be possessed; voices will come out of him. The teraphim is this sort of thing. The supreme example is Saul. Do you remember when he turned his back on God? and there was no answer from God to his questions? So Saul went to the 'witch' of Endor and told her to bring up a man: Saul silenced her protests that God Himself had forbidden such practices; and she brought up Samuel!

Is all this relevant? Well, it is relevant to people who are caught up in spiritism; who turn away from the word of God and tell us that they have a better source of information about how to live, about how to make a fortune, about health and about the future, and so on. Spiritualists, spiritists, mediums, and teraphim! The comfort they gave was false, in vain, and the Jews went their way and ended up in Babylon because they chose false gods.

So verse 2 is a picture of deluded Israel, and the central cause was that they had no shepherd! All through the Old Testament, God is the Shepherd of Israel; all through the New Testament, Christ is the Good Shepherd, the Chief Shepherd; and He looked upon the masses and had compassion upon them, because they were sheep without a shepherd, torn and afflicted, and that is the picture of the whole of Israel until its dispersion. And why? because they had unfaithful princes; unfaithful priests like Caiaphas and Annas; unfaithful rabbis who would not see; unfaithful Pharisees who would deny the word of God just because they wanted to keep their own position and privilege.

You know we have men like that in the Church. The people of England have not many shepherds: we have plenty of ministers, bishops, and leaders but they can lead us astray. The great sin of the leaders of Israel in the old days was that, with all their study of Scripture they would not believe it themselves! they would not obey God; and they would not let others obey God. They 'muddied the waters' for others, and that is the mark of a false shepherd; he does not believe in Christ; he does not believe in Heaven and Hell; he does not believe in salvation. Not only does he not believe himself, but he persuades or convinces everyone else to go his way! Let us refer to Isaiah 6 verses 9 to 13 and read again what God, when He appeared to Isaiah in that wonderful vision, ordered him to predict about what was going to happen after him:

> And he said, Go, and tell this people, Hear ye indeed, but understand not; and see ye indeed, but perceive not.
> Make the heart of this people fat, and make their ears heavy, and shut their eyes; lest they see with their eyes, and hear with their ears, and understand with their heart, and turn again, and be healed.
> Then said I, Lord, how long? And he answered, Until cities be waste without inhabitant, and houses without man, and the land become utterly waste,
> And the Lord have removed men far away, and the forsaken places be many in the midst of the land.
> And if there be yet a tenth in it, it shall again be eaten up ...

When there are false shepherds; when people reject the word of God; then God confirms them in their rejection, and this is their punishment. God never punishes anyone in a sense; men punish themselves. If I say to God, No! I do not believe it, I do not want to see it, I can see it with my eyes but I will not receive it, then God says, Very well, I will leave you to your judgment! As I have said earlier, in theological terms this is known as judicial blindness. When people hear the Gospel and understand mentally; and listen and see Christ and appear to go along with it, and then; for various reasons they say, No! and keep on saying, No! then God says: All right, say No! and they then become blind. They have chosen to be blind; it is a judicial blindness, and God keeps such people blind lest they be saved.

Do you see what I mean? It is justice in action. When mercy is rejected then justice will simply take its course. Our Lord repeats the very same thing as Isaiah: He talked in parables deliberately to provoke this; if people had any spiritual understanding they would know what He was getting at. Jesus said: If you are sincere you will see through this picture language that I am using. He never spoke in anything but parables, and the disciples would come and ask what He meant. The great theologians of that day should have seen through it immediately, but they did not want to see; they still do not want to see! So, says God, it is their choice and not mine. You get this continually in the parables and in the doctrine of Scripture. And so that had happened to Israel. But now we come to a happy change in verse 3:

> Mine anger is kindled against the shepherds, and I will punish the he-goats: for the Lord of hosts hath visited his flock the house of Judah, and shall make them as his goodly horse in the battle.

God is going to punish these wretched leaders, rulers, rabbis, and priests (he-goats is just another picture of them, these tough men). And what of this poor people who have been led astray by their shepherds? they will be punished too, but a tenth will remain: there will always be a remnant, for God's purposes are never mocked. And once again, because of His covenant with the fathers, God will make the little flock His goodly horse.

Isn't that good? God is never defeated and this actually happened, as I have said, under the Maccabees. There was quite a revival under Judas Maccabaeus at the time when the Jews were ruled by Antiochus Epiphanes of the Seleucid dynasty, which followed on the death of Alexander the Great. The Jews were squeezed between the Seleucids in the North and the Ptolemies in the South. They were an oppressed people and the Seleucid ruler offered a swine on the altar of the Temple and this roused the Maccabees to action. This feeble remnant of the Jews rose and fought off the stronger Syrian army; and it was at that same time that the Hassidic movement started. People were on fire for God, and God, as it were, used them as a goodly horse in battle against all odds. That was the physical and historical fulfilment - the immediate fulfilment. But it is going to happen again! Remember, one event of today is the precursor of the Final Event; one deliverance speaks of the Final Deliverance.

Then one of the greatest texts in Scripture, if you accept Scripture as truth, this magnificent verse 4:

> From him shall come forth the corner stone, from him the nail, from him the battle bow, from him every exactor together.

Exactor means 'ruler': in a bad sense it means a despotic ruler. The Hebrew words mean 'all rule in one', or, 'all command in one', or, in other words, Absolute Monarchy. Verse 4 is a tremendous Messianic verse: the corner stone is coming from Judah; the nail is coming from Judah; the battle bow is coming from Judah; the absolute ruler is coming from Judah, and this is backed up everywhere in the Bible. Read again Micah 5 verse 2, and compare it with Jeremiah 30 verse 21:

> And their prince shall be of themselves, and their ruler shall proceed from the midst of them; and I will cause him to draw near, and he shall approach unto me: for who is he that hath had boldness to approach unto me? saith the Lord.

Notice how scripture supports scripture in 'their prince shall be of themselves', and that Jeremiah agrees with Micah and with Zechariah in what may appear to be these minor details. But they are not minor details! And then, no one can approach God; but this Ruler will approach Him! and this is because God is going to bring this Ruler out of their own nation, and that is the whole history of Christ. He came out of the tribe of Judah, and out of Bethlehem, and of the family of David: and although it may seem obvious to you, the whole of Scripture endorses this in all sorts of ways.

In chapters 9 and 10, the conqueror has come in the person of Alexander the Great; and the Conqueror has come in the Just One riding on an ass and on a colt the foal of an ass; and the Conqueror will come as the Absolute Monarch. The question that the last prophet in the Old Testament asks is, But who may abide the day of his coming? Think seriously of what is going to happen when Christ appears again. We talk in religious language, and we look forward to the Coming of Christ and, I think, we sometimes get rather silly about it. Imagine what is going to happen when Christ comes - to the tremendous surprise of every unbelieving God-resisting person and nation on the face of the earth! It is one thing to sing about that Great Day; but, A Great Day for whom? you may ask. It will not be a Great Day for the majority of people; it will be a dreadful day for, 'who may abide the day of his coming?'

To my mind, I am afraid, evangelical Christians are sometimes stupid. They play around with great jewels of truth as though they were marbles; they toss truths to and fro until they seem of little value in our eyes, whereas they should be of great value. When He comes it will be an awesome Day and one we should give great thought to.

Let us look again at verse 4. The corner stone is imagery, a metaphor for Christ the Messiah. Now compare Isaiah 28 verse 16:

> Therefore thus saith the Lord God, Behold, I lay in Zion for a foundation a stone, a tried stone, a precious corner stone of sure foundation: he that believeth shall not make haste.

No one else says this: only the Lord God is saying this. Look at 1 Peter 2 verses 5 and 6:

> Ye also, as living stones, are built up a spiritual house, to be a holy priesthood, to offer up spiritual sacrifices, acceptable to God through Jesus Christ.
> Because it is contained in scripture, Behold, I lay in Zion a chief corner stone, elect, precious: and he that believeth on him shall not be put to shame.

Peter then goes on to quote: The stone which the builders rejected, the same was made the head of the corner. The significance of a corner stone is that it joins together two walls. The corner stone of the old Temple in Jerusalem has been found; it is sunk in rock and it joins two walls together; it is not only a foundation but it unites two walls. Paul talks about this in Ephesians 2 verses 19 to 21 - it is interesting to note how the New Testament is so centred on the Old; there is very little in the New Testament which is not taken directly or by implication from the Old Testament:

> So then ye are no more strangers and sojourners, but ye are fellow-citizens with the saints, and of the household of God,
> Being built upon the foundation of the apostles and prophets, Christ Jesus himself being the chief corner stone;
> In whom each several building, fitly framed together,

groweth into a holy temple in the Lord;

It is Christ who is the Corner Stone and He joins together Jew and Gentile; He is both the foundation stone, and the stone of the corner and that is wonderful. He is also the Nail. Now read Isaiah 22 verses 22 to 24:

> And the key of the house of David will I lay upon his shoulder; and he shall open, and none shall shut; and he shall shut, and none shall open.
> And I will fasten him as a nail in a sure place; and he shall be for a throne of glory to his father's house.
> And they shall hang upon him all the glory of his father's house, the offspring and the issue, every small vessel, from the vessels of cups even to all the vessels of flagons.

Isaiah is speaking of the Messiah, and the first of these three verses is quoted also in Revelation. Now these magnificent verses were spoken in the first place of Eliakim. Do you remember him? There was a treasurer named Shebna who was not a good man, and God swept him aside saying, This is not the man I want: it is Eliakim that I choose and upon him I will hang all the destiny of Israel! The verse speaks of a tent nail on which you hang everything; everything! In the first place it was Eliakim in the history of Israel; but it is looking forward to the Christ on whom hangs everything in the world. We hang burdens small and great on Christ; we hang all the Glory on Christ; our sins, our talents, our worship, our offerings small and great are all hung on Christ and He is a Nail in a sure place. Our whole salvation, our whole destiny, the Church, our whole health, our everything be it small, great, personal, - all hangs on Jesus Christ!

But, you might say, in verse 25 Isaiah says that the Nail that was fastened in a sure place shall give way! Yes indeed, in one breath it is prophesied that someone will be the Nail upon whom everyone will hang; and yet in the same breath Isaiah prophesies that the Nail will break. But remember, there is no perspective in prophecy: in verse 24 we are looking at Christ in His glory; though in the next verse we are also looking to the fact that He shall be cut off and everything that was hung upon Him will fall to the ground. But our Lord Himself, on that long Emmaus walk, expounds this matter of strength and weakness, of suffering and victory of the Messiah, from the Old Testament. This was His theme in answer to the sad observation, 'But we hoped that it was he which should redeem Israel'. Verse 25 of Isaiah does not undermine what has been previously said.

So you have the double picture: you build on Christ and you hang on Christ; but He is also the Battlebow, and here is a very serious picture of the Messiah. Turn to Isaiah 63 verses 1 to 6:

> Who is this that cometh from Edom, with dyed garments from Bozrah? this that is glorious in his apparel, marching in the greatness of his strength? I that speak in righteousness, mighty to save.
> Wherefore art thou red in thine apparel, and thy garments like him that treadeth in the winefat?
> I have trodden the winepress alone; and of the peoples there was no man with me: yea, I trod them in mine anger, and trampled them in my fury; and their lifeblood is sprinkled upon my garments, and I have stained all my raiment.
> For the day of vengeance was in mine heart, and the year of my redeemed is come.
> And I looked, and there was none to help; and I wondered that there was none to uphold: therefore mine own arm brought salvation unto me; and my fury, it upheld me.
> And I trod down the peoples in mine anger, and made them drunk in my fury, and I poured out their lifeblood on the earth.

Now that is indeed another picture of Christ! We build on Him; we hang on Him; but He is also this Battlebow, and this is again absolutely put into perspective in Revelation 19 verses 11 to 16 which, if I may say, ought to shake a few evangelicals and stop them leaping about in pious joy:

> And I saw the heaven opened; and behold, a white horse, and he that sat thereon, called Faithful and True (this is Christ); and in righteousness he doth judge and make war.
> And his eyes are a flame of fire, and upon his head are many diadems; and he hath a name written, which no one knoweth but he himself.
> And he is arrayed in a garment sprinkled with blood: and his name is called The Word of God.
> And the armies which are in heaven followed him upon white horses, clothed in fine linen, white and pure.
> And out of his mouth proceedeth a sharp sword, that with it he should smite the nations: and he shall rule them with a rod of iron: and he treadeth the winepress of the fierceness of the wrath of Almighty God.
> And he hath on his garment and on his thigh a name written, KING OF KINGS, AND LORD OF LORDS.

Note that! here is none of your Gentle Jesus, meek and mild! I am a conservative evangelical myself but you know ... we so often get carried away with romantic and simpering ideas of our Blessed Lord. Note also, that in 'a garment sprinked with blood', St John is repeating Isaiah. These magnificent verses should raise our silly little sermons to a level where they take account of the majesty, the symphony, the awesome destiny of this world! The Christ who saved us is going to come again and will fill us with such tremendous awe and wonder that men, says Revelation, will say to the mountains, Fall upon us; and to the hills, Cover us!

I am just trying to get things into perspective: He is the Battlebow as well as being the Gentle Jesus; and then of course He is the autocratic Ruler. In the bad sense this means the oppressor, and in the good sense it means a complete command, all rule in one; and the answer to this concept must of course be Psalm 2, which shows once again how scripture supports scripture. Read the Psalm in full and note especially that awesome verse 12 which I must repeat for you:

> Kiss the son, lest he be angry, and ye perish in the way, for his wrath will soon be kindled ...

There is your autocratic Ruler; there is the Christ of God; and so it brings into perspective the majesty of the Christian faith. If only we could preach more like this we might get more men to listen! What I am trying to say is that we major so much on the passive side of things that we leave out this awesome wonder, and men are not impressed. It's for the wife and the kids, they say; it is all lovey-dovey and it does not matter. But it does matter! The day is coming when an autocratic Ruler will come and it will be the Christ of God in righteousness; it takes this to move the hearts of sinful men to some sort of consideration. Let me say again, what a wonderful verse this verse 4 is.

And then the glorious prospect in store for Israel begins with verses 5 to 7:

> And they shall be as mighty men, treading down their enemies in the mire of the streets in the battle; and they shall fight, because the Lord is with them: and the riders on horses shall be confounded.
> And I will strengthen the house of Judah, and I will save the house of Joseph, and I will bring them again, for I have mercy upon them; and they shall be as though I had not cast them off: for I am the Lord their God, and I will hear them.
> And they of Ephraim shall be like a mighty man, and their heart shall rejoice as through wine: yea, their children shall see it, and rejoice; their heart shall be glad in the Lord.

Just imagine the Jews, downtrodden over the centuries, becoming mighty men and becoming victorious because the Lord is with them. Then there is the great promise to the returned Israel that the Lord will strengthen and save the nation, which will again become one nation; no longer will there be ten tribes in the North and two in the South; we are talking now of the whole house of Israel.

Then the prophecy 'I will bring them again', or 'cause them to dwell'. Now what does that mean? It means just what it says. If the Dispersion is a fact in the Old Testament; if you look at world history and admit that this was prophesied from Deuteronomy onward, and that it has taken place; then I would ask of any Bible scholar why is the regathering to be regarded as something spiritual and not factual? Do you see what I am trying to say? If the Dispersion is a fact and you admit that God said that it would happen, then why do you jib when God says: I will bring them back, and I will cause them to dwell, and they shall have children in My land? Why do you stop short and say God cannot bring them back again?

The fact is evident today that God is indeed bringing them back: in unbelief, in bitterness still, not praising them, but He is bringing them back and He has mighty things to do for them. It astounds me the way that men can accept the first Coming of Christ as being in all the Scriptures; but when you say, What about the second Coming? they then try to spiritualise and will not take it literally. But why not? If you take one literally, if you take the Dispersion literally, then why do you not take the regathering literally? The logic is bad, quite apart from the theology.

And then those words of balm 'and they shall be as though I had not cast them off' or, 'as though I had not loathed them'. Now they **have** been loathed by God: they crucified the Son of Glory; and God does not pat the Jew on the back. God said: I shall cast you off and call you 'Not My people'. God abhorred them yet, for His Holy Name's sake, for His oath to Abraham, He is going to turn it round one day and bring them again, and have mercy upon them as though He had never loathed them; and will hear them again.

As for the men of Ephraim, they were a 'naughty' tribe and were always causing trouble. Joshua was fed up with them in his day, and he was one of them. Do you remember that Joshua told them they were a hard lot? Ephraim has grey hairs and does not know it, says Hosea. Do you recall that particlar text? It meant that the tribe were morally and spiritually on the decline but they did not know it. But in the Great Day, the men of Ephraim will change, and they and their children will rejoice.

Then, after all the Jews have been 'in the pit' for so very long, God says that He will whistle for them, in verse 8:

> I will hiss for them, and gather them; for I have redeemed them: and they shall increase as they have increased.

That is a wonderful picture of a shepherd: in Palestine that is just what a shepherd does; Arab shepherds still play their reed pipes and the sheep collect around them. So will God 'whistle' or 'pipe' His people back again. God is going to say to the Jews: I am whistling for you! They are leaving America now, leaving England now, leaving South Africa now, leaving the other countries now, because they can hear a whistle. The Jew cannot understand; when you ask them why they are going back to a land of trouble they say, Well, I am a Jew ... but in fact they are listening to the whistling of God; He is whistling them and gathering them and, my goodness, how they have increased! for in verse 9:

> And I will sow them among the peoples; and they shall remember me in far countries: and they shall live with their children, and shall return.

They have indeed been sown in far countries: in America, Ireland, England, Germany, South Africa, Australia, Argentine, and they have indeed multiplied in those countries.

Do you know that in the sixteenth century there were about one million Jews, and today they number about fourteen million. God has multiplied them. Do you remember when the Israelites went down into Egypt and why Pharaoh ordered the midwives to appear before him? because they were increasing: they went down into Egypt as seventy souls and they came out as over one million!

Again, one small picture (such as that in Egypt) is the precursor of what is going to happen. The Jews, once nearly exterminated, have now increased to almost fourteen millions, and some of them are hearing the whistle, the piping. 'And I will have mercy, and I am Jehovah their God' ... When? when Messiah comes; when they look upon Him whom they have pierced; when the fulness of the Gentiles comes in.

The words in verse 9, 'and they shall remember me in far countries' require us to turn to Ezekiel 6 verses 6 to 10;

> In all your dwelling places the cities shall be laid waste, and the high places shall be desolate; that your altars may be laid waste and made desolate, and your idols may be broken and cease, and your sun-images may be hewn down, and your works may be abolished.
>
> And the slain shall fall in the midst of you, and ye shall know that I am the Lord.
>
> Yet will I leave a remnant, in that ye shall have some that escape the sword among the nations, when ye shall be scattered through the countries.
>
> And they that escape of you shall remember me among the nations whither they shall be carried captives, how that I have been broken with their whorish heart, which hath departed from me, and with their eyes, which go a whoring after their idols: and they shall loathe themselves in their own sight for the evils which they have committed in all their abominations.
>
> And they shall know that I am the Lord: I have not said in vain that I would do this evil unto them.

The passage refers to Palestine in the absence of the Jew and in the days of the Turks; judgment will take place as the Lord has warned and the land will be desolated. But then comes the doctrine of the remnant and some will escape in the countries where the Lord has scattered them; and then the words 'shall remember me ... ' This is Zechariah again! how congruous it all is. Then the self-loathing: if you do not want God to loathe you, loathe yourself! it is a very good thing to do. Now read Ezekiel 37 verses 11 to 14:

> Then he said unto me, Son of man, these bones are the whole house of Israel: behold, they say, Our bones are dried up, and our hope is lost; we are clean cut off.
> Therefore prophesy, and say unto them, Thus saith the Lord God: Behold, I will open your graves, and cause you to come up out of your graves, O my people; and I will bring you into the land of Israel.
> And ye shall know that I am the Lord, when I have opened your graves, and caused you to come up out of your graves, O my people.
> And I will put my spirit in you, and ye shall live, and I will place you in your own land: and ye shall know that I the Lord have spoken it, and performed it, saith the Lord.

Isn't it great? Can you possibly see any other reasonable interpretation of this Book? of course not - unless you invent anonymous authors for chapters 9 to 14 as some of the critics do!
And verse 10:

> I will bring them again also out of the land of Egypt, and gather them out of Assyria; and I will bring them into the land of Gilead and Lebanon; and place shall not be found for them.

Gilead is the Golan Heights, and as for Lebanon ... well, you could hardly be more up to date. There will be so many of them there will not be room. If all the Jews went back to Israel could they all get in? Today in Israel there are nearly four million Jews, but would it be impossible? You know, the old writers staked everything on the fact that this would come true, and they were mocked. The writers of one hundred years ago staked everything on the simple fact that this prophet was true, and that unbelievers were untrue. The Jews **will** go back to Palestine: it says so in the Word of God; Darby, Newton, Guinness and other great prophetic students of Scripture all said this at a time when there was no Jew in Israel; Lord Salisbury in particular was a firm believer in the prophecy and the return of the Jew; people scoffed at these men but now it is taking place!

Scripture in every part confirms the drift and message, one prophet agreeing with another, and that is the point I am making. God did indeed bring them out of the land of Egypt: Egypt and Assyria were the world powers in those days, and they may well become important powers again, I suppose. But just as Israel went through great affliction in those early times to get out of Egypt, so they are going through great affliction now. And verse 11:

> And he shall pass through the sea of affliction, and shall smite the waves in the sea, and all the depths of the Nile shall dry up: and the pride of Assyria shall be brought down, and the sceptre of Egypt shall depart away.

But affliction shall pass; and then that lovely last verse 12:

> And I will strengthen them in the Lord; and they shall walk up and down in his name, saith the Lord.

So they, the remnant, the converted Jew (remember that we are looking towards the end, and still have the process of their repentance and coming to Christ to go through in the next chapters) - they shall walk up and down in His name, or for the sake of His name. They will become evangelists! that is what it means; they will have freedom; freedom to walk up and down in His name. Today they walk up and down in the name of money, and might, and tanks, and power, and they are despised and disliked. But in that day they will walk up and down in His name; His name, saith the Lord; the Name that is above every Name: the Name of Jesus.

14 ISRAEL CAST OFF: THE IDOL SHEPHERD

If chapter 10 of the book of Zechariah was one of hope, in that Israel is to regathered and blessed and strengthened, and the Jew is to be on fire for the Lord, then chapter 11 plunges us back into gloom. Someone has written that this is to prevent the abuse of the proclamation of salvation, and so once again we are brought face to face with Israel's sin and guilt and anger; we are swung from the happy promises for a while 'lest any man boast himself'. This is exactly what happened to the scribes and Pharisees in our Lord's day. They were full of self-esteem; nothing could happen to them, they thought; and this at the very time when something was indeed going to happen to them. Again, you have to see that there is no perspective in prophecy; there is a juxtaposition always of the first and the second Coming.

Chapter 11 of Zechariah may be divided into three sections: verses 1 to 3, verses 4 to 14, and verses 15 to 17. The first section (and how appropriate it is) deals with the attack from the North:

> Open thy doors, O Lebanon, that the fire may devour thy cedars.
> Howl, O fir tree, for the cedar is fallen, because the goodly ones are spoiled: howl, O ye oaks of Bashan, for the strong forest is come down.
> A voice of the howling of the shepherds! for their glory is spoiled: a voice of the roaring of young lions! for the pride of Jordan is spoiled.

This incidentally is exactly what is happening in 1984 as I

write. Open your doors, O Lebanon, says the spirit of God through the prophet, because an attack is coming! It is a literal attack; there is an actual sweep, coming down from the North. Today, for instance, Israel is in south Lebanon. The Lebanese president is talking to the Syrian president; the Americans have been expelled from Beirut; and the French and the British have pulled out. And, (this is the point) the **final** attack on Israel will come from the North. As I have previously said, if you could have lived one hundred years ago and have seen and read about this, you would have remarked how wonderful it all was. But today we do not turn a hair; we are not amazed because we are no longer caught up with the wonder of prophecy.

In verse 2, the fir trees are the lesser ones: in other words, everyone is going to be involved in this final attack. 'The cedar is fallen, because the goodly ones are spoiled', is simply metaphor, and 'oaks of Bashan' are the Golan Heights, Gilead, and Bashan. I travel with a party around that area every year; we go to the Golan Heights and stand and look over to Damascus, and to the north, and south to the sea of Galilee. So what the prophet is saying is that from the North, in the future, there is to come upon Israel a tremendous attack down the steep paths from Lebanon, destroying everything; the great and mighty cedars, the great men, the armies; nothing and nobody will escape.

The 'oaks of Bashan' remind me of something that happened years ago. A clergyman came to Israel from St Leonards on Sea; he was a man with a dream. His church had been bombed in the war and he wanted to rebuild it and to have a pulpit looking like the prow of a ship; but the point was that he wanted the pulpit to be made of Israeli oak! He stayed with me whilst I was living in Jerusalem and he made his request to the Israeli government. You see, the oaks of Bashan are famous, but very rare as are the cedars of Lebanon, and are being conserved. The oaks of Bashan had almost disappeared, but he got special permission from the government to have the pulpit made to his design. It was made in a Bashan kibbutz in Gilead and when it was finished, I took a large party of Arabs to see the pulpit standing in the yard of the kibbutz; and I harangued them from the pulpit! A little later I came home to England, and preached from that very same pulpit in the clergyman's church; that pulpit made in Bashan and of that precious Bashan oak, and I related the story of preaching to Arabs from the pulpit before it was shipped from Israel - much to the amusement of the congregation.

Verse 3 emphasises the massive destruction of flocks of sheep. Sheep are very numerous there with flocks often numbering more than a thousand sheep, and Scripture is saying that all will be destroyed. The reference to the pride of Jordan is very interesting. Ancient writers tell us that the river Jordan was so lined with thick bushes and undergrowth that lions were numerous; in fact there were lions in Palestine up to two centuries ago. But the picture is that this incoming army is irresistible. It will sweep down, and everything will be burned up; the shepherds will run; the lions will roar; and the bushes and undergrowth which sustain them will be destroyed. A voice of the howling for Jordan indeed!

Now the Temple in Jerusalem was often called in Scripture, the House of Lebanon. The word Lebanon comes from the Hebrew word Leban, meaning white (the moon in Hebrew is called Or Levan, the white light) and the rabbis almost always referred to the Temple as the House of Lebanon, because it was constructed of cedars and the beautiful white dome stood on the hill of Moriah. So you have two things here: an actual attack is to come on the land of Israel, says Zechariah, which will come from Lebanon and sweep everything before it; and secondly, it will get to the House of Lebanon, to the Temple of the Lord, to Jerusalem itself!

The rabbis were aware of this, for an extraordinary thing happened forty years before the fall of Jerusalem which is recorded in the Babylonian Talmud. As you know, the Talmud (meaning The Learning) is the writings of rabbis after the death of Christ; and there are two writings, the Jerusalem Talmud, and the Babylonian Talmud which was written in Mesopotamia. The Talmud is the book which the Jews feed on to this very day and which teaches Jews how to live the Jewish life without a Temple, without a priesthood, and without a land. It gives advice about every facet of life, even of: how to lie in bed; the matter of alimony if you divorce a wife for making bad toast! how to cut your finger-nails (the parings of which are not even to be thrown into the fire), and so on. Everything that you can think of is in the Talmud, all mixed up, including exegesis of various texts and sermons and the like.

In the Babylonian Talmud it says that, forty years before the destruction of the Temple under Titus, the lot or dice cast for the goat to be sacrificed on the Day of Atonement did not come out on the right side; and also the scarlet tongue which was put on the horn of the scapegoat did not turn white as it should have done. Perhaps I should recall for you what was done on the Day of Atonement. On that day, one goat was killed as a sacrifice and another goat, the 'scapegoat', was sent into the wilderness; attached to its horn was a scarlet tongue or ribbon which always turned white to denote the symbol of sins forgiven. How this was done we do not know, but on this particular occasion the ribbon failed to turn white: in addition, the western lamp failed to burn and the doors of the Sanctuary opened of their own accord. All these were omens of disaster, said the rabbis.

The dark picture becomes more dark in verse 4. Now in Scripture the personages often change. Don't worry about it. Sometimes it is God speaking directly; sometimes it is God speaking through the prophet; sometimes it is God speaking through the prophet, in the words of the Messiah. These different modes of speaking are all mixed up, and can change quickly from one text to another. For example, God is speaking (as in verse 4); then suddenly in the next text it can be 'But he' meaning the Messiah, and of course the prophet is relaying it all. But it is one message and it is coming through the Messiah and the prophet is saying: I did this ... when what he actually means is that it is going to happen through the Messiah; that this is the word of God. Do you see? We often get this in Scripture; so the prophet speaks in the Divine Voice in verse 4 and he is speaking predictively of Israel given over to judgment:

> Thus said the Lord my God: Feed the flock of slaughter;

'The Lord my God' is the prophet's God and also the Messiah's God; it is one message from the same source. So we have first of all the impression of the imminence of a mighty invasion from Lebanon. Secondly you have God saying: Feed the flock of slaughter; feed the people who are about to be slaughtered. Now who is this One? It is the lowly King of chapter 9 who rides on an ass on Palm Sunday and who is rejected; it is the Good Shepherd of chapter 10 coming to the lost sheep of the house of Israel. And what does verse 5 say?

> Whose possessors slay them, and hold themselves not guilty; and they that sell them say, Blessed be the Lord, for I am rich: and their own shepherds pity them not.

What the Messiah is saying here, what God is saying here, what the prophet is saying here (and it is all synonymous), is that the people of Israel are now destined to slaughter. Those who possess Israel, that is, the nations and specifically Rome at the time of Christ, do Israel great harm but say to themselves: We are not guilty of anything; these Jews are terrible people and we can exploit them as much as we like. So the house of Israel is doomed to slaughter and those who slaughter them will feel no guilt. Look at Jeremiah 50 verses 6 and 7:

> My people hath been lost sheep: their shepherds have caused them to go astray, they have turned them away on the mountains: they have gone from mountain to hill, they have forgotten their resting place.

> All that found them (the nations) have devoured them: and their adversaries said, We offend not, because they have sinned against the Lord, the habitation of justice, even the Lord, the hope of their fathers.

And if we look at verses 17 to 19 of the same chapter:

> Israel is a scattered sheep; the lions have driven him away: first the king of Assyria hath devoured him; and last this Nebuchadrezzar king of Babylon hath broken his bones.
> Therefore thus saith the Lord of hosts, the God of Israel: Behold, I will punish the king of Babylon and his land, as I have punished the king of Assyria.
> And I will bring Israel again to his pasture, and he shall feed on Carmel and Bashan, and his soul shall be satisfied upon the hills of Ephraim and in Gilead.

The very places named in Zechariah are here. So, looking forward, Zechariah says, Before the great blessings that are to come, the Messiah will feed the flock of slaughter; the lost people; they are ripe for slaughter and those who rule them will feel no guilt; and worse, their own shepherds shall let them down and will not pity them. Then come those terrible words in verse 6:

> For I will no more pity the inhabitants of the land, saith the Lord: but, lo, I will deliver the men every one into his neighbour's hand, and into the hand of his king: and they shall smite the land, and out of their hand I will not deliver them.

The Jewish nation is to be attacked, pitied neither by the nations; nor by their own rulers; but sadly enough God Himself will feel no guilt about it. This is terrible; they will be given over to each other, and will not be delivered. Why? you ask. Because there comes a point in everybody's life, and in every nation's life where God finds no remedy to cure our sins; He goes so far but He cannot go any further. You get that in 2 Chronicles 36 verse 16, talking about the first exile when the Temple was destroyed and people were taken off to Babylon:

> But they mocked the messengers of God, and despised his words, and scoffed at his prophets, until the wrath of the Lord arose against his people, till there was no remedy.

Note how the picture builds up of this flock of slaughter 'until there was no remedy'. People who tell you that there is infinite everlasting mercy with God on the one hand are wrong. There is not! There comes a time when we can reject the Word, and scoff at the prophets of God, and scoff at the Christ of God, and still think that we can get away with it. We will not, because there is no further remedy; God has given His best; He has given all the light that He can possibly give. That is the dark undertone of the Gospel. The reason why the Gospel is not biting today is because the dark undertone is never mentioned. We all believe that we can spit at God; spit at Christ; and go on doing it and think that one day God will be kind to us all. Certainly not! There will be no remedy and we will be destroyed.

Now verse 6 says God will deliver every man into his neighbour's hand and also into the hand of his king. There was no king in the time of Zechariah; there was no king in the time of Christ, was there? But do you remember what the Jews said to Pontius Pilate in the time of Christ? Pilate said, Behold your King. And what did they reply? We have no king but Caesar ... and the Jews were delivered into Caesar's hands. Caesar was their king because they rejected the King of Israel; it was self-chosen; they actually went into apostasy. Very well, said Pilate, then put this Man to death. So the Jews chose their own king who turned out to be the most cruel king they could ever have had; and it is all there in John chapter 19. It resulted from scoffing at God's prophets, turning their back on God's Word, falsifying God's worship, facing God's Son and denying Him to His face; calling bad, good; good, evil; light, darkness; and saying, It is better that one man should perish than the whole nation perish; and choosing Caesar, with the result that the whole nation did indeed perish. They thought they were escaping the slaughter, but forty years after Christ the whole nation perished as a nation.

This is a terrible picture of apostasy, desolation, punishment, and tremendous destruction. It is all here in Zechariah verse 6: they had reached the fulness of sin against God who says, I will no more pity the inhabitants of the land.

The statement of God that He would not deliver them has led to the view the the Jew is finished, and both Jerome, sixteen hundred years ago, and Dr Pusey of the last century held this view that the dereliction upon the Jew was forever. 'I will not deliver them' was the last word, they both said; the Jew has no future. But you see how silly that point of view is: it takes into account only part of prophecy, the Dispersion, and forgets the whole weight of the restoration. These two illustrious men thought that the destruction of the Jew was definitive; that the Jew would never again have a place before God; but we are seeing what is happening and how this view is quite wrong; the Jew is indeed going to have a place. And in verse 7:

> So I fed the flock of slaughter, verily the poor of the flock. And I took unto me two staves; the one I called Beauty, and the other I called Bands; and I fed the flock.

Now this is the Messiah speaking: the only sense you can make of this is that it can refer only to Christ. Zechariah is writing five hundred years before Christ and of whom is he writing? It is so redolent of the New Testament; it is so true of Christ; you would have to be very dull to think that this has no particular significance and that it might be some little incident. 'So I fed the flock doomed to slaughter'. Christ came and indeed saw Israel as sheep scattered and torn; as sheep without a shepherd. He healed them, He pleaded with them, and He fed them. He fed them with Truth, with actual bread, and with miracles. He fed them with words, and what did they do? They rejected Him at the last and let Him be crucified. My contention is that you cannot interpret this except in the light of Christ.

The two staves are rod and staff. The equipment of any good shepherd is his rod and staff; the one to beat off the wild beasts and to defend his flock, and the other to gently curb his flock and to keep them together. 'Thy rod and thy staff, they comfort me', and that was the equipment of the Eastern shepherd in those days. Beauty means 'pleasant' and Bands means 'binders'. Beauty is to keep off the marauders; Bands is to keep the flock together; and that is the picture of Christ, His protection, His provision, and His compassion. It is the parable of the Good Shepherd. My sheep hear my voice, says Christ in John 10, and they go in and out and find pasture. But the thief (and we will see soon who the thief is) cometh not but to kill and to steal and to destroy. Christ also says: I am come that ye might have life.

The words 'poor of the flock' remind us that Christ was not without some who believed in Him whilst He was feeding the flock of Israel doomed to slaughter. He had His disciples and others who believed in Him; this is the poor of the flock; this is the doctrine of the remnant which goes right through Scripture. Read Romans 11 verses 1 to 5, and note particularly verses 4 and 5 which are:

> But what saith the answer of God unto him? I have left for myself seven thousand men, who have not bowed the knee to Baal.
> Even so then at this present time also (and this was at the time of, or just after the fall of Jerusalem) there is a remnant according to the election of grace.

And in verse 7 of that chapter:

> What then? That which Israel seeketh for, that he obtained not; but the election obtained it, and the rest were hardened.

Absolutely consistent! Our Lord comes to this flock, a nation: He pours out the Divine Love, He gives His works of healing, He raises the dead, He speaks the Truth, He speaks in the Temple; but the majority of those who heard hardened. They hardened and they plotted and they began to say, Away with this fellow, we will have no king but Caesar. But there were some, and that is the point, who listened; a Godly remnant; and from that remnant of course sprang the life of the Church, the life of Resurrection and, because of that remnant the Israelites are still on the earth.

We now come to a very difficult verse, verse 8, and the inspired writer says:

> And I cut off the three shepherds in one month; for my soul was weary of them, and their soul also loathed me.

Now what does that mean? Many interpretations have been given to this text: in a way it is one of the most disputed texts in Scripture. Who are the shepherds that this Messiah-figure cut off? Many say that they are the Babylonian, the Medo- Persian, and the Greek empires. In a sense that is not a bad guess because it says 'cut off in one month' or thirty days. If one day stands for a year and you multiply thirty by seven you get two hundred and ten years; and the time span from the Babylonian empire to the end of the Greek empire is two hundred and fifteen years - which is interesting. Others think that the three shepherds whom the Messiah cut off are Antiochus Epiphanes, Antiochus Eupator, and a man called Demetrius, all in the times of the Maccabees. Again, some men say that they are pre-exilic shepherds, Moses, Aaron, and Miriam. I believe that all these ideas are wrong.

What does the Messiah, when looking at the flock of

slaughter and feeding them and guiding them with His two staffs, suddenly say? He says: My soul wearied of them, and they loathed Me. So I would suggest, using Jewish metaphor, that the three shepherds are the leaders of the nation which, in old terms, are prophet, priest, and king. These were indeed the shepherds of Israel and in the time of Christ those offices still went on, though under different names. There were the prophets, there were the priests who were in the Temple, and there were the authorities of the nation (the civil authorities). You might say that there were no prophets at the time of Christ, and my reply is, No, but there were scribes. The scribes, says Christ, sit in Moses' seat (who was the great prophet); listen to them; do not deny what they say, but do not do as they do.

So the three great shepherds of Israel - prophet, priest, and king or, the scribes, the priests, and the civil authorities - were the very people who loathed Christ: and His soul was weary of them too. He used to argue with the scribes: He could say with reference to Herod, Go tell that fox ... So the three shepherds are the leaders of the nation, and this is not my thought in isolation; this is in the commentaries of all the very early fathers. The leaders straitened Christ's soul; He was disgusted with them; so at the end of three years of ministry, what does He say in verse 9:

> Then said I, I will not feed you: that that dieth, let it die; and that that is to be cut off, let it be cut off; and let them which are left eat every one the flesh of another.

In other words, He is saying: I have had enough of this nation; I am sick to death of this nation; I will not feed you.

That is a terrible condemnation. But our Lord said this on the Mount of Olives when He looked at Jerusalem; He said these very things in, 'You will not see me until you say, Blessed is he ... ' and, 'You have rejected the day of your salvation'. He wept over Jerusalem; He prophesied the most appalling disaster coming upon Jerusalem forty years before it happened; He was sick to death of the total hypocrisy of the authorities, be they civil, priest, or scribal - clever men and lawyers who insidiously got into His company to deny Him or to trip Him up. Do you see the point?

The reference to every one eating the flesh of another is exactly what happened in AD 70 when Titus surrounded the city. All the local Jews from the provinces round about crowded into the city of Jerusalem to take refuge; they should not have done so, but they were not to know. The city was under siege; there were warring factions inside; and even there the untrue shepherds divided the people man against man and caused, in a sense, the fall of Jerusalem. Jew was fighting Jew inside the city whilst the Romans were all around it; cannibalism took place, and one million one hundred thousand Jews died in the fall of Jerusalem. But the extraordinary thing is that the poor of the flock, the remnant, the people that believed in Jesus and who remembered His words, separated themselves from the city and ran away across the river Jordan and were saved.

But now the prophet says a remarkable thing in verse 10, and the Messiah is speaking:

> And I took my staff Beauty, and cut it asunder, that I might break my covenant which I had made with all the peoples.

The staff represented God's covenant with the nations, that while Israel obeyed Him and followed His steps He would prevent the nations from touching Israel. The Jews were quite safe while the Messiah had that staff in His hand, but now the prophet is saying: This is what God is going to do; He is going to break His covenant with the nations; He had told the nations to keep off but now He breaks that covenant and the nations can now come. And of course they did come; Titus and the Roman armies. You get this idea of God making a covenant in Hosea 2 verse 18:

> And in that day will I make a covenant for them with the beasts of the field, and with the fowls of heaven, and with the creeping things of the ground: and I will break the bow and the sword and the battle out of the land, and will make them to lie down safely.

You see, when God loves us He makes a covenant with all our enemies and says to them: You stay back; do not touch My people; leave them alone. He says that even on behalf of Christians! When God makes a covenant no one can break that covenant. When we are in the favour of God, when we are trusting and believing, God makes a covenant and says to everyone else: Do not touch My people; they are the apple of My eye. Thus God imposes His rule upon the others. But here, with the Jew, God is going to let the nations come in through Lebanon, to sweep in; He is going to break the staff! And in verse 11:

> And it was broken in that day: and thus the poor of the flock that gave heed unto me knew that it was the word of the Lord.

As I have said, when the Christians saw what was happening to Jerusalem and saw the Jews being slaughtered, they knew it was the word of the Lord. In a sad way it was the greatest thrill of their lives to see all that God had said come true. They remembered the words of Jesus: I tell you Jerusalem, not one stone will stand upon another ... and the remnant who believed in Jesus saw His predictions come to pass in their lifetime. Notice how the New Testament is essential to the understanding of Zechariah. The Messiah then speaks again in verse 12:

> And I said unto them, If ye think good, give me my hire; and if not, forbear. So they weighed for my hire thirty pieces of silver.

Through the prophet the Messiah speaks to these people who loathe Him and who have tired Him to death. Putting it in terms of our Lord's ministry, He is saying to them: Well, I have worked, I have fed the flock of Israel; now what are you going to pay me? He asks for His wages: in other words, here is a Man who has fed His flock the chief people of which loathe Him; He is fed up with them; so He comes to an end and says He is not going to do it any more and asks for His wages. So what do they give him? They give Him thirty pieces of silver!

Now what is the significance of that? Look at Exodus 21 verses 31 and 32:

> Whether he have gored a son, or have gored a daughter, according to this judgment shall it be done unto him.
> If the ox gore a manservant or a maidservant; he shall give unto their master thirty shekels of silver, and the ox shall be stoned.

If an ox gored a slave, thirty shekels of silver was demanded by the master. That is what thirty pieces of silver means: the price of a dead slave. Zechariah's words were all written five hundred years before Christ. The prophecy speaks of Christ the Messiah feeding the flock of Israel, coming to an end of His work because of their obduracy and saying to their leaders, Give me my money; I have finished; I will not feed you any more. So they gave Him the price of a dead slave! It is a contemptuous act: and so He is equally contemptuous, and God's voice in Christ says, in verse 13:

> And the Lord said unto me, Cast it unto the potter, the goodly price that I was prised at of them. And I took the thirty pieces of silver, and cast them unto the potter, in the house of the Lord.

Such irony! the price of a dead slave; that was all He was worth in their eyes; the very Shepherd of Israel. And the details are fascinating: Christ as it were, through Judas Iscariot, cast the thirty pieces of silver, where? in the Temple!

It is interesting to examine the theme of the potter. They were the poorest of people; they were paid the least; they made pots that broke, and they were not skilled men like the silversmiths. The Messiah, this Person who fed the flock and is now being estimated as not being worth more than a dead slave, says, Throw it down; I do not want your money. And the money is flung down openly before others in the house of the Lord. The potters, incidentally, lived in the valley of Hinnom, the Valley of Slaughter, just outside Jerusalem. Let us read Jeremiah 18 verses 1 to 7. This is very important:

> The word which came to Jeremiah from the Lord, saying,
> Arise, and go down to the potter's house, and there I will cause thee to hear my words.
> Then I went down to the potter's house, and, behold, he wrought his work on the wheels.
> And when the vessel that he made of the clay was marred in the hand of the potter, he made it again another vessel, as seemed good to the potter to make it.
> Then the word of the Lord came to me, saying,
> O house of Israel, cannot I do with you as this potter? saith the Lord. Behold, as the clay in the potter's hand, so are ye in mine hand, O house of Israel.
> At what instant I shall speak concerning a nation, and concerning a kingdom, to pluck up and to break down and to destroy it.

These words came to Jeremiah, the great prophet, who is far better known than Zechariah. Now read the first five verses of chapter 19 of Jeremiah, and then note verse 6 particularly, which says:

> Therefore, behold, the days come, saith the Lord, that

> this place shall no more be called Topheth, nor The valley of the son of Hinnom, but The valley of Slaughter.

Do you see the way it all fits in? The prophet is looking ahead to a time when the Messiah shall come and feed His people. They will take no notice; they will persecute Him and gang up against Him until His soul is absolutely wearied with them, and they hate Him. They will only give for Him (in the prophet's day metaphorically, but in the case of Judas Iscariot actually) thirty pieces of silver, the price of a dead slave. That is all they thought of Christ; He was not worth any more; it was their contempt for Christ. And He, equally contemptuous, throws it down and refers back to Jeremiah saying: This place shall be called the Valley of Slaughter because you are a flock destined for slaughter. Going on to verse 14, we read:

> Then I cut asunder mine other staff, even Bands, that I might break the brotherhood between Judah and Israel.

Remember, He had two staffs: one representing the covenant that God made with the nations not to touch His people until He broke that staff, and the other meaning that God would keep the whole Jewish nation together in good fellowship. And now He breaks that staff. So the Jewish nation is now dispersed, hated, and at odds, with no common centre, and no mutual love.

Let us read a great chapter in the New Testament, Matthew 27 and verses 1 to 10:

> Now when morning was come, all the chief priests and the elders of the people took counsel against Jesus to put him to death:
> And they bound him, and led him away, and delivered him up to Pilate the governor.
> Then Judas, which betrayed him, when he saw that he was condemned, repented himself, and brought back the thirty pieces of silver to the chief priests and elders,

> Saying, I have sinned in that I betrayed innocent blood. But they said, What is that to us? see thou to it.
> And he cast down the pieces of silver into the sanctuary, and departed; and he went away and hanged himself.
> And the chief priests took the pieces of silver, and said, It is not lawful to put them into the treasury, since it is the price of blood.
> And they took counsel, and bought with them the potter's field, to bury strangers in.
> Wherefore that field was called, The field of blood, unto this day.
> Then was fulfilled that which was spoken by Jeremiah the prophet, saying, And they took the thirty pieces of silver, the price of him that was priced, whom certain of the children of Israel did price;
> And they gave them for the potter's field, as the Lord appointed me.

Now try to put all this into context. Think of Jeremiah and the potters' valley just outside Jerusalem where all the poor potters worked. Think of Jeremiah going there and God giving him parables about making pots and remaking them and so on; and how that valley where they worked would soon become the Valley of Slaughter. Think of all this as you read Matthew. Notice the false shepherds in verse 1, the three shepherds whom I discussed in verse 8 of Zechariah. Notice how Judas cast down the thirty pieces of silver in the Sanctuary openly before all the people, in the house of the Lord, exactly as Zechariah had said. He flung them down in front of all the people and went out and hanged himself. And then the priests bought with the thirty pieces of silver the potter's field; a plot of land in the very Valley of Slaughter.

Now at this point all the critics jump to their feet and say, Aha, Jeremiah did not say what is written in verses 9 and 10 of Matthew. But he did say it. There is no mistake here. The prophecy which Matthew quotes was from a very famous prophecy by Jeremiah: that the valley would become the Valley of Slaughter; that the house of Israel would be treated like a pot and crushed; that they would reject their Messiah. Everybody knew about Jeremiah and the potters. Zechariah's prophecies refer back to Jeremiah's great prophecy; they retrace the beginning of these events, the foretelling, the overthrow of Jerusalem; and then he adds more details. In Zechariah, the potter, the house of the potter, the rejection of the Shepherd of Israel, the potter's field, a field of blood - all this is from Jeremiah; then Zechariah adds: They priced him for thirty pieces of silver. This is the detail Matthew picks out, but his fundamental reference is to the prophecy of the great Jeremiah.

Christ's generation there filled up the sins of the whole history of Israel. They had rejected the prophets; they had talked of stoning Moses; they had put other prophets to death; they had disobeyed God and had gone their arrogant course of thinking that they were more righteous than anyone else. They had defied God and when the Christ of God came Himself, they hated Him. The only value they set on the Christ of God was that of a dead slave. They had got, in a sense, to a point of no return. And so He broke His other staff. He broke the unity of Israel: He abandoned all the care and the gentleness for the family of God, for Judah and Ephraim. He broke the brotherhood and it happened forty years after Christ was put to death.

And continuing with verses 15 and 16, which are again full of images:

> And the Lord said unto me, Take unto thee yet again the instruments of a foolish shepherd (or idol shepherd). For, lo, I will raise up a shepherd in the land, which shall not visit those that be cut off, neither shall seek those that be scattered, nor heal that that is broken; neither shall he feed that which is sound, but he shall eat the flesh of the fat, and shall tear their hoofs in pieces.

God does not only raise up good men; He also raises up bad men, and through the prophet God is saying: You have rejected the true Shepherd; you have crucified the Lord of Glory; you have chosen Caesar as your king and you can have Caesar. Remember that, in prophecy, Caesar is only a picture of the Antichrist, the Man of Sin, and that one evil man is only a picture of the final great manifestation of evil. In rejecting Christ the Jews chose Caesar. They said: His blood be upon us and upon our children. Since then they have had evil rulers right down the years; evil rulers who have torn them to pieces (torn their hoofs in pieces) and were it not for the grace of God, not one of them would have survived. When you look at the mystery of Israel, you must look at it in the light of the above; it is no use simply saying 'anti-semitism'. What is 'anti-semitism'? It is the outworking of Zechariah; the outworking of Christ's words; the outworking of their own words when they said: We have no king but Caesar; put this Man to death. And they have gone on, broken, battered, and punished to this very day.

But as I say, the verses are predicting the total evil: a worse evil is to come. Read Daniel 7 verses 7 and 8. Here is your **Idol** Shepherd (Elil in Hebrew is often used to mean idols and images which were worshipped by apostate Israel); here is your Caesar in the last days; here is the personification of evil, because that is what we are working up to:

> After this I saw in the night visions, and behold a fourth beast, terrible and powerful, and strong exceedingly; and it had great iron teeth: it devoured and brake in pieces, and stamped the residue with his feet: and it was diverse from all the beasts that were before it; and it had ten horns.
>
> I considered the horns, and, behold, there came up among them another horn, a little one, before which three of the first horns were plucked up by the roots: and, behold, in this horn were eyes like the eyes of a man, and a mouth speaking great things.

Read also Daniel 9 verse 26:

> And after the threescore and two weeks shall the anointed one be cut off, and shall have nothing: and the people of the prince that shall come shall destroy the city and the sanctuary; and his end shall be with a flood, and even unto the end shall be war; desolations are determined.

'The anointed one' is the Good Shepherd, the Christ, the Shepherd of Zechariah; 'shall have nothing' is the Nail ripped out; and 'the prince' is the Evil Prince. The verses go on to merge the first desolation of AD 70 with the last desolation in the Last Days, which we are now approaching. This is a picture of the Antichrist; the Idol Shepherd; the thief 'who cometh only to kill and destroy'. Go back to Daniel 7 verses 19 to 26:

> Then I desired to know the truth concerning the fourth beast, which was diverse from all of them, exceeding terrible, whose teeth were of iron, and his nails of brass; which devoured, brake in pieces, and stamped the residue with his feet;
> And concerning the ten horns that were on his head, and the other horn which came up, and before which three fell; even that horn that had eyes, and a mouth that spake great things, whose look was more stout than his fellows.
> I beheld, and the same horn made war with the saints, and prevailed against them;
> Until the ancient of days came, and judgment was given to the saints of the Most High; and the time came that the saints possessed the kingdom.
> Thus he said, The fourth beast shall be a fourth kingdom upon earth, which shall be diverse from all the kingdoms, and shall devour the whole earth, and shall tread it down, and break it in pieces.
> And as for the ten horns, out of this kingdom shall ten kings arise: and another shall arise after them; and he shall be diverse from the former, and he shall put down three kings.

> And he shall speak words against the Most High, and shall wear out the saints of the Most High: and he shall think to change the times and the law; and they shall be given into his hand until a time and times and half a time.
> But the judgment shall sit, and they shall take away his dominion, to consume and to destroy it unto the end.

'And another shall arise after them', refers to the Antichrist. And 'they shall be given into his hand' means power shall be given to him. No wonder that Daniel says in verse 28, 'Here is the end of the matter. As for me Daniel, my thoughts much troubled me, and my countenance was changed in me: but I kept the matter in my heart'. It is a picture of the Man of Sin; it is a picture of bestiality. Instead of Jesus Christ the Jews chose the kings of this world; but God is determined to bring an election out of them and that election began with the first few believers in Jesus Christ.

And now we are approaching the day when Lebanon is opening her doors; the Jew is back in the land, still blaspheming God; evil is still building up; and the Caesar will come in the form of what? Look at 2 Thessalonians 2 verses 1 to 10:

> Now we beseech you, brethren, touching the coming of our Lord Jesus Christ, and our gathering together unto him;
> To the end that ye be not quickly shaken from your mind, nor yet be troubled, either by spirit, or by word, or by epistle as from us, as that the day of the Lord is now present;
> Let no man beguile you in any wise: for it will not be, except the falling away come first, and the man of sin be revealed, the son of perdition,
> He that opposeth and exalteth himself against all that is called God or that is worshipped; so that he sitteth in the temple of God, setting himself forth as God.
> Remember ye not, that, when I was yet with you, I told

> you these things?
> And now ye know that which restraineth, to the end that he may be revealed in his own season.
> For the mystery of lawlessness doth already work; only there is one that restraineth now, until he be taken out of the way.
> And then shall be revealed the lawless one, whom the Lord Jesus shall slay with the breath of his mouth, and bring to nought by the manifestation of his coming;
> Even he, whose coming is according to the working of Satan with all power and signs and lying wonders,
> And with all deceit of unrighteousness for them that are perishing; because they received not the love of the truth, that they might be saved.

In other words, all the scriptures are in accord with each other. The Jew rejected Christ; they rejected His ministry as the Good Shepherd of Israel so that He no longer pitied them. He handed them over; He broke His covenant with the nations; He broke the unity of the Jewish nation; and He handed them over to the Gentiles. The Jews chose their king and they have lived under him. But the end is not over yet. Someone else is coming: the little horn (in Daniel), the Antichrist, the Man of Sin, the Beast in Revelation; these are all synonymous terms for the one person. We are moving to a period when some mighty person will come, who will perform miracles, signs, and wonders, and who would deceive the very elect - even the very elect - were God not to keep us.

Do not make light of this. Christians can go astray: they too can be caught up in the charismatic signs and wonders of some brilliant man who will make an agreement with the Jews, who will rule universally in many ways, and who will have enormous power. But what is he? He is against everything that is called God. He will sit in the very Temple of God; he will sneer at the Christians; he will persecute true Christians; but he will sweep with him many, many, weak believers. And the Jew? The Jew is going to meet his ultimate and final persecution. We will read about this in the next chapters. And in verse 17:

> Woe to the worthless shepherd that leaveth the flock! the sword shall be upon his arm, and upon his right eye: his arm shall be clean dried up, and his right eye shall be utterly darkened.

The right arm is the arm of power, Yad Yammin; the Antichrist will rule with power. The right eye means his intelligence. This man who is coming is a man of mighty power and God will smite his right arm; he is a man of mighty intelligence and God will smite his right eye; or rather Christ will smite him, as we shall see.

Do you see the meaning of this wonderful prophecy? It is confused is it not? But it is great! It is a great challenge to you. People will say, Surely this interpretation is a bit far-fetched. But is it? Can you interpret this chapter in any other way? Can you interpret the thirty pieces of silver and the Temple, and the potters, and the valley, and so on in any other way? Can you tell me who the Shepherd is or why God has cast off His people, not pitying them?

Pusey and Jerome are wrong. God has left His people; He has left them in darkness for two thousand years but, because of His oath, because of His covenant, He is drawing them back; and we are reaching an apex of history which will be in terms of great personalities, and great evil. It will all be consummated by the Coming of Christ and the destruction of Israel and, what has always been a Biblical principle, the saving of the remnant of Israel. This remnant will be saved simply because they believe. They will look upon Him whom they pierced and wail because of Him and say: This is our God. A wonderful thought! the Jew one day will say of Christ as He comes in glory: This is our God. They have rejected Him for all that time and that is the cause of world trouble today.

I think that we are living in days which are so significant that it is unbelievable: the Lebanon; the gathering of the Jew which was not a fact even eighty years ago; the obstinacy of the Jew; the hatred of the nations; the seeking for someone to lead us. And the only answer is the Coming of Christ which will smite the right arm of wickedness, and smite the right eye, the high intelligence of wickedness. He is called a foolish shepherd because, as one wise Puritan says, if you are opposed to God, the more clever you are the more foolish you are. It is a fact: if you deny God, you might be clever; but you are a bigger fool that the ordinary ignorant man because you have got brains; you are absolutely a fool, for 'a fool hath said in his heart, there is no God'. So the foolish shepherd is not foolish in the sense of lacking in intelligence; he has all the brains in the world; but he does not see the Truth. He does not know God!

15 GRACE AND SUPPLICATION FOR THE REMNANT

The heavy tidings in chapter 11 concerning the fate of Israel continue in chapter 12 as 'the burden of the word of the Lord'. Notice the repeated use of the words 'in that day'. The phrase occurs fifteen times in these last three chapters of Zechariah. Other prophets render the phrase as 'the day of the Lord'. In Hebrew the words are Yom Hahu meaning, His Day. The phrase used by Zechariah means 'In His day' or 'The Day of the Lord' or 'The Day of His Glory'.

In chapter 12 of Zechariah a very particular point of view is presented to us, and you have got to relate all these things to the rest of the scriptures. Israel is in view, the nation of Israel 'in that day'. We are not talking about the world; nor about the final apostasy of the nations; nor about the worldwide events and disasters that are chronicled in graphic form in Revelation; we are not talking even about the reign of the Idol Shepherd at the end, the Antichrist. There are many questions to be packed in between, such as, What is the great tribulation? Will the Temple be rebuilt in Jerusalem? When is the fulness of the Gentiles to be recognised? and so on, and much of Daniel and much of Revelation is to be related to what we are saying, such as the seals, the trumpets, and the vials.

But here, it is Israel in view, and chapter 12 is talking entirely about the physical people of God. It is 'the time of Jacob's trouble' as Jeremiah calls it, and the final two chapters amplify what we are now going to discuss. I want to say this: the events in this chapter have never known fulfilment; not at the fall of Jerusalem under Nebuchadnezzar, nor at the fall of Jerusalem at the time of Titus, nor during the time of the Maccabees when they drove the Syrians out of the city in 165 BC. None of these events contain what is being said in chapter 12; for example, when did they look upon him whom they pierced? What we are talking about in verses 1 to 9 is the sudden, final deliverance of the Jew by a Divine Intervention, and a Divine Appearance. Indeed, in chapters 10 to 14 of Zechariah we are talking about the national mourning, the repentance, and the conversion of the Jew that have so far never taken place.

But first I would just like to look back, because Scripture is rather wonderful, to Deuteronomy 32 verses 36 to 43 about this judgment, repentance, mourning and conversion. These are the closing verses of the song that Moses, when he was about to die, taught the children of Israel. The order was given that they should never forget it; they had to teach their children this song:

> For the Lord shall judge his people, and repent himself for his servants; when he seeth that their power is gone, and there is none remaining, shut up or left at large.
> And he shall say, Where are their gods, the rock in which they trusted;
> Which did eat the fat of their sacrifices, and drank the wine of their drink offering? let them rise up and help you, let them be your protection.
> See now that I, even I, am he, and there is no god with me: I kill, and I make alive; I have wounded, and I heal: and there is none that can deliver out of my hand.
> For I lift up my hand to heaven, and say, As I live for ever,
> If I whet my glittering sword, and mine hand take hold on judgment; I will render vengeance to mine adversaries, and will recompense them that hate me.
> I will make mine arrows drunk with blood, and my sword shall devour flesh; with the blood of the slain and the captives, from the head of the leaders of the

> enemy.
> Rejoice, O ye nations, with his people: for he will avenge the blood of his servants, and will render vengeance to his adversaries, and will make expiation for his land, for his people.

The whole of Scripture is consistent. God reigns. Though Israel is cast off, and though Israel has been in the pit and has lived on in bitterness and in The Hope, nevertheless chapters 10 to 14 point to a national mourning and repentance and conversion of this people, who at this very moment are filling the town of Tel Aviv. Do you realise that one million Jews live in Tel Aviv? Do you realise that that is a miracle? There is a big square in Tel Aviv (Dizzengoff Square) and Jews sit in the cafés in that square and say: Here we are back in the Land, with only Jews all around us! You know, they can hardly believe it; it is a miracle.
And so to verse 1 of chapter 12:

> The burden of the word of the Lord concerning Israel. Thus saith the Lord, which stretcheth forth the heavens, and layeth the foundation of the earth, and formeth the spirit of man within him:

Now that is a very impressive beginning. Who is speaking? Read Isaiah 42 verse 5:

> Thus saith God the Lord, he that created the heavens, and stretched them forth; he that spread abroad the earth and that which cometh out of it; he that giveth breath unto the people. upon it, and spirit to them that walk therein:

The same great titles. In other words, the one who is speaking now concerning this great promise is none other than God the Creator, the Mighty God who inhabiteth eternity. What He is saying is: I who stretch forth, lay, form ... it means that God's creative works do not stop at

Genesis 1; they go on now, every morning; 'New every morning'.

You probably know the two theories about the beginning of the earth: one is a 'big bang' theory, and the other is continuous creation. I believe they are both right as far as one can understand physics; that it began, but it is always being renewed; there is a continuous creation. And this is the picture here, of God who created, God who night by night calls out every star and not one fails to appear; every star appears by name and everything is being renewed. Our Lord takes this up when He talks about the sabbath day. He takes them into the realms of real wonder and glory in, 'My father worketh hitherto ... and I work'. Our Lord is always known in Scripture as the One who not only created, but sustaineth, and upholdeth. So in a wonderful sense this world of ours and this glorious universe of ours is not like a clock running down; we are not, as the pessimists say, going to revert to an ice age in five hundred million years or so, or be drawn into a vortex and be burnt up; we are not like a mechanical clock. No! say the Old and the New Testament; God not only created the world, He is sustaining it. And our Lord who is the Agent of creation asks: What does God do on a Sunday? Does He work? Of course He works, in the sense of sustaining His wonderful creation. And our Lord takes up this marvellous theme with the Jews.

So here we are not dealing with some small idea of God. We are dealing with God the Creator, God the Sustainer, God that renews; and while this earth remains, seed time and harvest, winter and summer, will go on because God is doing it, so have no fears, good folk. And it is God who will deliver His people Israel. It is important to get that: the eschatology (which means words about the Last Day) of the Bible depends entirely on the Old and the New Testament; on God and His Christ. There is no dichotomy; we do not have a sort of Christian eschatology (well, we do, but it is totally related to all the words of the prophets); Jewish and Christian eschatology all merge into the same God, God and His Christ.

And continuing with verses 2 and 3:

> Behold, I will make Jerusalem a cup of reeling unto all the peoples round about, and upon Judah also shall it be in the siege against Jerusalem.
> And it shall come to pass in that day, that I will make Jerusalem a burdensome stone for all the peoples; all that burden themselves with it shall be sore wounded; and all the nations of the earth shall be gathered together against it.

The word 'cup' here in Hebrew means 'a large cup'. The country Israelites of Judah, as distinct from the Jerusalem Israelites (or the townsfolk), will share this cup of reeling; that is, share in the suffering in the siege against Jerusalem. We are dealing with the final agonies of Jerusalem, which is encompassed about by world armies. Now again, this would have seemed absurd a hundred years ago. Is it absurd now? If Russia were to come down from the North, if the Arabs were to close in, if Iran and Iraq and Pakistan and North Africa were to join in an attack on Jerusalem, where would we all be? It is not impossible: we all know that the cockpit of the world now is Israel, the Middle East; we all have our eyes on it anxiously; who is going to be drawn in? Will America come in?

So this is the final agony of Jerusalem. Will the Jew be finally exterminated? Is this the final solution? Many people would like it to be, you know: they **are** a bit of a curse; they cause an awful lot of trouble; many people regret that Balfour signed anything at all in favour of the Jews; and their history in the last thirty-five years, and the troubles that have flared up are frightening. Is it the last judgment?

Well, yes and no! It is the last judgment ... but God ... but God! how I love those two words. Paul used them a lot; I use them a lot. Things are hopeless for you and for me as Christians in our personal relationship with the Lord. But when things are hopeless in bigger circumstances, in bigger contexts, then 'you are shut up unto faith' says the inspired writer. When you have no way to turn, when all you have left is your faith, then that is the safest thing to have. But God ... But God! and God remembers Abraham, Isaac, and Jacob; there is a sudden intervention against the exulting nations - because Israel will appear to have come to the end of its time, and can no longer stand against the nations.

Those nations have gone beyond their mandate. God gave them licence to attack His people in order to chastise them; but people given such permission often go beyond their brief, and the nations have indeed done this. Therefore, instead of Israel reeling and stumbling like a drunken man, the nations now begin to reel. Look at Isaiah 51 verses 21 to 23:

> Therefore hear now this, thou afflicted, and drunken, but not with wine:
> Thus saith thy Lord the Lord, and thy God that pleadeth the cause of his people, Behold, I have taken out of thine hand the cup of staggering, even the bowl of the cup of my fury; thou shalt no more drink it again:
> And I will put it into the hand of them that afflict thee; which have said to thy soul, Bow down, that we may go over: and thou hast laid thy back as the ground, and as the street, to them that go over.

And in Jeremiah 25 verse 15:

> For thus saith the Lord, the God of Israel, unto me: Take the cup of the wine of this fury at my hand, and cause all the nations, to whom I send thee, to drink it.

See how consistent the scriptures are. What amazes me about Scripture, if I may say so after years and years of reading it, is its complete congruity: even the metaphors, used by one prophet and then another, all come to one fine thread. To me it is a mark of complete inspiration. So much for the people who talk about stylistic analysis and so on! You have to read Scripture as we are trying to do; and realise that there is only one Author behind the sixty-six authors if you like; that He is the Holy Ghost; that He brings all things, even the very words, to have that one purpose.

The words 'all that burden themselves with it' in verse 3, mean 'try to lift it'. Notice that it is now 'all the nations of the earth' that shall be gathered against Jerusalem. See the accuracy of Scripture? In That Day it is not just going to be peoples round about; the text amplifies it to 'all the peoples of the earth'. Now do not skip over this; it is essential to see that Scripture lays emphasis on this point. There have been local attacks on Jerusalem, local wars as it were, but in the last day, In That Day, all the peoples of the earth are going to be involved in this mighty battle. And those who try to lift the burdensome stone will, in the Hebrew, be cut to pieces. Now oddly enough, Jerome, who died in AD 420 and who translated the Bible from Hebrew and Greek into the Roman Catholic Vulgate version, says that in Palestine in his day every village had a big stone. The young men of the village would test their strength on this stone by lifting it. This, he says, was a very strong Palestinian custom. Jerome also says that when he went to Athens he saw a huge round thing by the gates of the city. He tried to lift it but could not move it and enquired as to what it was. He was told that it was the stone that all the wrestlers had to be able to lift before they were allowed to enter the games.

So you have a picture. God will make Jerusalem a burdensome stone, and all the nations of the earth will be gathered there to try to lift it, or burden themselves with it, and this is 'The Day of the Lord'. According to Amos, when the people asked him about this in 800 BC, The Day of the Lord is darkness and not light. Amos calls God a Lion, and The Day of the Lord is called 'The Roar of the Lion'. And you get the final catastrophes in Revelation 16 verses 13 and 14; I know this cross-referencing is tedious, but it is essential in the interests of truth and accuracy:

> And I saw coming out of the mouth of the dragon (that is Satan, the inspirer of evil), and out of the mouth of the beast (that is the Antichrist), and out of the mouth of the false prophet (that is the religious genius who makes everybody worship the Antichrist, and note again the triunity of evil based upon the Trinity of God), three unclean spirits, as it were frogs:
> For they are spirits of devils, working signs; which go forth unto the kings of the whole world, to gather them together unto the war of the great day of God, the Almighty.

You see it? The nations will come and what ultimately brings them will be (but only superficially) economic or historical or political reasons and so on; but behind it all is the Dragon, and the Beast, and the False Prophet who want to destroy the people of God. And why? Because, if this ancient people of God, this fleshly people of God - abhorrent in some ways as they are - were ever destroyed, then all God's covenants would be made to look a laughing- stock! The gathering of all the nations, the attack, is an inspired attack by Satan himself, as Revelation says. Read Joel 3 verses 9 to 16:

> Proclaim ye this among the nations; prepare war: stir up the mighty men; let all the men of war draw near, let them come up.
> Beat your ploughshares into swords, and your pruning-hooks into spears: let the weak say, I am strong.
> Haste ye, and come, all ye nations round about, and gather yourselves together: thither cause thy mighty ones to come down, O Lord.
> Let the nations bestir themselves, and come up to the valley of Jehoshaphat: for there will I sit to judge all the nations round about.
> Put ye in the sickle, for the harvest is ripe: come, tread ye; for the winepress is full, the fats overflow; for their wickedness is great.
> Multitudes, multitudes in the valley of decision! for the

> day of the Lord is near in the valley of decision.
> The sun and the moon are darkened, and the stars withdraw their shining.
> And the Lord shall roar from Zion, and utter his voice from Jerusalem; and the heavens and the earth shall shake: but the Lord will be a refuge unto his people, and a strong hold to the children of Israel.

What I am saying is that Zechariah is the quintessence of the prophets. He does not write, as it were, from his own head; he is gathering together all the truths of the other prophets and putting them in one pithy, marvellous, small prophecy. Read Ezekiel 38 verses 8 and 9 for this purpose:

> After many days thou shalt be visited: in the latter years thou shalt come into the land that is brought back from the sword, that is gathered out of many peoples, upon the mountains of Israel, which have been a continual waste: but it is brought forth out of the peoples, and they shall dwell securely, all of them.
> And thou shalt ascend, thou shalt come like a storm, thou shalt be like a cloud to cover the land, thou, and all thy hordes, and many peoples with thee.

And we could go on. Chapter 39 of Ezekiel too is fascinating; in other words, this is the day that the Lord hath made. Refer to Psalm 118 (which is a national hymn, remember, as well as a personal prayer) and verses 10 to 26:

> All nations compassed me about: in the name of the Lord I will cut them off.
> They compassed me about; yea, they compassed me about: in the name of the Lord I will cut them off.
> They compassed me about like bees; they are quenched as the fire of thorns: in the name of the Lord I will cut them off.
> Thou didst thrust sore at me that I might fall: but the Lord helped me.

> The Lord is my strength and song; and he is become my salvation.
> The voice of rejoicing and salvation is in the tents of the righteous: the right hand of the Lord doeth valiantly.
> The right hand of the Lord is exalted: the right hand of the Lord doeth valiantly.
> I shall not die, but live, and declare the works of the Lord.
> The Lord hath chastened me sore: but he hath not given me over unto death.
> Open to me the gates of righteousness: I will enter into them, I will give thanks unto the Lord.
> This is the gate of the Lord; the righteous shall enter into it.
> I will give thanks unto thee, for thou hast answered me, and art become my salvation.
> The stone which the builders rejected is become the head of the corner.
> This is the Lord's doing; it is marvellous in our eyes.
> This is the day which the Lord hath made; we will rejoice and be glad in it.
> Save now, we beseech thee, O Lord: O Lord, we beseech thee, send now prosperity.
> Blessed be he that cometh in the name of the Lord: we have blessed you out of the house of the Lord.

Our Lord Himself refers to this Psalm. It is very thrilling. Scripture is for personal use, for personal strength, for personal application; there is no doubt about that because Paul uses it that way. But it is also for the great events of history.

And continuing with verse 4:

> In that day, saith the Lord, I will smite every horse with astonishment, and his rider with madness: and I will open mine eyes upon the house of Judah, and will smite every horse of the peoples with blindness.

All nations are gathered around Jerusalem; this is the picture. The big thing is that God is opening His eyes once again; God is looking in mercy towards this people who have defied Him and gone their own way; this stubborn, hard-hearted people who crucified the Lord of Glory, His own Son. Notice the words 'bewilderment' (or astonishment), 'madness', and 'blindness': this is the content of the cup of reeling; these are the very three things that God said, through Moses, that He would give to Israel. In Numbers and Deuteronomy He says: If you leave me I will give you madness, blindness, and bewilderment. I will make you drink the dregs of a cup of wine. But now, in that day, at the end of this terrible period of suffering, He is taking the cup from them and giving it to the nations round about! He is going to smite the nations; He is going to hand out to them the same punishment that He gave, as it were, to His own people. This is the cup of reeling: and He will do it on the day that the armies of the nations surround Jerusalem to destroy Israel once and for all.

But what takes place? Israel is suddenly inspired, and in verses 5 and 6:

> And the chieftains of Judah shall say in their heart, The inhabitants of Jerusalem are my strength in the Lord of hosts their God.
> In that day will I make the chieftains of Judah like a pan of fire among wood, and like a torch of fire among sheaves; and they shall devour all the peoples round about, on the right hand and on the left: and Jerusalem shall yet again dwell in her own place, even in Jerusalem.

They are going to get enormous inspiration and courage and fighting ability. Jerusalem is not going to be totally destroyed by any means. And in verses 7 and 8:

> The Lord also shall save the tents of Judah first, that the glory of the house of David and the glory of the

> inhabitants of Jerusalem be not magnified above Judah. In that day shall the Lord defend the inhabitants of Jerusalem; and he that is feeble among them at that day shall be as David; and the house of David shall be as God, as the angel of the Lord before them.

'Tents of Judah' means the countryside around (tents signify a sort of temporary dwelling place), that is, the land around Jerusalem down on to the plain, to Tel Aviv and so on. The glory of the house of David and of Jerusalem will not be magnified over the rest of the country; even the feeble shall be as David the great warrior.

It is going to be a tremendous thing: Jerusalem is surrounded but suddenly the cup of reeling passes to the nations; and what causes all this? It is because the Divine gaze is on His people. It is not them: it is God; God is intervening at the last moment; 'But God ...' God is returning to this despised and outnumbered people; He is jealous for His people; He is returning. The people will become as a pan of fire; each one will become a David and the clan of David will become like God Himself; like the angel of the Lord who led the Israelites through the wilderness and gave them strength in all their past history, and why? Because the Divine gaze is once again turned on the ancient people, to defend them, to restore, and God is in the midst. And verse 9 says:

> And it shall come to pass in that day, that I will seek to destroy all the nations that come against Jerusalem.

That is what we might call a great understatement; 'I will seek'! When we talk of seeking to do something we speak within the limits of our ambitions and strength. But when God says, I will seek to destroy the nations, this does not mean that He will fumble or fail at any point; it just means that it is well within His power.

So up to verse 9 we have the Jewish nation surrounded, the land attacked, but God opening His eyes, God smiting the nations, and now seeking to destroy all the nations that come against Jerusalem. This is THE great deliverance; it is the greatest deliverance that Israel has ever had or ever will have. We can talk about Egypt; we can talk about the Red Sea; great deliverances indeed. We can talk about Babylon and the return; we can talk about the Maccabees; but nothing matches up to this. You have got to be honest in the interpretation of the Word: this man Zechariah had lived through it; he knew; nothing had ever happened in Jewish history like this; but In That Day, on His day, everything else pales into insignificance. This is going to be a deliverance of deliverances; and it is because God has once again turned His eyes with favour upon the ancient people.

But now the mood changes. You might say, Well, happy people they are; but let me just add in passing (because we have not yet reached chapter 13), that defending Jerusalem does not mean that Jerusalem is inviolate altogether. As we have seen in the prophecy, many Jews will die in that siege: in fact as we get to the next two chapters we shall see that only one third will come through; a remnant. So it is a very real thing, and whilst this chapter can give the impression that Jerusalem is totally defended, it does not mean that; it means **ultimately** defended; in the midst of the tremendous siege and battle - then God delivers. And in verse 10:

> And I will pour upon the house of David, and upon the inhabitants of Jerusalem, the spirit of grace and of supplication; and they shall look unto me whom they have pierced: and they shall mourn for him, as one mourneth for his only son, and shall be in bitterness for him, as one that is in bitterness for his firstborn.

Now Adolf Saphir, a great Jew, a Christian, and a great student of the scriptures, says that this is one of the most pathetic (in the Victorian sense of the word), touching, and moving texts in the whole of Scripture. The simple unadorned beauty of the text: They shall look upon me, says

God in that day, whom they have pierced. Then extraordinarily, the pronoun alters: And they shall mourn for **him.** In other words, although they are delivered, there is no spirit of shouting when they come out of the agony; there is no spirit of triumph, or boasting or singing; just bitter, almost unconsolable mourning; that is what Scripture is saying here. So you have a mighty deliverance here, and when it is achieved the people break down; they are totally broken-hearted because God is pouring out upon them at the same time the spirit of grace and of supplication; and to see what that means let us read Joel 2 verses 28 to 31:

> And it shall come to pass afterward, that I will pour out my spirit upon all flesh; and your sons and your daughters shall prophesy, your old men shall dream dreams, your young men shall see visions:
> And also upon the servants and upon the handmaids in those days will I pour out my spirit.
> And I will shew wonders in the heavens and in the earth, blood, and fire, and pillars of smoke.
> The sun shall be turned into darkness, and the moon into blood, before the great and terrible day of the Lord come.

Peter uses part of that prophecy: you often get part prophecy used in the New Testament. This is it! The last days have begun, Peter is saying. And here is the pouring out of the Spirit. But he is not saying that it is the end of the last days; we have not yet seen the moon turn to blood or watched all those dramatic events; but the last days have begun, and 'in these last days God hath spoken unto us by His Son'. But the last days come to an end with the return of Jesus Christ, and in that very last day God will pour out the spirit of grace and of supplication.

I have lived among the Jews and they are always boasting about what they have achieved with their armies: they have done this, and they have done that; our pride, our law, our nationalism have done this for us, they say.

But it will not be like that at all 'in that day'. They will recognise sheer unmerited grace in action and supplication which is the fruit of grace. They will plead with God and 'they shall look unto **me** whom they have pierced' (then that extraordinary change) 'and they shall mourn for **him**'. The Hebrew word used for 'look unto' means 'sustained looking', the same word used when the Israelites 'looked upon' the brazen serpent in, 'Whosoever looketh upon it shall be healed'. Do you remember that in the wilderness? The word means looking, not glancing; looking with expectancy; a sustained looking; and they shall look upon Him just as the Israelites did in that desert. If they wanted to be healed, they crawled out of their tents and 'looked upon' the brazen serpent that Moses lifted up.

Let us revert to what Adolf Saphir said about verse 10. He said that this simple unadorned truth of our Lord Jesus Christ should be apparent to every man; but as one writer has said, this is the most controversial text in Scripture because the Jews have tried with all their force to turn it away from what it means. The Jews are caught up: Who is it they shall look upon whom they pierced? and they give all sorts of explanations because it is terribly difficult for the rabbis to get over the text. It is so Messianic, so obviously a reflection of what happened at Calvary; yet the Jews and the rabbis such as Rashi, Ben Ezra, indeed all the famous rabbis, have all tried to get round it. They have interpolated words; they have given various explanations. One is that it is the nation; another is that the Jews will be fighting so well, that even if one Jew falls hurt in the battle, 'they shall look upon him (the wounded Jewish soldier) whom they (the enemy) have pierced and look to me ... ' It is fantastic nonsense.

Remember these people are in unbelief; they have a very uneasy conscience about Jesus Christ to this very day. They try to change Isaiah 53; I touched on this in Vision 4. They try to change the pronouns to make **Israel** the suffering servant in, 'Surely he hath borne our griefs and carried our sorrows ... '. That is Israel, they say; but then they are up against the change in, 'Yet we did esteem him stricken **...** ' and if **him** and **we** are the same there is no point in the prophecy, if you see what I mean.

Nevertheless there are one or two honest rabbis (I have been reading them) and they say that this is no other than the Messiah; and Messiah is always connected interchangeably with God; He is the Metatron. Do you know that word? Messiah is the one who shares God's throne; to look upon Him is to look upon Me, the One who layeth out the universe and rolleth it out. Messiah is His Fellow; to look upon One is to look upon the Other; and some of the rabbis in an honest exegesis have admitted this. But we know what it means, don't we? It is the Christ of God. Now read John 19 verses 36 and 37:

> For these things came to pass, that the scripture might be fulfilled, A bone of him shall not be broken.
> And again another scripture saith, They shall look on him whom they pierced.

So it is not James Ayre, it is John the divine; it is not the rabbis, it is the Bible itself. Look at Revelation 1 verse 7 and just stand amazed at the congruity of Scripture:

> Behold, he cometh with the clouds; and every eye shall see him, and they which pierced him; and all the tribes of the earth shall mourn over him. Even so, Amen.

It is the triumph, in other words, of the Crucified; it is **that day** which the prophet is always talking about; it is His day. Look at Matthew 24 verses 29 and 30; this is our Lord speaking:

> But immediately, after the tribulation of those days, the sun shall be darkened, and the moon shall not give her light (there is Joel you see, not yet completed at the day of Pentecost, which was a partial fulfilment), and the stars shall fall from heaven, and the powers of the heavens shall be shaken:

> And then shall appear the sign of the Son of man in heaven: and then shall all the tribes of the earth mourn, and they shall see the Son of man coming on the clouds of heaven with power and great glory.

That Day! The Jewish nation is going to be overcome in the day of deliverance with an overwhelming sense of guilt and of sorrow; it will be so intense as to be hardly believable. Their stubborn opposition to their God as a nation; their stubborn opposition to their Messiah whom they crucified and pierced - literally pierced; their incredible and insufferable pride; their self-worship and their Babylonish spirit and activities which they will recognise as a shame and a curse. Yes, they will be overcome with terrible sorrow as they think of these things, terrible grief, as one who is in bitterness for his firstborn son. Some of you have met Jewish people and you know the value that they put on their children and particularly on sons. Read Amos 8 verse 10:

> And I will turn your feasts into mourning, and all your songs into lamentation; and I will bring up sackcloth upon all loins, and baldness upon every head; and I will make it as the mourning for an only son, and the end thereof as a bitter day.

An only son! And in verse 11 of Zechariah:

> In that day shall there be a great mourning in Jerusalem, as the mourning of Hadadrimmon in the valley of Megiddon.

Do you know whom they mourned for there? Look at 2 Chronicles 35 verses 22 to 25:

> Nevertheless Josiah would not turn his face from him, but disguised himself, that he might fight with him, and hearkened not unto the words of Neco, from the mouth of God, and came to fight in the valley of Megiddo.

> And the archers shot at king Josiah; and the king said to his servants, Have me away; for I am sore wounded. So his servants took him out of the chariot, and put him in the second chariot that he had, and brought him to Jerusalem; and he died, and was buried in the sepulchres of his fathers. And all Judah and Jerusalem mourned for Josiah.
> And Jeremiah lamented for Josiah: and all the singing men and singing women spake of Josiah in their lamentations, unto this day; and they made them an ordinance in Israel: and, behold, they are written in the lamentations.

So the mourning began then in the valley of Megiddo with Jeremiah lamenting for Josiah. This man was an extraordinary king, and there was enormous lamentation for him which was written into Jewish prayerbooks. Now in the Last Day, instead of shouting 'we won the war', the Jews are going to mourn as they did then, and as for their firstborn son.

Do you realise that Christ is the firstborn of Israel? Do you realise that Revelation talks of Israel as the woman who gave birth to a Son? Christ is truly Israel's firstborn Son; Israel brought forth the Messiah; this barren nation brought forth the Christ of God; and then killed Him; and they are going to mourn when they realise what they have done. But He is not only Israel's firstborn Son, He is God's only Son. Do you know all the parables? - I will send my own beloved son; I will send my only son to them: I have sent servants, now I will send my son to the vineyard; surely they will respect him ... but they said: Let us kill him and the inheritance will be ours.

That is Jewish sin: they have taken election upon themselves. Instead of being thankful to God for being elect in order to serve the nations, they say: We are elect because we are better; the inheritance shall be ours and not God's. When I first went to Israel, the Chief Rabbi admitted that Israel's sin is that they worship Israel instead of the God of Israel. Herzog said, while I was still living there: God is just a cypher 'up there' to add glory to us. But not in This Day! not in the Last Day! So with Jacob the supplanter: you see how he supplanted his brother Esau; but he also supplanted God too - Jacob is a villain really! (though I like him).

But there is going to be, it says, national and family and personal mourning; great mourning as in Hadadrimmon in the valley of Megiddo. And verses 12 to 14:

> And the land shall mourn, every family apart; the family of the house of David apart, and their wives apart; the family of the house of Nathan apart, and their wives apart;
> The family of the house of Levi apart, and their wives apart; the family of the Shimeites apart, and their wives apart;
> All the families that remain, every family apart, and their wives apart.

All that is meant here is that the great men in the royal tribe of Judah (the Davids) are going to mourn for the Christ of God; and the lesser-known names in the tribe (Nathan was a younger son of David) are also going to mourn. And Levi, chosen to be the High Priest, he is going to mourn; and (look up Numbers 3 verse 18) Shimei, son of Gershon, the son of Levi, and virtually unknown, even he is going to mourn. So what the verses are saying is that both great and small, royal and priestly, all are going to mourn, and they are going to mourn apart when they see Him whom they have pierced. But to apply a word of comfort in all this, let us read Isaiah 66 verses 8 to 13:

> Who hath heard such a thing? who hath seen such things? Shall a land be born in one day? shall a nation be brought forth at once? for as soon as Zion travailed, she brought forth her children.
> Shall I bring to the birth, and not cause to bring forth? saith the Lord: shall I that cause to bring forth shut the womb? saith thy God.

> Rejoice ye with Jerusalem, and be glad for her, all ye that love her: rejoice for joy with her, all ye that mourn over her:
> That ye may suck and be satisfied with the breasts of her consolations; that ye may milk out, and be delighted with the abundance of her glory.
> For thus saith the Lord, Behold, I will extend peace to her like a river, and the glory of the nations like an overflowing stream, and ye shall suck thereof; ye shall be borne upon the side, and shall be dandled upon the knees.
> As one whom his mother comforteth, so will I comfort you; and ye shall be comforted in Jerusalem.

Oddly enough, the women's liberation armies which 'bestride this narrow world' claim this text in order to say that we should not call God 'Him', we should call God a Person, because God is a Mother as well as a Father. Apparently we should address God nowadays not as Our Father, but as Our Parent in Heaven, or some such term. They quote this text to insist upon the Motherhood of God. They do not appear to have noticed that this is said **in the last day** when Jerusalem is delivered from the nations, and not today to these ladies - even if there were the slightest validity in their claim.

God comes in; and instead of boasting and exulting, 'They shall look upon Me and they shall look upon Him whom they pierced, and they shall mourn'. This is the beginning of the conversion and the total transformation of the world. We are getting close to the climax, good people: Keep believing, the Lord is at hand.

16 ISRAEL: SCATTERED, CLEANSED, AND RECONCILED

Chapter 13 of Zechariah begins with that magnificent phrase, 'In that day'. We are still watching the effects of 'I will open mine eyes upon the house of Judah' in verse 4 of the last chapter. We have seen what will happen to the Gentiles; but what about the Jew? He is still in unbelief; he is coming to the end of the history of his iniquity; and in verse 1:

> In that day there shall be a fountain opened to the house of David and to the inhabitants of Jerusalem, for sin and for uncleanness.

Let me repeat: there is no glorifying of the Jew; there is no glorifying of human beings; there is no pat on the back. The effect on the unbelieving Gentiles is wholesale destruction; on the Jew, it is that God is going to open a fountain for sin and uncleanness.

Go back to verse 9 of chapter 3 (Vision 4) and note the words 'and I will remove the iniquity of that land in one day'. Now this goes right through Scripture. Look again at Isaiah 66 verse 8; you know this so well but it is necessary to connect all these texts:

> Who hath heard such a thing? who hath seen such things? **Shall a land be born in one day**? shall a nation be brought forth at once? for as soon as Zion travailed, she brought forth her children.

That is what happens when God opens His eyes upon Israel. The awful day of destruction is for them a tremendous day of cleansing, and forgiveness, and rebirth, and God is going to remove the iniquity of that land 'in one day'.

It is stupendous! Think of the Jews living all over the world; think that for two thousand years they have led a life in deliberate antipathy to Christ. Do not tell me that the Jews are good moral people: they are, but that is to fall into the trap of thinking that God is well pleased with good moral people. God is pleased with no one outside Jesus Christ; our morality, our righteousness, are as filthy rags to God. Unless we are in Christ, you see, God has no eye to us; no eye to any man; so think of what is going to happen to this ancient people who have lived all around us for so long. They (especially the orthodox) actually call Him 'Jeshu', and spit as they say it. Jeshu means 'curse', and is very close to 'Jeshua' (Jesus). Yes, the word 'Jeshu' is very close and the Jew spits and goes around in his own righteousness. Some of them may say, Well, Jesus is a good man. But He is not just a good Man! They crucified the Lord of Glory: but having said that, so have we; so have we! We do not stand aside ... In America they persecute Jews for being Christ's killers: that is unfair, because it was not only the Jews, but also Pontius Pilate and the nations who crucified Him. But back to chapter 13 which is in two parts; verses 1 to 6, and 7 to 9, still dealing with the effects of when God turns His eyes on the nation. It is interesting to trace the word 'fountain' in verse 1. You get the word as a very popular image; Look at Jeremiah 2 verse 13:

> For my people have committed two evils; they have forsaken **me** the fountain of living waters, and hewed them out cisterns, broken cisterns, that can hold no water.

Note the phrase, 'me the fountain of living waters'. This is the point; this is the significance. This, in a sense, is the fountain that is going to be opened. Now read Revelation 21 verse 6:

> And he said unto me, They are come to pass. **I am** the Alpha and the Omega, the beginning and the end. **I** will give unto him that is athirst of the **fountain** of the water of life freely.

Again, that same metaphor 'the fountain of the water of life'. And of course this is absolutely Messianic, because our Lord uses this in John 4. It strikes me more and more as I read the Bible that nothing is put in as a sort of incidental, as though they were 'just writing'. It is all connected up with the language of the Holy Ghost of previous ages and through previous men. Our Lord goes to the well in Samaria and says: Give Me to drink ... if you had asked Me I would have given you living water. And the woman in her blindness or misunderstanding says: Give me, so that I do not have to come here to draw water. It is in this very chapter around the fountain of living water that she says, sort of cynically: When Messiah comes we will know all these things. And Christ's answer? I who speak unto you am He.

Do you see the point? The fountain metaphor and the Person of the Messiah are consistently connected right through Scripture. You must not read John and say, That is a nice little way of saying it. It is! But it is more than that: it goes back to Zechariah; it goes back to Jeremiah; it goes back to Psalm 36 where the fountain of life is mentioned, and so on. In other words there is a total coherence in Scripture. But here in Zechariah it is a fountain for sin and uncleanness and for that you have to look at Numbers 8 verse 7; this is God speaking to Aaron:

> And thus shalt thou do unto them, to cleanse them: sprinkle the water of expiation upon them, and let them cause a razor to pass over all their flesh, and let them wash their clothes, and cleanse themselves.

This is Israel being cleansed; the waters of expiation. This had to happen to lepers too: as many commentators have said, sin is the leprosy of the soul. So here in the command to Aaron, in the Levitical commands, here is the sprinkling of water to wash away sin. You get it again in that great piece of prophecy in Ezekiel 36 verses 24 and 25, and there is no doubt what these verses are referring to:

> For I will take you from among the nations, and gather you out of all the countries, and will bring you into your own land.
> And I will sprinkle clean water upon you, and ye shall be clean: from all your filthiness, and from all your idols, will I cleanse you.

I hope once again that you do not find this cross-referencing boring, but you have got to see the thread that runs through the prophetic Scriptures; they are not just incidentals and accidentals; it is all connected up. Again, you get it in Numbers 19 verse 9:

> And a man that is clean shall gather up the ashes of the heifer, and lay them up without the camp in a clean place, and it shall be kept for the congregation of the children of Israel for a water of separation (or impurity): it is a sin offering.

So Zechariah now is binding together this theme from the whole of the Bible. **In that day** what is God going to do? He is going to do what He has promised right through the Bible. He is going to, as it were, cleanse the Jewish nation from all sin and uncleanness: it is not a sprinkling now; it is a fountain, a dug out thing; they are going to be absolutely cleansed.

How can we apply this today? We can of course only apply it today for ourselves. But is something different going to happen to the Jew in the Last Day? Not a bit. The fountain is the Cross of Christ: of course it is, and that fountain was opened two thousand years ago. When you think of the Cross and when you accepted Christ, that Cross became real to you; it became a contemporary thing, didn't it? Although Christ died two thousand years ago, when we accept Christ the Cross becomes instantly relevant; and this is going to happen to the Jew; it is the perennial effect of the Cross. Two thousand years ago they said, His blood be upon us and upon our children; but 'in that day' that Cross is going to be made manifest; they are going to be cleansed by the sacrifice of Calvary. For two thousand years the blood of Christ has been on the Jewish nation, upon them and upon their children. We cannot escape that, no matter how unpleasant it is to modern ethicists, who hold that it is unworthy of God to have allowed so many generations to suffer because of what happened long ago. This is not the point: the Jewish nation is essentially a corporate body; they think the same; they link themselves with all the acts of their fathers; and 'His blood be upon us and upon our children' has literally and historically become true.

But now in chapter 1 of Zechariah God says: I am returned with mercies and will comfort Zion. In that day the fountain will be opened; the Jews will see Jesus Christ as their Saviour; the Jews will come to the once and for all sacrifice that is referred to in Hebrews 9 verses 13 and 14 which, as it were, brings together in one small passage everything from the old covenant and the new covenant:

> For if the blood of goats and bulls, and the ashes of a heifer sprinkling them that have been defiled, sanctify unto the cleanness of the flesh:
> How much more shall the blood of Christ, who through the eternal Spirit offered himself without blemish unto God, cleanse your conscience from dead works to serve the living God?

The first verse refers to the text in Numbers quoted above. So you see, the cleansing of the Old Testament, the cleansing in the New Testament, and the open fountain in Zechariah in the very last day are all one and the same thing, and are brought together by the blood of Christ, who through the eternal Spirit offered Himself to the

Father.

And continuing with verses 2 and 3, which show another effect of what happens when God opens His eyes on Israel:

> And it shall come to pass in that day, saith the Lord of hosts, that I will cut off the names of the idols out of the land, and they shall no more be remembered: and also I will cause the prophets and the unclean spirit to pass out of the land.
>
> And it shall come to pass that, when any shall yet prophesy, then his father and his mother that begat him shall say unto him, Thou shalt not live; for thou speakest lies in the name of the Lord: and his father and his mother that begat him shall thrust him through when he prophesieth.

In that day, not only does He cleanse the nation through faith in Christ, through the effect of Calvary, but all idolatry will go; all false prophets will go; and all unclean spirits will pass out of the land, never to be remembered. Some people say that this points to the fact that these chapters are really pre-exilic, because in the day of Zechariah after the return from Babylon, the Jews were not idol worshippers; they had learned their lesson and were not like their fathers. So, say the critics, this must surely have been written beforehand. But you know that this argument is quite unnecessary. These people who came back from Babylon were at first in danger of idolatry: remember that at the time of Nehemiah, many of them (even the high priest's sons) married foreign wives. Potentially they were very much in danger of going back to the old sins committed by their fathers and mothers until disciplined and taught by Ezra and the Synagogue.

The argument also ignores the fact of that **last day** when there will be the very incarnation of idols and evil spirits. Read once again Revelation 13 verses 1 to 4. We have referred to this before, but you have got to see it in this context:

> And he stood upon the sand of the sea. And I saw a beast coming up out of the sea, having ten horns and seven heads, and on his horns ten diadems, and upon his heads names of blasphemy.
> And the beast which I saw was like unto a leopard, and his feet were as the feet of a bear, and his mouth as the mouth of a lion: and the dragon gave him his power, and his throne, and great authority.
> And I saw one of his heads as though it had been smitten unto death; and his death-stroke was healed: and the whole earth wondered after the beast;
> And they worshipped the dragon, because he gave his authority unto the beast; and they worshipped the beast, saying, Who is like unto the beast? and who is able to war with him?

So you see, that is the position in the last day: the whole of the idolatry will be reincarnated in the Beast, the Idol Shepherd in chapter 11 verse 17 of Zechariah. What we have read in Revelation is simply the reincarnation of all idolatry and all false prophecy personalised in the Beast. And in the last day men everywhere, and especially the Jew, will enter into a covenant with the Idol Shepherd, with the Antichrist. Read 2 Thessalonians 2 verse 4:

> He that opposeth and exalteth himself against all that is called God or that is worshipped; so that he sitteth in the temple of God, setting himself forth as God.

Again, we are talking about the Man of Sin, the Antichrist, The Last Day. And so when God cuts off idolatry and utterly exterminates the unclean spirits, then, for the first time in its history, Palestine will become the Holy Land. Today we call it the Holy Land when in fact it is the most unholy land in the whole world, for at present it is a Christ-less land.

Another thing that happens when God turns His eyes on Israel is the remarkable zeal of the people, the indignation, the shame, the repentance. For example, if a man is intoxicated by the evil spirists (as many will be) and begins to prophecy, even his parents will call him a liar and be prepared to kill him. Again, this is linked with Deuteronomy 13 verses 6 to 11:

> If thy brother, the son of thy mother, or thy son, or thy daughter, or the wife of thy bosom, or thy friend, which is as thine own soul, entice thee secretly, saying, Let us go and serve other gods, which thou hast not known, thou, nor thy fathers;
> Of the gods of the peoples which are round about you, nigh unto thee, or far off from thee, from the one end of the earth even unto the other end of the earth;
> Thou shalt not consent unto him, nor hearken unto him; neither shall thine eye pity him, neither shalt thou spare, neither shalt thou conceal him:
> But thou shalt surely kill him; thine hand shall be first upon him to put him to death, and afterwards the hand of all the people.
> And thou shalt stone him with stones, that he die; because he hath sought to draw thee away from the Lord thy God, which brought thee out of the land of Egypt, out of the house of bondage.
> And all Israel shall hear, and fear, and shall do no more any such wickedness as this is in the midst of thee.

So once again, you see, Zechariah is gathering together the whole spiritual atmosphere of the Bible. If a man should prophesy, then even his parents shall fulfil the Deuteronomic law. In that day, no false prophets will be even tolerated: and they themselves will drop all pretence, says verse 4:

> And it shall come to pass in that day, that the prophets shall be ashamed every one of his vision, when he prophesieth; neither shall they wear a hairy mantle to deceive:

You know Elijah used to wear a hairy mantle; and John the Baptist, we read, wore a hairy mantle and our Lord refers to it; but in that day there will be no pretence, no prophecy. and I would like to link this up to our own day.

I am very worried about the Church today claiming to have prophets. Now some of you know all about this; some of you have been mixed up with churches which claim to have prophets, and which boast about prophecy; only recently I passed by a church called Church of the Prophecy of God. This new movement claims that prophecy is one of the gifts of the Spirit, and that there are men who are prophets today, and this alarms me greatly. This whole thing is coming up again: men claiming to have direct communication from God; people laying aside Scripture and acting directly on extra-revelation. In a sense this is what is being condemned in our present chapter. **In that day** no one shall do that: no one shall claim to be a prophet; no one shall claim to have a Word from God; and they will take off their special garb and marks of being a prophet. So I sometimes wonder how much this new movement is of God. Now, I am not going to condemn people who are involved in it, but I am going to question very much whether such revelations claiming to be the Word of God are true or untrue. Think about that when you hear of present-day prophets. These prophets in our verse will utterly deny any connection with prophecy; there will be so much popular revulsion against such men that there will be hot denial, as in verse 5:

> But he shall say, I am no prophet, I am a tiller of the ground; for I have been made a bondman from my youth.

You see, he will claim to be just a slave labourer such as the Jews had in those days. And then in verse 6:

> And one shall say unto him, What are these wounds between thine arms? Then he shall answer, Those with which I was wounded in the house of my friends.

Now in the old days the false prophets, especially Baal prophets in the time of Elijah, used to cut themselves to bring on orgies and ecstasies (remember Carmel and the priests of Baal). The word in Hebrew, is to cut 'between thy hands' though the cuts might be on the chest. In That Day, people will gather round a man who claims to be a prophet and say, Now what are these wounds? you say that you are not a prophet but just a labourer, a farm worker; but what are these wounds on your hands or on your chest? And the man will deny any link with prophecy and claim that the wounds were received in the house of his lovers! This is an important text that has been misquoted time and time again. The false prophet will say how he has received the wounds and, though we do not like it, it may refer to the cuts of debauchery. You get that sort of thing nowadays; he will even go that far, even to admit homosexuality, in order to deny any connection with false prophecy, such is the indignation of the people. The spirit of God has come upon them; the fountain has been opened; the idols have been swept away; and the prophets will deny any links with their past. So do not apply that text to our Lord: I have heard the text applied as though it is our Lord speaking, but is is not Christ speaking at all; the text can only apply to false prophets.

So far, we have seen effect after effect happening when God turns His eyes, In That Day, once again on Israel. We have seen cleansing, grace, supplication, mourning, a fountain for sin and uncleanness opened, remarkable indignation, and the land purged of falsehood and of all evil. But now from verse 7, it moves significantly from the false prophets - the evasive man who claims to have been wounded in the house of his lovers or his friends, and who is trying to escape retribution - it moves to the True Shepherd:

> Awake, O sword, against my shepherd, and against the man that is my fellow, saith the Lord of hosts: smite the shepherd, and the sheep shall be scattered; and I will turn mine hand upon the little ones.

Against my shepherd! Against the Man who did not escape; the Man who was smitten of God and afflicted - literally in the house of His friends! and what does Isaiah say in chapter 53: But He was wounded for our transgressions, He was bruised for our iniquities; the chastisement of our peace was upon Him ... Yet it pleased the Lord to bruise Him; He hath put Him to grief; when thou shalt make His soul an offering for sin ...

This is the great mystery of our redemption. Read again Acts 2 verses 22 and 23; these things become so well known to us that we do not stop to ponder:

> Ye men of Israel, hear these words: Jesus of Nazareth, a man approved of God unto you by mighty works and wonders and signs, which God did by him in the midst of you, even as ye yourselves know;
> Him, being delivered up by the determinate counsel and foreknowledge of God, ye by the hand of lawless men did crucify and slay:

Note the words, 'Him, being delivered up by the determinate counsel and foreknowledge of God'; now that is one side of our redemption. 'Smite the Shepherd': this God speaking; Christ is the object. This is the mystery of our salvation, the mystery of Christian redemption that God Himself planned; God in Christ laying down His life for us. Although men put Christ to death, yet it was the Father who gave Him to death. We have to bring these two things together; we should never separate them; and though they mystify us, this is the outpouring of the Divine Love; it is a Divine mystery; it is Divine love that God was content to give His own Son to death. And you have it here in verse 7: Awake, O sword, against my shepherd, and against the man that is **my** fellow.

It is the Shepherd of Zechariah 11 verse 4, who was told to feed the flock of slaughter; the One who was sold for thirty pieces of silver; the Shepherd of John 10 verse 11 in, 'I am the good Shepherd'; it is God's true Shepherd that is being talked about now. And the Hebrew for 'the man who is my fellow' means 'the one who is nearest to me'. Read Ezekiel 34 verses 20 to 24:

> Therefore thus saith the Lord God unto them: Behold, I, even I, will judge between the fat cattle and the lean cattle.
> Because ye thrust with side and with shoulder, and push all the diseased with your horns, till ye have scattered them abroad;
> Therefore will I save my flock, and they shall no more be a prey; and I will judge between cattle and cattle.
> And I will set up one shepherd over them, and he shall feed them, even my servant David; he shall feed them, and he shall be their shepherd.

You get the picture now, don't you? that Christ is the Shepherd, He is God's Fellow, He is related, He is God's Representative; He is as close to God as He can possibly be, says the Hebrew. And our Lord says: I and My Father are one; I am the good Shepherd who giveth His life; My sheep know My voice and the stranger they will not follow. Again, our Lord is not using just a pretty metaphor: He is using the great picture of God being the Shepherd of Israel, and our Lord Himself is claiming that very title in, 'I am the good Shepherd'. And of course this peculiar relationship between Messiah and God as it is here - the Man that is My Fellow, My Shepherd - comes right through the prophets in, 'unto us a child is born; unto us a son is given; His name shall be called Wonderful, Counsellor, the Mighty God, the Everlasting Father; the Prince of Peace', and so on.

So what is in view in the words 'and the sheep shall be scattered' is the sheep of slaughter that we read about in chapter 11 of Zechariah, and this is exactly what happened when our Lord came. He was put to death and in AD 70 the whole Jewish nation, the sheep of slaughter, was scattered. As we have previously noted, over one million died in Jerusalem at that time and half a million died under the Bar Kokhba rebellion of AD 130, and from AD 70 right through to modern times, Jews have died - the sheep of slaughter - in their millions. 'Smite the shepherd and the sheep will be scattered'; they have indeed been scattered and killed; in the sixteenth century there were only one million Jews left because of the persecutions, and they wondered if they ever would survive. But with God there is always that doctrine of the remnant, and it comes here in verse 7, 'and I will turn mine hand upon the little ones'.

It is an extraordinary thing that happened at the Cross: the Christ was put to death, but the disciples, the little ones, the patient, the humble, the poor of the flock, were saved. Read Matthew 26 verse 31, where you get, not my interpretation, but our Lord's interpretation:

> Then saith Jesus unto them, All ye shall be offended in me this night: for it is written, I will smite the shepherd, and the sheep of the flock shall be scattered abroad.

This is the very text of Zechariah! and from a chapter which the critics say was not written by the prophet! Our Lord endorses this Messianic prophecy; Our Lord is using it Himself; He is using these very words that we have meditated upon. And our Lord continues: But after I am raised up, I will go before you into Galilee. In other words the little ones, the humble ones, the sheep, are going to be scattered - and they were - but our Lord rose and He led His own believing handful of men and women who believed in Him into Galilee.

You see, that was true then and a remnant was saved and, says verse 8, it is also going to be true in the last days, though we could almost say that between verses 7 and 8 two thousand years have intervened:

> And it shall come to pass, that in all the land, saith the Lord, two parts therein shall be cut off and die; but the third shall be left therein.

It is true that the Jewish nation has been decimated right

down the centuries; it is true that possibly two thirds have been cut off and only a remnant of one third have been saved. Let us read Ezekiel 5 verse 12. Remember that Ezekiel was the prophet who prophesied in Babylon about the Jewish nation:

> A third part of thee shall die with the pestilence, and with famine shall they be consumed in the midst of thee; and a third part shall fall by the sword round about thee; and a third part I will scatter unto all the winds, and will draw out a sword after them.

Do you see how tremendously consistent Scripture is? So when our Lord was smitten of God and afflicted, the nation was scattered; millions died; but our Lord kept His hand on the remnant; He went before them into Galilee and He has been going before them ever since. And now we are coming right over that period into the final days, In That Day, and it is still true that in this enormous battle of Jerusalem, in this enormous battle in the Holy Land, two thirds or two parts shall be cut off and die, and one third will be brought through and refined and redeemed.

What an inheritance the Jews have had, and how wonderfully history bears it all out. What a tremendous destiny: it is only against this sort of background that we can put the holocaust into perspective. You know, when they talk about the holocaust of Hitler, they talk of it in terms of anti-semitism; but what they are actually dealing with is a Divine Mystery, and they just do not or cannot realise it - except a few Jewish commentators who are very uncomfortable in Zechariah. Most Jews do their best to switch away from Messiah; but some of them do say, We cannot switch, it is Messiah! But when you look upon Jewish affairs, Jewish suffering, and the great holocaust, and you say, What does it all mean? it is only this book of Zechariah that can explain it; human reasoning cannot.

So we have two thirds possibly killed in AD 70; and a great scattering of the flock of slaughter from that day, until 'in that day'. And if it is true of the Dispersion, it is going to be true in the very last day because of the phrase used, 'And it shall come to pass, that in all the land ...' This destruction of the Jew and this smiting of the flock of slaughter started in the land; and it will end in the land, as we shall see in chapter 14 - a terrible purging, a day of darkness and not light, says Amos, and this particular day is referred to in Jeremiah 30 verses 6 and 7:

> Ask ye now, and see whether a man doth travail with child: wherefore do I see every man with his hands on his loins, as a woman in travail, and all faces are turned into paleness?
> Alas! for that day is great, so that none is like it: it is even the time of Jacob's trouble; but he shall be saved out of it.

And that is precisely what Zechariah says, and in verse 9:

> And I will bring the third part through the fire, and will refine them as silver is refined, and will try them as gold is tried: they shall call on my name, and I will hear them: I will say, It is my people; and they shall say, The Lord is my God.

Do you remember the great phrase from Hosea? God said that they would be called 'Not My people'. But now they are going to be restored to 'My people' and, speaking of the Shepherd that has been smitten, they are going to recognise the Christ of Calvary and say, This is our God.

17 THE LAST DAYS FOR ISRAEL AND FOR THE WHOLE WORLD: THE DAY OF THE LORD

So we turn to the last great chapter of this tremendous book, which Luther very rightly called the quintessence of the prophets. It ties up in these fourteen simple chapters 'multum in parvo', much in little: all that Isaiah says, all that Jeremiah says, all that Ezekiel says, all the strands; in fact in many ways it draws together all that Revelation says, although it is specifically centred on Israel.

It is the climax of Israel's apostasy (We will not have this Man to reign over us), and of the awesome consequential sorrow which followed - two thousand years of it. 'His blood be upon us and upon our children'; 'Away with Him, crucify Him'; 'If He be the king of Israel let Him come down from the cross'; it teaches us all that we cannot mock God; not even the people of God can escape! So a hardening in part happened to Israel and a blinding of their eyes, and there was this scattering throughout the world and they became 'Not my people'. What did the Jew become for two thousand years? nothing really! No king, no priest, no sacrifice, no altar, no people, say the prophets. But here is the climax, the regathering, the repentance, the cleansing, and the coming of Messiah.

In chapter 14 we are looking at the day of Jacob's trouble. No day like it, says Jeremiah in chapter 30 verse 7. We are looking at Isaiah's vision of this from afar, long beforehand, the day when a nation is born **in one day.** In one day a whole people will come to birth, says Isaiah in chapter 66 verse 8. This day too is the day Amos speaks of, 'The day of the Lord is darkness not light', before Christ intervenes. It is the day of Jacob's trouble - the day of vengeance of our God. It is the day the whole world is slowly moving towards.

Liberal thinkers are always optimistic; they are always going to work out their Utopia by their own religiosity and political skills and their economic know-how! 'The day of the Lord' is always going to be great, it is going to be a Golden Age, they say. But the Bible just writes across the whole of that, 'Nonsense!' Scripture is not against man; it is against the false optimism of 'man without God'. We have so many liberally-minded men like that today: in fact every government promises a Golden Age, doesn't it? The Bible says, Not so! While men's backs are turned to the Christ of God, while men are living in their own strength, The Day of the Lord will be darkness and not light.

I want to make one or two comments at this point. Zechariah is a marvellous book, but it is not the main strand of evangelism. I do not preach this from my pulpit in Cheadle Parish Church but I allude to it; I do not preach it as I preach it to you. Secondly, I would have to say in all intellectual honesty, that there is a division of opinion about prophecy held by good men, converted men: there is a division of interpretation, and it should be no man's task to divide the Church. This is why I do not preach Zechariah in a dogmatic way - simply because other believing men read these chapters and put a different interpretation to them, and it is not our job to divide believer from believer. The important facts of the Gospel in **this** day - the day of the Gentile, this day of Grace - are the Cross, the Lordship of Christ, the Holy Spirit, the bringing in of the Gentiles, and the mission of the Church to go into all the world and preach the Gospel. The disciples wanted Zechariah's prophecies fulfilled on the day of Pentecost when they asked: Lord, wilt thou at this time restore the kingdom to Israel? and our Lord rebuked them and ordered them to go into the world and preach the Gospel, that men might be saved and be forgiven by faith in Christ. But our Lord was in no way abrogating the great prophets; He was saying in effect, that now is the period when the emphasis has got to be put on the essential facets of the Gospel.

Remember too when you read prophecy that there **is** always the factor of anti-semitism. There is a natural distaste for the Jew; we would not express it crudely by shooting them or putting them to the fires; but it is a theological attitude. It is a thing which is one of the essential weapons used by Satan to turn our hearts against this people. It is in my heart, it is in everybody's heart, this natural distaste for the Jew, especially when reading the Gospels and when we consider seriously how they were hardened and blinded, and are described as enemies of the Gospel. They crucified the Lord Jesus, said Paul, and he himself has often been called an anti-semite! but 'Love them for the Father's sake', is Paul's plea. If you cannot love them any other way, then love them for the Father's sake, for the sake of the great promises: they gave you Abraham, Isaac, and Jacob; they gave you the Law; they gave you the prophets and the Word of God; love them for that. God knows them to be hard-hearted, stiff and stubborn, 'a thornbush of a nation' - that is what He calls them in Micah; but love them, for in so many ways they represent the faithfulness of God; their presence as distinctly Jews will support your faith.

So remember the danger of anti-semitism and remember that this book of Zechariah, which we can easily get out of perspective, is at the apex of a world tribulation. Remember the four horsemen of the Apocalypse; the white, the black, the red, and the pale one which is death and hell. If you have read Revelation, you will realise that Zechariah is dealing with only one aspect of world tribulation - the Jewish aspect: there remain the seven seals, the seven trumpets, the release of evil spirits upon the earth; the armies of the East in chapter 9 coming in to the great conflagration; the Man of Sin who will bemuse and dazzle all the nations of the earth; the war in heaven of Revelation 12; the seven last plagues; and Armageddon of chapter 16 verse 16. What I am trying to say is that you have to put Zechariah into the broader picture of world distress, of real convulsions, real wars, real famines, and disasters on a world scale and magnitude involving all the nations. In our case we are looking at a people who are largely ignored in the total picture of the End Times. They are only a little part of the scene today, of only modest importance in the world newspapers; but there is going to be a cataclysmic convulsion at the end which will involve all men and every aspect of living, including the Jew. And today we see so many signs of it: pollution, wars, nuclear arms, missiles, famine, over-population; and we are simply blind and foolish if we do not know what they are leading to.

At the same time, as F. F. Bruce warns us, we have to be very wary of identifying too quickly world events with specific prophecy. Take for instance the Common Market. When it was composed of ten nations, some people asked whether it was the age of the little horn who elevates himself over the ten kingdoms? Is the Common Market, in a sense, the rise of the spirit of the old Roman empire which many of the Schofieldites and the Plymouth Brethren spoke of a hundred years ago? Even if it is not, what I would like to say to you is, the fact that the Common Market does exist today shows at least the credibility of that prophecy. It **could** happen; and that is the point. A century ago the idea of a federation of ten nations in Europe was unheard of; but we have seen this happen today. So when I say, Beware of saying this means that, nevertheless as you look at world events, as you see the astonishing ease of travel, the enormous firepower of the nations in the Common Market, then all the things that Revelation says and all the things that the prophets say could now be on our doorstep. It is no longer fantasy. A hundred years ago people wrote prophecy off, but no sober thinker can do so any longer.

A final comment I would like to make before starting on the last chapter of Zechariah, is the element of not knowing in the Church today. Nobody wants to know! It is all right saying that these things are in the Bible, but people are simply not interested. Even Christians are not interested; I am amazed at the lack of interest in

Christian minds. They 'major' on the Cross and on Conversion, and their Gospel seems to stop there and in the end it all becomes a bit tedious. Be honest, do you not feel like that sometimes? They are so limited and narrow! This book of Zechariah is not the Gospel per se, admittedly, but at the same time there is an amazing lack of interest in prophecy, and when it all happens there will be an enormous element of surprise. Our Lord says, 'They shall say in that day, Peace, peace', then suddenly Christ will burst in, and people will say, Why were we not prepared, why did we not know about all these things? ... But it is all here in the Bible if we will only take the time and trouble to study it.

So now we are going to Jerusalem and we will begin with verses 1 and 2:

> Behold, a day of the Lord cometh, when thy spoil shall be divided in the midst of thee.
> For I will gather all nations against Jerusalem to battle; and the city shall be taken, and the houses rifled, and the women ravished: and half the city shall go forth into captivity, and the residue of the people shall not be cut off from the city.

I have said it many times and I will say it again, Jerusalem today is a real fact! There is a real nation in existence and there is a real danger on our doorstep because of Jerusalem. Jerusalem has become the centre of the most volatile and dangerous area in the world. The Middle East is simmering, waiting to explode, and when it does it will mean nothing less than a world war. What was dismissed as apocalyptic dreaming is now a fearful possibility, and at the heart of it all is Jerusalem!

It amazes me, although I will not criticise my brethren who differ from me in their interpretation of prophecy, but it amazes me how they can get over the fact that the Scripture tells us these things, and what we have before our eyes appears to be the fulfilment of them. Yet they keep saying, 'But it has no significance', and 'Israel is a political accident' - and yet even the Verger in Chester Cathedral 'woke up' when I was preaching on this theme! The assumptions of Zechariah are now the facts of our day and generation.

The return has taken place. In 1917 the Balfour Declaration saw something very remarkable in the annals of the history of the Jew. For the first time in two thousand years they were officially restored to their land under the mandate of Great Britain. Then they became a nation, a land, a sovereign people, and the subsequent history from 1917 to the events of 1948, 1956, 1967 to 1973, and 1983 to 1985, are living history, a history of enormous achievement, but also of blood and tears, wars and uncertainty. They have returned in unbelief and are very anti-Christian. They worship Israel and not the God of Israel, as the Chief Rabbi said in the 1950's in Jerusalem.

The scriptures say that there will be an interval when the people are regathered, when the land is restored, and that when the people come back there will be an interval of prosperity. Ezekiel predicts that the Northern powers will say, Ah, here is a land with unwalled villages, at ease, prospering ... that is the indication! we will go, we will take the spoil; it is worth capturing ... It is rather like saying that Iran is worth capturing for its oil. So Israel will have a period, a coming-back in unbelief before the great night of anguish.

In that period lots of things will happen. As I have said, the Beast will appear; the Man of Sin will appear, and the Jews will make a pact with him, as stated in Revelation. If another shall come in his own name, says Christ, you will receive him; you will not receive me. It is the Idol shepherd of Zechariah, the false shepherd; and this will take place. We see now Israel regathered, reconstituted, a language re-learned, a culture restored; but who knows what is going to happen? Are they going to build a Temple? Are they going to take the Mosque of Omar (The Dome of the Rock) from the Arabs? They could take it tomorrow. Will they do it? Can they resist doing it?

Now we are not adding to the events of chapter 12.

One of the principles of Scripture, sometimes, is to state a case generally and then fill it in particularly. Have you ever heard the argument that Genesis 2 is a new thing from Genesis 1 and therefore you must not believe Genesis 1? That argument is nonsense: people who say such things do not understand the scriptures. Genesis 1 describes the Creation; Genesis 2 fills in the details. Zechariah 14 is a repetition of chapters 12 and 13, but fills in the details; it is very important to appreciate this point.

Now the events are fairly simple. The allied armies are going to attack Jerusalem. There will be terrible destruction and dreadful suffering and it is all put in one compressed verse. All the convulsions of the earth, the great Armageddon, the great Last Day is now pouring upon and is centering upon the Holy Land. When I cross the plain of Megiddo, which is something I have done a hundred times, I am reminded that all invading armies come through that plain. It is on the Via Maris, you see: you can get down from the North right into Egypt this way. East of the plain you are soon in the desert and so an invader from, say, Baghdad goes north from that city, round the Fertile Crescent, and down through this great plain. It is the only way; the Crusaders all went that way; it is the only way for armies to come to Jerusalem. In the south and to the east you have deserts, and on the west you have mountains to climb; so from the North they come, says Ezekiel, and so it is from Mount Scopus (from the word telescope) in the north of Jerusalem that the enemy can be seen advancing from the North. And in verse 3 is the Great Day:

> Then shall the Lord go forth, and fight against those nations, as when he fought in the day of battle.

Now read Joshus 10 verses 12 to 14:

> Then spake Joshua to the Lord in the day when the Lord delivered up the Amorites before the children of Israel; and he said in the sight of Israel, Sun, stand

> thou still upon Gibeon; and thou, Moon, in the valley of Aijalon.
> And the sun stood still, and the moon stayed, until the nation had avenged themselves of their enemies. Is not this written in the book of Jashar? And the sun stayed in the midst of heaven, and hasted not to go down about a whole day.
> And there was no day like that before it or after it, that the Lord hearkened unto the voice of a man: **for the Lord fought for Israel.**

The same thought is expressed in the Song of Moses (look up Exodus 15) where the Lord is the Warrior. And this is the picture in Zechariah; the whole of Scripture is utterly consistent. The Lord will fight in this last day at Jerusalem as He fought particularly in the Exodus from Egypt, the one great event which dominates all Jewish thinking. But we are talking now of THE momentous event: this day is the end of the rainbow of promise; this is the day **when our Lord Jesus shall return**; and so **we** have a vested interest in this. We are looking at Israel, but we have an enormous vested interest. And in verse 4:

> And his feet shall stand in that day upon the mount of Olives, which is before Jerusalem on the east, and the mount of Olives shall cleave in the midst thereof toward the east and toward the west, and there shall be a very great valley; and half of the mountain shall remove toward the north, and half of it toward the south.

Note, it is the Lord Jesus referred to here; no one else. **This is the day of Christ's coming.** Then verse 5:

> And ye shall flee by the valley of my mountains; for the valley of the mountains shall reach unto Azel: yea, ye shall flee, like as ye fled from before the earthquake in the days of Uzziah king of Judah: and

> the Lord my God shall come, and all the holy ones with thee.

Compare this verse with Matthew 24 verses 29 to 31, and with Acts 1 verse 11, and with 1 Thessalonians 4 verse 15. This is nerve-tingling! This is the day of Christ's second Coming. This is also the day of Israel's great tribulation, the day of Jacob's trouble; there is no day like it; a day of terrible gloom and sadness for them, terrible convulsions in the world, terrible wickedness. And if you read Revelation, the saints will be involved beforehand. We, if we live to that day, will be persecuted; we will find ourselves under the iron, under the fire; but this day of Israel's deliverance will be our day too. I do not believe in any secret rapture of the Saints.

You will note that He comes to the Mount of Olives. What does Ezekiel 10 verses 18 and 19 say?

> And the glory of the Lord went forth from over the threshold of the house, and stood over the cherubim.
> And the cherubim lifted up their wings, and mounted up from the earth in my sight when they went forth, and the wheels beside them: and they stood at the door of the east gate of the Lord's house; and the glory of the God of Israel was over them above.

You will remember that when the city was doomed and was being captured by Nebuchadnezzar and being destroyed, and the holy city and the Temple of Solomon were under destruction and burning, the greatest calamity in the life of the nation was the Glory leaving the Temple. But as we read Ezekiel 11 verse 16 it says:

> Therefore say, Thus saith the Lord God: Whereas I have removed them far off among the nations, and whereas I have scattered them among the countries, yet will I be to them a sanctuary for a little while in the countries where they are come.

Israel was to be dispersed and the Times of the Gentiles were to begin. The Glory of God was leaving Israel; yet God makes the promise in the midst of this ban, this curse: I will be a little sanctuary wherever I move you. And then verses 22 and 23 of Ezekiel 11 say:

> Then did the cherubim lift up their wings, and the wheels were beside them; and the glory of the God of Israel was over them above.
> And the glory of the Lord went up from the midst of the city, and stood upon the mountain which is on the east side of the city (the Mount of Olives).

Ezekiel saw the Glory departing and yet in a vision he saw it return in the Last Day from the East, from the same Mount of Olives. But we must translate this into New Testament terms. We must read Acts 1 verses 4 to 12. Do not think that this is tedious; if you do not link it up, you will accuse me or anybody else of twisting Scripture:

> And, being assembled together with them, he charged them not to depart from Jerusalem, but to wait for the promise of the Father, which, said he, ye heard from me:
> For John indeed baptized with water; but ye shall be baptized with the Holy Ghost not many days hence.
> They therefore, when they were come together, asked him, saying, Lord, dost thou at this time restore the kingdom to Israel?
> And he said unto them, It is not for you to know times or seasons, which the Father hath set within his own authority.
> But ye shall receive power, when the Holy Ghost is come upon you: and ye shall be my witnesses both in Jerusalem, and in all Judaea and Samaria, and unto the uttermost part of the earth.
> And when he had said these things, as they were looking, he was taken up; and a cloud received him out of their sight.

> And while they were looking steadfastly into heaven as he went, behold, two men stood by them in white apparel;
> Which also said, Ye men of Galilee, why stand ye looking into heaven? this Jesus, which was received up from you into heaven, shall so come in like manner as ye beheld him going into heaven.
> Then returned they unto Jerusalem from the mount called Olivet, which is nigh unto Jerusalem, a sabbath day's journey off.

You see, the disciples did not deny the prophets; indeed they wanted the second Coming to happen immediately, and you will note that Jesus does not deny the second Coming either; yet the first job of the Church is to be His witnesses. He was taken up: here is the Glory departing again; here is Christ going to Heaven and here is the Jew about to go into the Great Dispersion. In a sense, as far as we are concerned, here is the Glory visibly and personally departing but, as with the Jews, there is the promise of its return, and for us, meanwhile, the gift of the Holy Spirit.

The prophecies of Christ about the fall of Jerusalem are about to take place. The words of Jesus to the Jews are about to be fulfilled: 'And you shall no more see me until you say, Blessed is he that cometh in the name of the Lord.' The Glory departed, and the Glory is still withdrawn from the Jewish nation: it has no Glory, and until the Lord returns to the beloved place He left, it will have no Glory. He prayed in the Mount of Olives; He wept in the Mount of Olives over the impending destruction of Jerusalem; He taught the Lord's Prayer on the Mount of Olives: Thy kingdom come on earth as it is in Heaven. Why did He say, 'on earth', I wonder? According to some of our best theologians there isn't going to be a kingdom on earth! there isn't going to be one in the literal sense. Some of course keep telling us that with a little of education, and a little of liberal theology, the knowledge of the Lord shall cover the earth as the waters cover the sea! But I do not see that in Scripture: rather, I see the waters of Marx covering the earth as the waters cover the sea, and not the Glory of the Lord! This will come cataclysmically: but it will come! 'Thy kingdom come on earth' ... unless you empty meanings out of words you have got to face these words. Will it come on earth or is it a vain fiction?

But let us go back to verse 5. Who are the holy ones? The angels? Yes, but not only the angels but all believers as well. What does 1 Thessalonians 4 say? The Lord shall descend from heaven with a shout and the voice of the archangel and the trump of God, and the dead in Christ shall rise first; and we that remain shall be caught up together with the Lord **in the air.** Now as I have said before, the headquarters of the Devil's kingdom are **in the air.** He is the Prince of the powers **of the air**, says St Paul. Our Lord will come to his very headquarters; there will be no escape for Satan; he will be trapped like Hitler in a bunker, a kind of atmospheric bunker. He will be caught and ensnared.

The Lord will descend bringing with Him all the saints that have died. Isn't that wonderful? Angels and the saints who have died of every dispensation shall be caught up; and all this happens on the day that Israel, physical Israel is to be rescued. It will be a marvellous thing and we shall join Him to share His Glory; **In That Day.** This is truly the greatest honour. Do not envy Israel; some people, when they read prophecy, say that they wish they were Jews. I have just received a letter from a Jewess who was one of my youth group in Israel years ago, a beautiful girl who worked in a bank in Tel Aviv; and I often thought how difficult it would be for her to find a Christian to marry. She was a secret believer but God not only gave her a husband, a wandering soldier who was passing through Israel, but incidentally a Christian soldier! God has given her a son, and she closes her letters with, 'Shalom in our Messiah'; **Our Messiah**!

But do not envy Israel. She is hardened and blind and 'in purgatory'. Israel is living in the pit, yet she is clinging on to The Hope. She has been regathered but she has no immediate knowledge of God; she has no certainty of the forgiveness of sin; she still carries on all her shibboleths and the little things she prides herself in, her own righteousness. Israel is going to be surrounded and decimated. So the greatest honour in the world is to be a Christian and to be associated, whether Jew or Gentile, with Christ on this momentous day when He comes. We will not need to justify ourselves In That Day: **we** - His brethren, Jew and Gentile, bond and free, male and female, Greek and barbarian - shall be with Him. Even so come, Lord Jesus!

Now the effects of it. What is going to happen when our Lord comes and His feet stand on the Mount of Olives and we see the return of the Glory? Verses 4 and 5 state that a great physical convulsion will take place. Now again, because we are basically 'unbelievers', people will shrug their shoulders and say, Is it possible? The Jew will flee: the topographical particulars are not important to our understanding; they just give us the broad picture of what is going to happen.

God, in a sense, is going to create new mountains: the Mount of Olives is going to be divided, creating a great valley, and the remnant - the third part of Israel we spoke about before - will flee by the way of escape made by God. What a day it will be; can you imagine it? the armies massing around Jerusalem; a day of neither brightness nor darkness; tremendous earthquake convulsions such as are talked about by Amos in Uzziah's days in Amos 1. That particular earthquake left such an impression on the nation that they never forgot it, and it is going to be like that. I have in fact been in three minor earthquakes in Palestine. Thousands were killed in the earthquake of 1929. Palestine is in a rift valley which extends right down the Jordan and on into East Africa: so do not write this off as trivial fantasies of prophetical minds like Zechariah's. It is going to happen! and the remnant will flee through the great valley caused by these convulsions. You know, the Bible says, 'I will make all my mountains a way', and we often preach on that in a kind of airy-fairy poetical way when we speak of the problems of life. There is nothing wrong with that; but it is also true literally, that God will make His mountains a way for His people.

This dividing of the Mount of Olives is very much like the dividing of the Red Sea, and what did God do at the Red Sea? Another impossible act! He divided it and they crossed through and were redeemed. The Passover, the Lamb offering, the Red Sea, dominate everything Jewish, just as the Cross dominates us. Anything that happens in the future is reflected back and has a connection with these historical landmarks: the dividing of the Mount of Olives is going to be like the dividing of the Red Sea; it is the same God at work; if He can divide the sea I do not see why He should not divide the land. Is our God too small? The Mount is going to be divided; and we are going to get a little sanctuary again. Shall I lead you into an esoteric secret that I think might be true, though it is only an opinion? Look at Revelation 12 verses 1 to 6:

> And a great sign was seen in heaven; a woman arrayed with the sun, and the moon under her feet, and upon her head a crown of twelve stars;
> And she was with child; and she crieth out, travailing in birth, and in pain to be delivered.
> And there was seen another sign in heaven; and behold, a great red dragon, having seven heads and ten horns, and upon his heads seven diadems.
> And his tail draweth the third part of the stars of heaven, and did cast them to the earth: and the dragon stood before the woman which was about to be delivered, that when she was delivered, he might devour her child.
> And she was delivered of a son, a man child, who is to rule all the nations with a rod of iron: and her child was caught up unto God, and unto his throne.
> And the woman fled into the wilderness, where she hath a place prepared of God, that there they may nourish her a thousand two hundred and threescore days.

This is about the birth and the ascension of Christ, and about Israel's place of refuge in the Last Day. Now go back to Zechariah, to the remnant, to the Jewish people: are they all going to be slain when this confederate army, the allied armies, surround Jerusalem? No! the Mount of Olives is going to be divided and 'My mountains will make a sanctuary for her'. Where? I ask myself. And if you go to Isaiah 16 verses 1 to 6, it is fascinating; but remember what I said about not going overboard and insisting on what is only an opinion:

> Send ye the lambs for the ruler of the land from Sela which is toward the wilderness, unto the mount of the daughter of Zion.
>
> For it shall be that, as wandering birds, as a scattered nest, so shall the daughters of Moab be at the fords of Arnon.
>
> Give counsel, execute judgment; make thy shadow as the night in the midst of the noonday: hide the outcasts; bewray not the wanderer.
>
> Let mine outcasts dwell with thee; as for Moab, be thou a covert to him from the face of the spoiler: for the extortioner is brought to nought, spoiling ceaseth, the oppressors are consumed out of the land.
>
> And a throne shall be established in mercy, and one shall sit thereon in truth, in the tent of David; judging, and seeking judgment, and swift to do righteousness.
>
> We have heard of the pride of Moab, that he is very proud; even of his arrogancy, and his pride, and his wrath; his boastings are nought.

Now that is a little obscure passage, is it not? I, at some time, have written in my Bible, 'Moab, the last refuge!' Sela is a word for 'rock' and Sela in the above text is the identical word for Petra. So it is possible that Petra is the last refuge, but it is only my suggestion, and I do not insist on it because we must never press details and declare that this means that. Nevertheless, going back to Revelation, where the Devil is seeking to destroy this nation which gave birth to the Man who is to rule all the nations, the whole of Scripture states that there is a place prepared for the remnant.

We are now at that point when the mountains are being opened, and we are noting (Zechariah chapter 12) another effect of that glorious day - madness, astonishment, and bewilderment which will hit all the nations around Jerusalem. What an incredible surprise! Of course there will be general mocking at all this prophecy. And there is indeed general mocking: 'Where is this promised Return of Christ?' - this has been said right down the ages. Peter has told us that men would say, You have been promising this Return since the Fathers fell asleep; what a load of fantastic, apocalyptic rubbish! And Peter has to remind us that God is merciful and is only restraining His hand, that many might repent. But the nations around Jerusalem are going to be so overcome with this incredible surprise that they will be filled with astonishment and bewilderment, and, says Revelation 6 verse 16: 'They say to the mountains and to the rocks, Fall on us, and hide us from the face of him that sitteth on the throne, and from the wrath of the Lamb'. Look at Revelation 12 verses 7 to 10:

> And there was war in heaven: Michael and his angels going forth to war with the dragon; and the dragon warred and his angels;
> And they prevailed not, neither was their place found any more in heaven.
> And the great dragon was cast down, the old serpent, he that is called the Devil and Satan, the deceiver of the whole world; he was cast down to the earth, and his angels were cast down with him.
> And I heard a great voice in heaven, saying, Now is come the salvation, and the power, and the kingdom of our God, and the authority of his Christ: for the accuser of our brethren is cast down, which accuseth them before our God day and night.

What a day it is going to be, and according to verses 6

and 7 of Zechariah it is going to be the most mysterious day of all time:

> And it shall come to pass in that day, that the light shall not be with brightness and with gloom:
> But it shall be one day which is known unto the Lord; not day, and not night: but it shall come to pass, that at evening time there shall be light.

In the Hebrew it says that the bright ones shall contract themselves: there will be cold and frost. Let us look at Joel 3 verse 15 just to back up what this is saying:

> The sun and the moon are darkened, and the stars withdraw their shining.

And in Isaiah 13 verse 10:

> For the stars of heaven and the constellations thereof shall not give their light: the sun shall be darkened in his going forth, and the moon shall not cause her light to shine.

And in Isaiah 24 verse 23:

> Then the moon shall be confounded, and the sun ashamed; for the Lord of hosts shall reign in mount Zion, and in Jerusalem, and before his ancients gloriously.

'Ancients' mean elders or saints. All I am trying to do is to show you by cross-references, that our prophecy is not standing on its own authority; it stands on the authority of the whole Word of God; the marvel of the Bible is that all the sixty-six Books talk in the same way. And to bring the New Testament squarely into all this read also Mark 13 verses 24 to 27, and verse 32. Our Lord is speaking: if you disbelieve the prophets then beware that you do not disbelieve the Lord:

> But in those days, after that tribulation, the sun shall be darkened, and the moon shall not give her light,
> And the stars shall be falling from heaven, and the powers that are in the heavens shall be shaken.
> And then shall they see the Son of man coming in clouds with great power and glory.
> And then shall he send forth the angels, and shall gather together his elect from the four winds, from the uttermost part of the earth to the uttermost part of heaven.
> But of that day or that hour knoweth no one, not even the angels in heaven, neither the Son, but the Father.

And so says Zechariah in verse 7, 'It is one day known unto the Lord'. This is backed up by our Lord who says no man will know the day. When Jehovah's Witnesses and other people predict a precise date, it is folly! even our Lord does not know the day of His return.

That is no indictment of His deity; it is what is known as 'functional subordination'. He came as Man to redeem man and as Man He puts Himself in the position of subordination and He leaves everything to the Father. It is one day known unto God alone: make a note of that and remember that Christ's deity is not at all impugned, for He humbled Himself and made Himself of no reputation. He took upon Himself the form of a Servant and a servant does not know all the answers in his master's mind. Our Lord was obedient unto death and now God has highly exalted Him so that every one will call Him Lord. But when our Lord makes statements such as 'My Father is greater than I' and other sayings like that, it is an instance of functional subordination.

The phrase 'at evening time' is significant. It is true spiritually; everything that happens here can be translated into spiritual terms: all our fading hopes; our fading bodies; our fading loves; our sadness and gloom ... but God whispers to our soul, At evening time there shall be light. It is true spiritually because we have the Christ of God; even in the hour of death there is going to be light.

But it is supremely true of **This Day**; it is going to be true historically; it is going to be a strange day. As far as the Jew is concerned it is the final great day of Atonement, the most sacred day of the year. The day begins with the night before (the evening and the morning are the first day) and this is spent in mourning and lament. And This Day will be their Great Day of Atonement, not the ritual day that comes year after year, unfulfilled and never satisfied, but the great and final day in the history of the nation of the Jews. And how is it going to end? With great joy and light because their God and their Saviour, the Son of Righteousness, will arise with healing in His wings. What a day for the remnant, whether in Petra or between the mountains, for like Thomas, they will say, 'My Lord and My God', to the Christ they have rejected. When That Day comes, the remnant will actually see Him whom they pierced when His feet stand on the Mount of Olives. The nations will be destroyed around them and the Jews shall lament as we have seen before; filled with shame, filled with zeal, filled with joy and tears, filled with laughter **In That Day.** But for the Nations it will be a day of total confusion, and looking ahead to verses 12 to 15 we read of their fate:

> And this shall be the plague wherewith the Lord will smite all the peoples that have warred against Jerusalem: their flesh shall consume away while they stand upon their feet, and their eyes shall consume away in their sockets, and their tongue shall consume away in their mouth.
>
> And it shall come to pass in that day, that a great tumult from the Lord shall be among them; and they shall lay hold every one on the hand of his neighbour, and his hand shall rise up against the hand of his neighbour.
>
> And Judah also shall fight against Jerusalem; and the wealth of all the nations round about shall be gathered together, gold, and silver, and apparel, in great abundance.

> And so shall be the plague of the horse, of the mule, of the camel, and of the ass, and of all the beasts that shall be in those camps, as this plague.

What does verse 12 remind you of today? It speaks of a death that they could not have imagined; but we, standing in regathered Israel, can easily imagine the effects of a nuclear war. We do not know, but it could indeed take place! What an enormous stamp of credibility, of authority, on the Scripture.

And verse 13 is nothing else than the nations fighting among themselves. Now this again is Scriptural. That happened when the small remnant under Gideon fought against the Midianites: you see, everything is repeated in Scripture; that was prophetical. Three hundred men stood around the great camp of Midian and shouted, The sword of the Lord and of Gideon; then every man's arm was turned against his neighbour, and Gideon and his men simply stood and watched them killing each other. And this will happen In That Day on a great scale. As I have said before, just as Hitler leads to THE Antichrist, so these events in Scripture lead to, and are pictures of, the great day, That Day when the nations shall destroy each other.

And there shall be plague. The preposition 'against' in verse 14 is best rendered as 'at' Jerusalem. The means of warfare in those days were horses and mules, etc., so the Bible does not use the words tanks and aeroplanes, and so on. God is going to fight: God is the Man of War as in Exodus, the Man of War as in Joshua, the Man of War as with Gideon and Jehoshaphat and the rest of them, with the terrible plagues that we read about in Revelation attending their defeat. This fills in the picture concerning the Gentile nations. We now have a totally defeated foe: the Dragon, the Beast, the False Prophet and the Godless nations, and the unfaithful part of Israel too.
So we come back to verse 9:

> And the Lord shall be king over all the earth: in that day shall the Lord be one, and his name one.

'The Lord our God is one Lord' - the Jew says that every day. He shouts that at every service: Hear, O Israel, the Lord our God is one Lord; and yet they worship mammon, they worshipped idols; they worshipped everybody except the one Lord. But **in that day** the Lord, after a cataclysmic Coming, is going to reign over all the earth. Now you have your choice of believing that the Gospel is going to spread and convert the earth; or you have the choice of believing the Old Testament and the New Testament that the Coming of Christ will be cataclysmic, coming from outside, suddenly, to establish all this. And when He does establish this, the Lord shall reign over all the earth: but if there is no kingdom reign, then I think that the words must be entirely superfluous! And the words 'and his name one'; now that is very important to the Jew. There will be no competition; one Lord, one Name and no other Name; for, says the Acts of the Apostles, 'There is no other Name under heaven given among men whereby we must be saved'. See how consistent it all is? 'I have given him a name which is above every name, that at the name of Jesus every knee shall bow, and every tongue confess that Jesus Christ is Lord, to the Glory of God the Father'. One Name! and it is the name of the Saviour that we sing about and love.

Then follow verses 10 and 11 which are the introduction to the Kingdom:

> All the land shall be turned as the Arabah, from Geba to Rimmon south of Jerusalem; and she shall be lifted up, and shall dwell in her place, from Benjamin's gate unto the place of the first gate, unto the corner gate, and from the tower of Hananel unto the king's winepresses.
>
> And men shall dwell therein, and there shall be no more curse; but Jerusalem shall dwell safely.

I said that great convulsions are going to take place and that is true; great physical changes are going to take place in Palestine. First of all Jerusalem is going to be lifted up. At present Jerusalem is in a hollow with the various hills around it all higher than the actual city which, although on the hills, lies in a sort of basin. All that will change. The whole of the city is going to be lifted up in this convulsion. The rest from Rimmon to Geba is going to be a plain like the Arabah; and this wonderfully exalted city is going to dominate Palestine. I am not talking about a city being miles high, but about a very prominent and glorious city.

And a river will come from the city of Jerusalem and go down to the Dead Sea. Now some of you may have bathed in the Dead Sea. It is dead! but it is going to be fresh; it is going to become glorious! Some of you will remember that the Good Samaritan road, leading down from Jerusalem to the Dead Sea, is as dry as a bone; but it is going to be marvellously changed. The river from Jerusalem will purify the Dead Sea and fructify the desert of Judah. Read Isaiah 30 verses 25 and 26:

> And there shall be upon every lofty mountain, and upon every high hill, rivers and streams of waters, in the day of the great slaughter, when the towers fall.
> Moreover the light of the moon shall be as the light of the sun, and the light of the sun shall be sevenfold, as the light of seven days, in the day that the Lord bindeth up the hurt of his people, and healeth the stroke of their wound.

Let me ask you again, what do you make of this text if it is not literally true? If we think such texts are rubbish, why do we preach on them? Remember, half of the Old Testament is written in that sort of language. I say to my friends who do not accept this literal point of view, Well, what do you do in these cases? and they say, Well, James, you know ... But I do not know! and I say, You tell me, what do you do with it? And they do nothing with it except make pretty little sermons out of nonsensical metaphors. But what the Bible says about the second Coming of Christ is just as true as the things it says about the first Coming of Christ. Why should we suddenly twist these texts into some spiritualised nonsense? What are they writing about, these men? Why do we say that they are great if they were merely seeing apocalyptic visions which were never going to come to pass? But they **are** going to come to pass. This is truth! Read Isaiah 33 verses 20 to 22:

> Look upon Zion, the city of our solemnities: thine eyes shall see Jerusalem a quiet habitation, a tent that shall not be removed, the stakes whereof shall never be plucked up, neither shall any of the cords thereof be broken.
> But there the Lord will be with us in majesty, a place of broad rivers and streams; wherein shall go no galley with oars, neither shall gallant ship pass thereby.
> For the Lord is our judge, the Lord is our lawgiver, the Lord is our king; he will save us.

Well, what do you make of that? Poetical nonsense or truth? Read Ezekiel 47 verses 1 to 12 which is Ezekiel's vision of the last days when the ideal Temple and City are reconstituted and the Glory has returned:

> And he brought me back unto the door of the house; and behold, waters issued out from under the threshold of the house eastward, for the forefront of the house was toward the east: and the waters came down from under, from the right side of the house, on the south of the altar.
> Then brought he me out by the way of the gate northward, and led me round by the way without unto the outer gate, by the way of the gate that looketh toward the east; and behold, there ran out waters on the right side.
> When the man went forth eastward with the line in his hand, he measured a thousand cubits, and he caused me to pass through the waters, waters that were to the ankles.

Again he measured a thousand, and caused me to pass through the waters, waters that were to the knees.
Again he measured a thousand, and caused me to pass through the waters, waters that were to the loins.
Afterward he measured a thousand; and it was a river that I could not pass through: for the waters were risen, waters to swim in, a river that could not be passed through.
And he said unto me, Son of man, hast thou seen this? Then he brought me, and caused me to return to the bank of the river.
Now when I had returned, behold, upon the bank of the river were very many trees on the one side and on the other.
Then said he unto me, These waters issue forth toward the eastern region, and shall go down into the Arabah: and they shall go toward the sea; into the sea shall the waters go which were made to issue forth; and the waters shall be healed.
And it shall come to pass, that every living creature which swarmeth, in every place whither the rivers come, shall live; and there shall be a very great multitude of fish: for these waters are come thither, and the waters of the sea shall be healed, and every thing shall live whithersoever the river cometh.
And it shall come to pass, that fishers shall stand by it: from En-gedi even unto En-eglaim shall be a place for the spreading of nets; their fish shall be after their kinds, as the fish of the great sea, exceeding many.
But the miry places thereof, and the marishes thereof, shall not be healed; they shall be given up to salt.
And by the river upon the bank thereof, on this side and on that side, shall grow every tree for meat, whose leaf shall not wither, neither shall the fruit thereof fail: it shall bring forth new fruit every month, because the waters thereof issue out of the sanctuary: and the fruit thereof shall be for meat, and the leaf thereof for healing.

That is exactly what Zechariah says in verse 8:

> And it shall come to pass in that day, that living waters shall go out from Jerusalem; half of them toward the eastern sea, and half of them toward the western sea: in summer and in winter shall it be.

Can you imagine all that? Isn't it wonderful? Look up Isaiah 11 verses 1 to 9. These are very well-known Christmas readings, but they only really make sense when put into the context of the reign of Christ on earth.

And Jerusalem is going to become the centre of world worship: it is going to become the city of the great king; that is in verse 16:

> And it shall come to pass, that every one that is left of all the nations which came against Jerusalem shall go up from year to year to worship the King, the Lord of hosts, and to keep the feast of tabernacles.

In other words, Jerusalem is now becoming the centre of the world! Let us read Isaiah 2 verses 1 to 3, and my challenge to you at all times is, if this is not true then what is true?

> The word that Isaiah the son of Amoz saw concerning Judah and Jerusalem.
> And it shall come to pass in the latter days, that the mountain of the Lord's house shall be established in the top of the mountains, and shall be exalted above the hills; and all nations shall flow unto it (just as Zechariah says).
> And many peoples shall go and say, Come ye, and let us go up to the mountain of the Lord, to the house of the God of Jacob; and he will teach us of his ways, and we will walk in his paths: for out of Zion shall go forth the law, and the word of the Lord from Jerusalem.

Do you see the glory of all this? The Lord is going to set up His Kingdom; Jerusalem is going to be THE city of the earth; and the risen Christ, the reigning Christ will reign from Jerusalem; and His saints will reign with him.

People ask, Where will we be? What a silly question! If we have resurrection bodies, and if we are like Him, there is no hindrance to where we will be; you know what I mean. I do not know where we will be and I am not worried at all: there will constant communication from the Glory to the renewed earth, and the city of Jerusalem will be right at the heart. Read for yourselves Psalm 46 which is the Psalm of the exalted Jerusalem here on earth. I have listened to preachers preach on that Psalm and quote, 'He maketh wars to cease'; and I say: But not very often! what do you mean, brother? You see we skate over it. God is not doing it in El Salvador or in Africa or in other places: of course He is not, because this Psalm is the Psalm of the exalted Jerusalem **in that day.** You see Scripture is only understandable if you pay serious attention to it and do not allegorize all the time. This is marvellous: this Kingdom on earth, I believe, is the consistent witness of the prophets. This, I believe, you have got to face when you read the prophets.

Now verse 16 goes on to talk of the feast of tabernacles. Why pick on the feast of tabernacles? This is when the Jews go back into tents. It is the only feast of eight days; they put up pseudo-tents of branches on their balconies or in their gardens, and they all leave their houses and sleep outside. This was the order of the feast of tabernacles: they had to go back to when they were in the wilderness, when they dwelt in tents. So for a week they reside in these booths and it is a harvest festival. It reminds them that God brought them out of a dry desert into a glorious land flowing with milk and honey; a land of broad rivers and streams.

In Jerusalem it was the most glorious feast ever. The old rabbis say that if you had never seen Jerusalem at the feast of tabernacles, or at the feast of Sukkot as it is called, then you had never seen joy, you had never seen light, you had never seen wonder, because Jews came to it from everywhere. They had four great urns, candlesticks if you like, candlesticks full of oil, and do you know what they used to put in them? the old tunics and trousers of the priests to act as wicks! The light was glorious; the whole city was alight; every one was in booths; they massed in their thousands. They used to go to the pool of Siloam and take out water, and come and meet a priest in the middle of the Temple area with wine, and together they would pour water and wine into a silver bowl. It was a harvest festival thanking God for the rains, the water, and the wine, and joy. The water is the fructifying thing. They sang the great Hillel Psalms 111 to 118 (the last one is almost certainly a Psalm of the history of Israel) and went almost mad with delight. There was joy, there was water, there was light, there was everything.

And on the last great day of the feast, says John 7, our Lord Jesus in part of that multitude said: If any man thirst let him come unto me and drink, for out of his inner man shall go rivers of living water. You do not understand this properly unless you understand what we have been saying. Our Lord was caught up with the tremendous excitement in all these Jews, for in the Jewish mind was: Not only are we looking back to the desert and thanking God for bringing us to this wonderful land; not only are we thanking God for the rains that have made the land fruitful; but we are looking forward to the Day of Messiah, when we will be delivered from all our ills and pains, and the nation will be raised up, and Christ will be with us on that great eighth day of the Feast.

Now what is the eighth day in Christian theology? It is the Resurrection Day. On the first day of the week He rose from the dead (that is, the eighth day). Now do you see how the Christian Gospel fits into all this? Our Lord said: If any man thirst let him come unto me; - 'and this spake he of the Holy Spirit' which was not yet given because Jesus was not yet glorified, not yet put to death. The Jews believe that in the day of the Messiah, the Spirit of God will come upon them all in a special way:

'And your daughters, and your young men and your old men will dream dreams and see visions and your lives will be transformed'. It is going to happen; Jerusalem will be dwelt in; and to get the picture that Jesus looked forward to, look at Isaiah 65 verses 17 to 25:

> For, behold, I create new heavens and a new earth: and the former things shall not be remembered, nor come into mind.
> But be ye glad and rejoice for ever in that which I create: for, behold, I create Jerusalem a rejoicing, and her people a joy.
> And I will rejoice in Jerusalem, and joy in my people: and the voice of weeping shall be no more heard in her, nor the voice of crying.
> There shall be no more thence an infant of days, nor an old man that hath not filled his days: for the child shall die an hundred years old, and the sinner being an hundred years old shall be accursed.
> And they shall build houses, and inhabit them; and they shall plant vineyards, and eat the fruit of them.
> They shall not build, and another inhabit; they shall not plant and another eat: for as the days of a tree shall be the days of my people, and my chosen shall long enjoy the work of their hands.
> They shall not labour in vain, nor bring forth for calamity; for they are the seed of the blessed of the Lord, and their offspring with them.
> And it shall come to pass that, before they call, I will answer; and while they are yet speaking, I will hear.
> The wolf and the lamb shall feed together, and the lion shall eat straw like the ox: and dust shall be the serpent's meat. They shall not hurt nor destroy in all my holy mountain, saith the Lord.

This is the beginning of the kingdom age before going on into the greater age of joy and happiness. Children are not going to die at birth; there is to be great longevity; a child, for example, shall die a hundred years old. Sin is going to be strictly controlled: it is not going to be erased until the eternal state is ushered in; the punishment for the sinner is that he will not have these added years. It is significant that in the first part of Isaiah (chapter 11) this same glorious hope is given, and that here in the so-called Deutero-Isaiah or Trito-Isaiah, the same hope is repeated. Could it be that the same Isaiah wrote the whole book!

All nations shall flow into the city of Jerusalem. Malachi says that in chapter 1 verse 11, but it does not mean all the nations literally. It means representatives of all the nations. And, in verse 17 of Zechariah, if they do not come there will be no rain, and that is terrible punishment for the Middle East as everyone knows; when the rain fails there is untold suffering:

> And it shall be, that whoso of all the families of the earth goeth not up unto Jerusalem to worship the King, the Lord of hosts, upon them there shall be no rain.

Verses 18 and 19 mention Egypt especially, because she does not depend on rain. As I have said previously, Egypt depends on the river Nile which is fed by rain in other countries, and Egypt is the traditional enemy of Israel:

> And if the family of Egypt go not up, and come not, neither shall it be upon them; there shall be the plague, wherewith the Lord will smite the nations that go not up to keep the feast of tabernacles.
> This shall be the punishment of Egypt, and the punishment of all the nations that go not up to keep the feast of tabernacles.

Where? Here on earth! But now, to finish off.

The Lord is going to reign in Jerusalem; people will go up to Jerusalem to celebrate this marvellous joy. The millennial reign will begin. If you do not believe that, then you have got to explain to me Revelation 20 verses 1 to 5. This so impressed Litton, the great theologian, that he was a pre-millenialist; so is Professor Bruce, I believe; and so were all the very early Fathers, until Augustine, hypnotised by the Church, threw his considerable influence against it:

> And I saw an angel coming down out of heaven, having the key of the abyss and a great chain in his hand.
> And he laid hold on the dragon, the old serpent, which is the Devil and Satan, and bound him for a thousand years,
> And cast him into the abyss, and shut it, and sealed it over him, that he should deceive the nations no more, until the thousand years should be finished: after this he must be loosed for a little time.
> And I saw thrones, and they sat upon them, and judgment was given unto them: and I saw the souls of them that had been beheaded for the testimony of Jesus, and for the word of God, and such as worshipped not the beast, neither his image, and received not the mark upon their forehead and upon their hand; and they lived, and reigned with Christ a thousand years.
> The rest of the dead lived not until the thousand years should be finished. This is the first resurrection.

That is a very difficult passage for anybody to juggle with. It is either true or it is not; it is very difficult to spiritualise it. In the light of present world history, to suggest that this age is the millenium age and that Satan is bound today is ludicrous, if not total lunacy. The theologically minded should re-read Litton on this chapter.
So to the last two verses of the book of Zechariah:

> In that day shall there be upon the bells of the horses, HOLY UNTO THE LORD; and the pots in the Lord's house shall be like the bowls before the altar.
> Yea, every pot in Jerusalem and in Judah shall be holy unto the Lord of hosts: and all they that sacrifice shall come and take of them, and seethe therein: and in that day there shall be no more a Canaanite in the house of the Lord of hosts.

This simply means that there will be no trafficking, no unjust trading, and no spirit of Babylon. Nor is there going to be any distinction between the domestic, the profane, the holy, and the secular: we all are going to love the Lord. Your washing-up dishes will be as holy as the dishes on the altar; there will be no profane and holy; no distinction or separation. You see, the Jew was given laws in the books of Moses to make a distinction between the holy and the profane; but not **in that day.**

With the Lord upon us the lesson has been learned, that the whole of life will be sanctified. The Kingdom will come upon earth with a mighty demonstration of the power of Christ; on the very earth that rejected Him. And the earth that rejected Him will see Him reigning in Glory for a thousand years, which is the message of Revelation 20, and of Zechariah, and of all the prophets.

And so (as Paul exults in Romans 11 verse 26 onwards) **in that day** all Israel shall be saved - the elect of physical Israel and the believing Gentiles - all the Israel of God (Galatians 6) in the glorious fulfilment of God's promises to Abraham, 'And in thy seed shall all the nations of the earth be blessed; because thou hast obeyed my voice'. As we follow the day by day events in Israel and in the Middle East generally, I believe that they can only be explained in the light of the words of the great prophets, and in particular the words of Zechariah, the quintessence of the prophets. And that day is upon us. Let us close with the words of Revelation chapter 1 verse 7:

> Behold, he cometh with the clouds; and every eye shall see him, and they which pierced him; and all the tribes of the earth shall mourn over him.
> Even so, Amen.